NEW YORK AND AMSTERDAM

NEW YORK AND AMSTERDAM

Immigration and the New Urban Landscape

Edited by
Nancy Foner, Jan Rath, Jan Willem Duyvendak,
and Rogier van Reekum

NEW YORK UNIVERSITY PRESS
New York and London

NEW YORK UNIVERSITY PRESS
New York and London
www.nyupress.org

References to Internet websites (URLs) were accurate at the time of writing.
Neither the author nor New York University Press is responsible for URLs that
may have expired or changed since the manuscript was prepared.

Library of Congress Cataloging-in-Publication Data
New York and Amsterdam : immigration and the new urban landscape /
edited by Nancy Foner, Jan Rath, Jan Willem Duyvendak, and Rogier van Reekum.
pages   cm
Includes bibliographical references and index.
ISBN 978-0-8147-3809-2 (cl : alk. paper) — ISBN 978-0-8147-3844-3 (pb : alk. paper)
1. Immigrants—New York (State)—New York. 2. Immigrants—Netherlands—
Amsterdam. 3. New York (N.Y.)—Emigration and immigration. 4. Amsterdam
(Netherlands)—Emigration and immigration. 5. Cultural pluralism—New York
(State)—New York. 6. Cultural pluralism—Netherlands—Amsterdam.
I. Foner, Nancy, 1945– editor of compilation.
JV7048.N49 2014
305.9'0691209492352—dc23   2013028294

New York University Press books are printed on acid-free paper,
and their binding materials are chosen for strength and durability.
We strive to use environmentally responsible suppliers and materials
to the greatest extent possible in publishing our books.

Manufactured in the United States of America
c 10 9 8 7 6 5 4 3 2 1
p 10 9 8 7 6 5 4 3 2 1

Also available as an ebook

CONTENTS

ACKNOWLEDGMENTS

This book has its origins in a conference held at the University of Amsterdam in January 2011. Entitled "Amsterdam and New York: The Impact of Immigration in Two Global Cities," the conference brought together a distinguished group of scholars to explore—and compare—how immigration has dramatically changed Amsterdam and New York in recent decades and, at the same time, affected the lives of the hundreds of thousands of immigrants, and their second-generation children, who live there. The conference evolved out of the activities of the Center for Urban Studies at the University of Amsterdam, as well as earlier collaborations among many of the Dutch and American contributors to this volume. Through these collaborations as well as conversations at various workshops and meetings on both sides of the Atlantic, we became more aware of the effects of—and scholarly work on—immigration in each other's cities. It became clear that there was a need for a more systematic examination and comparison of the consequences of immigration in Amsterdam and New York, which is what led to the organization of the conference—and ultimately this book.

We would like to express our gratitude to the Center for Urban Studies at the University of Amsterdam for its support in making the conference possible. We are also grateful to the Institute for Ethnic and Migration Studies (IMES), also at the University of Amsterdam, for its additional support, and owe a special thanks to Aukje IJpma, who at the time of the conference was a research assistant at the institute. At the conference itself, a number of people served as discussants, and we are grateful for their excellent commentaries. These include many of the authors in this volume as well as Daniel Hiebert, Yvonne Leeman, Bowen Paulle, and Sharon Zukin. In New York, we thank the CUNY Graduate Center for providing a meeting place for the editors in the process of preparing the book, as well as serving as an intellectual home that has nurtured the work of several of the New York authors.

We have had the great good fortune to work with a wonderful editor at New York University Press, Ilene Kalish, who has been a source of support, wisdom, and advice at every stage of the publication process. We are also grateful to assistant editors Aidan Amos and Caelyn Cobb as well as managing editor Dorothea Stillman Halliday for their help along the way. Thanks, too, to the two anonymous reviewers for their suggestions, which, we believe, have made this a better book.

Finally, our appreciation to all the authors in the volume for their commitment to this ambitious transatlantic project, their responsiveness to requests for revisions from us and from reviewers, and for the high quality of their contributions.

Introduction

New York and Amsterdam: Immigration and the New Urban Landscape

JAN RATH, NANCY FONER, JAN WILLEM DUYVENDAK,
AND ROGIER VAN REEKUM

Immigration is dramatically changing major cities throughout the world. Nowhere is this more true than in Amsterdam and New York City, which, after decades of large-scale immigration, now have populations that are about a third foreign born. Amsterdam and New York City have had to deal with incorporating hundreds of thousands of immigrants whose ethnic, racial, and national backgrounds differ from those of many long-established residents, and who display a variety of different languages, religions, cultures, and lifestyles. How have the specific urban contexts of Amsterdam and New York shaped the fates of these newcomers? And—conversely—how has the massive recent immigration transformed New York City and Amsterdam? These are the central questions that will be addressed in this book.

A Transatlantic Comparison of Immigrant Cities

Amsterdam and New York City share more than a high proportion of foreign born. That the immigrants arriving there in the last half century have mostly come from outside of Europe is a new development in both cities. Newcomers have had to face a wide array of challenges of adjustment and accommodation, and these processes show remarkable *similarities* in the two cities. Immigrants have sometimes gotten a cold or even hostile shoulder, but at other times received a warm welcome. By the standards of their respective countries, Amsterdam and New York are relatively liberal cities with progressive elites.

The *differences* between the cities, however, overshadow the parallels. Among other things, Amsterdam lacks a large native minority presence, which is so significant in New York, as well as a continuous history as an immigrant city and the institutional legacy that this involves. New York, for its part, lacks (in American eyes) the generous welfare protections and services that are provided in Amsterdam.[1] The cities have different political and economic institutions. The immigrant flows also diverge dramatically. Owing to recent immigration, Amsterdam is now home to a large number of Muslims[2] while New York's nonwhite populations— Latino, West Indian, and Asian—have mushroomed. About 13 percent of the foreign-born population in the Netherlands lives in Amsterdam;[3] New York City has slightly less than 8 percent of the U.S. foreign-born population.[4] The naturalness of the way in which these migratory flows are commonly characterized and in which labels are attached to them—"Muslims" in Amsterdam, "nonwhites" in New York—also point to remarkable social, political, and discursive differences. And, finally, there are profound differences in scale. The population of Amsterdam's municipality proper as of 2012 was 790,044 and that of the agglomeration about one million,[5] whereas New York City's population was 8.2 million according to the 2010 census and the 31-county metropolitan region's about 22.1 million.[6] The surface area of New York City is six times that of Amsterdam and the population density three times as high. Notwithstanding the fact that Amsterdam is considered a "big city" in the Dutch context, Amsterdam compared to New York City sometimes seems barely more than a small picturesque European place.

Starting from the observation that Amsterdam and New York City simultaneously display similarities and local differences, this book explores the immigrant experience so as to be better able to describe, understand, and explain the nexus of immigrant incorporation and urban form and structure. Although the book focuses on two specific cases, old and "new" Amsterdam, we think it has implications that go beyond these cities.

Comparative studies on the immigration experience in cities, let alone transatlantic comparisons, are still quite rare. There is nonetheless a growing interest in comparisons of immigration in European and American cities. Within Europe, there have been some attempts to look at the effects of immigration in cities in the same or different countries (e.g., Alexander 2007; Body-Gendrot and Martiniello 2000, Garbaye 2006; Penninx et al. 2004); within the United States, comparisons of different gateway cities have risen on the research agenda, especially in light of large-scale immigration to new or emerging urban destinations (e.g., Singer, Hardwick, and Brettell 2008).[7] A central question has been understanding how cities differ as contexts of reception depending on the way geographic and historical particularities have shaped immigrant flows—including their skill levels, national origin composition, and timing of arrival—and the effects of particular social, economic, and political institutions and structures on the options available to newcomers from abroad (Brettell 2003; Foner 2005; Price and Benton-Short 2008; Waldinger 2001). New York has loomed large in cross-city comparative efforts in the United States, which have often tried to explain why Los Angeles—the other major U.S. immigrant city—has provided a different, and until recently a much less welcoming, reception for millions of immigrants who have moved there in the last half century (e.g., Sabagh and Bozorgmehr 2003; Foner 2005, 2007; Foner and Waldinger 2013; Mollenkopf 1999; Waldinger 1996). As Roger Waldinger (1996) has pointed out, the case of New York has been too often considered as a proxy for "the" immigrant experience in American cities. Certainly, many of the same kind of social relations and processes are found in different cities, but "the unique characteristics of each of the places and the differences in their respective immigrant flows highlight the way in which the urban context matters" (Waldinger 2001: 5).

Comparisons of European and American immigrant cities are also scarce. John Mollenkopf (2000) in a thought-provoking paper explored the fate of the second generation in Amsterdam and New York. Bowen Paulle (2005) has provided a comparative ethnographic account of schools in the Bronx (New York) and Bijlmer (Amsterdam) that focuses heavily on immigrant-origin youth, and Maurice Crul and Jennifer Holdaway (2009) have examined how the different educational systems in New York and Amsterdam shape the trajectories of the children of immigrants in schools. A number of edited collections—*Unraveling the Rag Trade: Immigrant Entrepreneurship in Seven World Cities*

(Rath 2002), *Immigrant Entrepreneurs: Venturing Abroad in the Age of Globalization* (Kloosterman and Rath 2003), *Bringing Outsiders In: Transatlantic Perspectives on Immigrant Political Incorporation* (Hochschild and Mollenkopf 2009), *The Next Generation: Immigrant Youth in a Comparative Perspective* (Alba and Waters 2011), and *The Changing Face of World Cities: Young Adult Children of Immigrants in Europe and the United States* (Crul and Mollenkopf 2012)—compare immigration's effects in Europe and the United States, but they put the spotlight on one topic (ethnic entrepreneurship, political incorporation, the second-generation experience) and include wide-ranging chapters on different countries and groups. Immigrant political incorporation and immigration policy in European countries and the United States have been the subject of several single-authored books—for example, *Immigration and the Nation-State: The United States, Germany, and Great Britain* (Joppke 1999) and *The Politics of Immigration in France, Britain, and the United States: A Comparative Study* (Schain 2008)—but there is, at yet, no systematic book-length analysis with an immigration focus on other topics through a transatlantic lens. In general, in U.S.-Europe comparisons, the nation-state is the unit of study, yet cities within them vary in significant ways—so that the urban context needs to be examined and its special features taken into account. When we speak of migration to countries what we often mean is migration to cities. It is usually in these urban contexts that migrant incorporation into host societies ultimately takes place and shape. Therefore, comparing cities of migration allows us to be more precise in our analysis.

By focusing on two urban contexts, this book represents an in-depth view of the impact of immigration as it affects particular places, with specific histories, institutions, and immigrant inflows, thereby contributing to our broader understanding of the transformations wrought by immigration and the dynamics of urban change. It provides material on issues that are at the heart of debates about immigration in the United States and Europe—from economic incorporation and immigrant access to political influence to racial and religious inequalities and barriers. And it offers new insights into how—and why—immigration's effects differ on the two sides of the Atlantic. We strongly believe that our comparative approach will bring us further for a number of reasons.

First, as has already been said, such comparative studies are thin on the ground and this is actually quite striking in a field as global as international migration to world cities. It is precisely because Amsterdam and New York are both so similar and so different that a book bringing together essays on them as immigrant cities is valuable. Juxtaposing essays on, and contrasting, immigration in the two cities helps to illuminate the contextual factors shaping immigration's effects. The transatlantic, trans-city comparison also calls attention to dynamics that might be missed or taken for granted if we focused on only one city. Scholars of immigration in New York, for example, often downplay the role of the state, while for Dutch academics it is central; in New York, race is at the top of the agenda, in Amsterdam it is not, but "Islamophobia" is a dominant theme in academic and public discourse. Those local particularities—both in everyday urban practice and in academic research—emerge more sharply and can be better identified in a comparative setting. Many social and cultural patterns that are seemingly "natural" in one setting—so natural that researchers don't even bother to pay attention to them—might seem unusual or out of place in another setting. Comparing one's own city with another one is therefore like looking into a mirror (cf. Bovenkerk, Miles, and Verbunt 1991). It is the strategy *par excellence* to learn about the self—and, in this case, about one's own city—and a more profound understanding is the result.

Second, comparing cities also serves to correct ideas about the immigrant experience in particular settings that are based on generalizations about national features or qualities. For as far as students of international migration are interested in the situation in countries other than their own—something that, unfortunately, cannot be taken for granted—there is a tendency to take commonsense assumptions about national characteristics or even "national models of integration" for granted (cf. Bertossi and Duyvendak 2012). Think for example of such notions as "In the U.S., the state and other regulatory institutions do not interfere with immigrants' integration into the mainstream" or "The Netherlands abandoned soft multiculturalism and embarked on a tough assimilationist approach." Such sweeping statements are problematic in general, but are definitely misleading when one focuses on local settings (Rath 2011). As the various chapters in this book show, both Amsterdam and New York are positioned in specific ways in terms of a broad range of real or alleged national developments.

While acknowledging that the immigrant experience is the product of a multitude of factors at various levels, Adrian Favell (2001) has been critical of national comparisons as these often reproduce national stereotypes and assumptions about the nation-state. What is needed, according to Favell, is an international comparative approach that appreciates local particularities. He has argued that the city is an excellent unit of analysis, as it represents a level of research that "enables both contextual specificity and structural comparisons that allow for the fact that immigrant integration might be influenced simultaneously by local, national and transnational factors" (2001: 349 ff.). All in all, the city constitutes a level of analysis that provides a way to appreciate and understand the complexities of everyday experiences and patterns of incorporation.

Third, and related to the previous points, a volume on Amsterdam and New York offers an opportunity to see whether theoretical perspectives and frameworks developed to explain the immigrant experience and immigration's impact in one urban context make sense to apply to the other. Or to put it another way, it reveals whether theoretical insights into immigration's effects in Amsterdam help to illuminate what happens in New York—and the other way around, as well. Ultimately, the analysis of immigration's role in the two cities can stimulate new research questions and lead to future comparisons and transatlantic interchanges.

Although our focus is on the two cities, it is clear—indeed obvious—that they do not exist in isolation from the countries in which they are located. The immigrant experience in both cities is affected by social, economic, and political developments in the nation-state as a whole, including laws passed and policies made at the national level and that apply nationwide. At the same time, as the chapters in this book bring out, Amsterdam and New York are distinctive immigrant gateway cities in the Netherlands and United States in many ways. In the United States, New York stands out for, among other things, the remarkable diversity of its contemporary immigrant flows and presence of historically based institutions that have shaped immigrant incorporation. In Amsterdam, the widely held international and perhaps cosmopolitan outlook as well as "live-and-let-live" mentality have fostered the development of an environment in which immigration and diversity are seen as a normal part of life, or at least as more normal than elsewhere in the Netherlands.

Introducing Amsterdam and New York

Before introducing the main themes and the structure of the book, let us first go a bit deeper into the characteristics of the two cities.

Amsterdam is the older of the two. It started as a small fishing village in the twelfth century, then rose to great power in the sixteenth and seventeenth centuries—the so-called Golden Age—due to its aggressive and innovative maritime trading strategies. Private investors and entrepreneurial traders, unbothered by traditional power structures, established a successful mercantile capitalist system and—for a relatively short period of time—a globally dominant empire (Chua 2007). The famous *grachtengordel* (the scenic ring of canals located in the heart of the city) dates from that period. Amsterdam lost its leading position to other cities, notably to London, in the late seventeenth and early eighteenth centuries, but it remained the Dutch capital. The Amsterdam economy has continued to depend on trade and commerce, although it did attract manufacturing industries in the nineteenth and twentieth centuries, including ship building and repair, tobacco, diamonds, car assembly, and garments. However, most of these industries were relocated at the closing years of the twentieth century, and a new economy emerged. Amsterdam is now the country's most important center for financial and cultural industries. In 2011, Amsterdam attained twelfth place on the Mercer list of the world's most livable cities—a ranking based on the availability of goods and services, safety, and infrastructure.[8] People from around the world are evidently attracted to Amsterdam, including approximately 30 million tourists and visitors each year. The city of Amsterdam nonetheless has felt the need to further boost its international image with the slogan (in English!) *I Amsterdam*, inspired by *I love New York* and *Je suis Paris*.[9]

As Leo Lucassen describes in his chapter in this book, these economic developments have coincided with international migration, although the migratory flows in various historical periods show sharp differences. Benton-Short, Price, and Friedman (2005), who explored the rise of global cities, point to the fact that globalization entails more than just economic developments, and they argue that immigration is a powerful example of "globalization from below." They claim that seen from such a perspective, Amsterdam is among the leading global cities in the world. This "globalization from below" is vernacularized within everyday urban practices. According to Nell and Rath:

> One senses the international mobility of capital and labour in the sky-boxes of the Amsterdam Arena—the grounds of the local soccer team Ajax—where international businessmen manage their affairs. One senses globalization in basements of the high-rises in the Bijlmer suburb where everything from food processing to hairdressing and weed dealing takes place, oftentimes informally, or at the Albert Cuyp Market in the southern part of the city where one can purchase imported ingredients for Surinamese and Ghanaian dishes. The globalization of popular culture can literally be smelled and tasted in the Chinese, Thai, Vietnamese, Japanese and Portuguese restaurants on the Zeedijk in downtown Amsterdam. This much is clear: international business people, travellers and migrants personify the global character of the city and bring new impulses to the urban social fabric. (2009: 12)

The international character of the city is obviously manifested in the composition of the population. In 2012, almost 29 percent of Amsterdam's inhabitants were first-generation immigrants. First- and second-generation immigrants together made up half the population (precisely 50.5 percent).[10] These proportions of immigrants bring Amsterdam on a par with global cities such as New York City.

After World War II, Amsterdam like many other places in the Netherlands, received many guest workers from Mediterranean countries such as Spain, Italy, Portugal, Yugoslavia, Greece, Tunisia, Morocco, and Turkey. They were attracted by manufacturing industries to fill the vacancies that upwardly mobile Dutch left behind. The guest workers were recruited between the late 1950s and the early 1970s, initially on a short-term basis, but gradually also on a more permanent basis, to do dirty, dangerous, and dull jobs such as meatpacking, cleaning, assembly line production, and so forth. Being selected on the basis of their physical strength rather than educational qualifications, and being hired mainly for low-level jobs, they got stuck in the bottom tiers of the labor market. Things took a serious turn for the worse when the manufacturing industries downgraded and one factory after the other had to close its doors. As Kloosterman describes in his chapter, unemployment skyrocketed in the 1980s, and especially the poorly educated guest workers and their children found it hard to get reconnected to the new urban economy.

Amsterdam was also a magnet for immigrants from former colonial areas, notably immigrants from Suriname. This "small" country—squeezed between French and British Guiana and (measured in square kilometers) still four times the size of the Netherlands—was part of the Dutch kingdom until November 25, 1975, when Suriname became an independent republic. Until the early 1970s, only small numbers of Surinamese moved to the Netherlands, mainly people from the elites who came to study. In the early 1960s, there were some attempts to recruit Surinamese as guest workers, but those programs failed (Schuster 1999). Things changed in the early 1970s when negotiations about impending independence were being held. People in Suriname feared political (and ethnic) strife and one after the other decided to move to the Netherlands before it was too late. This migration took the form of a true exodus as eventually one-third of the total Surinamese population had left for greener pastures. Amsterdam received large numbers, especially those of African origin—the so-called Creole Surinamese.[11] Many flocked to the southeastern part of the city, the Bijlmer, a satellite city built on the basis of Corbusian principles, with a strict separation of functions and many anonymous high-rise buildings. In the 1990s, immigrants from other parts of the world, notably from Ghana, Nigeria, and other African countries, settled in Amsterdam, and many joined the Surinamese community in the Bijlmer.

Amsterdam also has a relatively sizable population of "expatriates," an utterly amorphous and heterogenous category comprising well-educated professionals, students, and businessmen from both advanced and less-advanced economies. This is related to the fact that Amsterdam hosts a number of international or European headquarters (including Starbucks, Cisco, and various financial companies) and higher educational institutions, that it is adjacent to the international Amsterdam

Schiphol Airport, and that it continues to be an appealing place for life-style migrants from all walks of life.

While it is important to note that numerous immigrants and members of the second generation are following the example of the native Dutch middle class and moving to the suburbs, the Amsterdam population is still becoming more and more diverse. In 2012, foreign-born Moroccans comprised 4.3 percent of the Amsterdam population, Turks almost 3 percent, and Surinamese almost 6 percent, while another nearly 16 percent came from the rest of the world (more than half of them originating in Western countries).[12] However, if we count the second generation as well, we get a different picture: first- and second-generation Moroccans comprise 9 percent of the Amsterdam population, Turks more than 5 percent, Surinamese nearly 9 percent, and more than 25 percent have other origins.

The immigrant population is not equally distributed over all neighborhoods. The canal area in downtown Amsterdam and the area around the Vondelpark are predominantly native white. Surinamese and Africans are strongly represented in the Bijlmer, while Moroccans are to be found in great numbers in the Western part of the city, notably the garden-park neighborhoods built in the early 1960s.

The Dutch government categorizes immigrant groups primarily on the basis of a combination of ethnocultural characteristics and socio-economic disadvantage, even though in policy making other labels play an important role as well, such as "autochthones" and "allochthones"; the latter group, defined as people born abroad or with at least one parent born abroad, is subdivided into "Western allochthones" and "non-Western allochthones." Recently, non-Western allochthones often have been equated with Muslims, who are the subject of government interventions, as the chapter by Uitermark, Duyvendak, and Rath shows.

Across the Atlantic, *New York City*—originally called New Amsterdam—was settled by the Dutch as a trading post in the early seventeenth century, and evolved into the nation's major center of maritime trade and later of manufacturing. As manufacturing declined after World War II, the city's economy became dominated by financial and other producer services (for an overview of the history of the city's economy, see Drennan 2010). Although New York City was the first capital of the newly formed United States in 1788, it lost this role only two years later, never to regain it. New York is, however, the financial capital of the country and one of the world's two premier financial centers. A global corporate hub, it is home to Wall Street and the New York Stock Exchange as well as major corporate services in commercial and investment banking, securities, insurance, accounting, advertising, management consulting, and law. Among other things, it is the most important center for book and magazine publishing and the arts in the United States.

New York is also the classic city of immigrants, the major historical gateway for the country's new arrivals and a major receiving center today. It is fitting, as Nancy Foner notes in her chapter, that America's two most powerful symbols of immigration—Ellis Island and the Statue of Liberty—stand in New York's harbor. Many of the millions of southern and eastern European immigrants who passed through Ellis Island's halls a hundred years ago remained in New York. In 1910, one out of seven of the nation's immigrants lived in New York City—and 41 percent of the city's residents were foreign born. A smaller fraction (7.6 percent) of the nation's immigrants live in New York City today—and a smaller percentage of the city's population is foreign born (37 percent)—but the actual number of immigrants has never been larger, just over three million in 2010. Adding on the children of immigrants, the figure rises to about 4.5 million, or an estimated 55 percent of the city's population (Lobo and Salvo 2013).

Since the late 1960s, New York City has received millions of people from abroad, and the influx shows no signs of abating. Changes in U.S. immigration law at the federal level in 1965 opened the doors to mass immigration by ending the national origins quotas that had restricted inflows since the 1920s as well as severe limits on Asian immigration in place since the late nineteenth century. As long as the doors to the United States remain relatively open—and the federal government continues to allow hundreds of thousands of immigrants into the country every year—New York is likely to continue to receive large numbers if only because of the networks that link newcomers to settlers.

New York City's immigrant population today is extraordinarily diverse. Before the 1960s, the overwhelming majority of immigrant New Yorkers were from Europe, and earlier massive waves were dominated by two groups—the Irish and Germans in the mid-nineteenth century and Russian Jews and Italians at the turn of the twentieth century. Even the enormous internal migration in the twentieth century was a two-group phenomenon: African Americans who arrived from southern states between World War I and the 1960s and Puerto Ricans from the island (U.S. citizens by birth and not classified as immigrants) in the first few decades after World War II (see Foner, this volume; Foner 2000). Today, no two—or three or four—groups dominate, and most immigrants come, not from Europe, but from Latin America, Asia, and the Caribbean. In 2010, the top three immigrant groups—Dominicans, Chinese, and Mexicans—were 30 percent of all the foreign born, and no other group accounted for more than 6 percent (Foner, this volume). Immigrants are also diverse in their socioeconomic origins; while many have low levels of education and skills, a substantial proportion—26 percent in 2010—have a college degree or more.

The huge immigration of the past half century is a major factor behind the dramatic transformation of the city's ethnic and racial composition. Between 1980 and 2010, non-Hispanic whites went from 52 to 33 percent of New York City's population, Hispanics from 20 to 29 percent, Asians from 3 to 13 percent, and non-Hispanic blacks, reinforced by immigration from the Caribbean and, to a lesser extent, from Africa, held fairly steady, 24 percent in 1980, 23 percent in 2010 (Lobo and Salvo 2013). Not surprisingly, views of race and ethnicity have changed as well—"Asian," for example, no longer means Chinese in New York City but also Indian, Korean, Filipino, and Bangladeshi, to name a few, and Puerto Ricans, who several decades ago equaled "Hispanic," are now outnumbered by a combination of Dominicans, Mexicans, Colombians, and Ecuadorians, among others (Foner 2000, 2005, 2013; see Waters, this volume).

Because successive waves of immigrants over the past 200 years have left an indelible imprint on the city, it is not surprising that their impact on New York's institutions, politics, and culture looms large in the chapters in this book on New York City. What comes out from these chapters is the legitimacy of ethnicity—and appeals to ethnicity—and that New Yorkers, both old and new, are used to ethnic succession. Writing about second-generation New Yorkers, Philip Kasinitz and his colleagues observe, "While these young people feel the sting of disadvantage and discrimination, they move in a world where being from somewhere else has long been the norm. For them, being a New Yorker means being both ethnic and American. . . . In this feeling they are reaping the benefits of New York's long history of absorbing new immigrants" (Kasinitz et al. 2008: 360).

Comparative Complications

It is clear that both Amsterdam and New York City have been undergoing dramatic changes owing to the large-scale immigration of recent decades. As the chapters show, both cities try to be welcoming, failing and succeeding in different ways. But this book is not about winners and losers, about which city is better. Rather, it brings together a distinguished—and interdisciplinary—group of American and Dutch scholars to examine and compare the impact of immigration on these two major world cities.

In so doing, the authors and editors encountered several complications. Migration and assimilation/integration studies are internationalizing: international scholars publish more often in the English language, go to the same international conferences and workshops, invite each other back and forth, embark on joint research projects, and exchange empirical data and theoretical ideas. They communicate intensively with each other and use the same terms and concepts and speak to the same theories. For those involved in such exchanges it is very tempting to believe that they are really on the same page. But is it really true that terms, concepts, and theories have exactly the same meaning at both sides of the Atlantic?

Take the term "race," which is commonplace in American parlance. The Dutch equivalent would probably be *ras*, although even that seems debatable (see Bovenkerk 1984), and in the Netherlands the term *ras* is rarely if ever used. Yet social scientists and others from outside the Netherlands frequently refer to the concept of "racism" in discussing the Amsterdam context, a concept associated with a set of assumptions about the superiority or inferiority of "races" marked by visible physical differences. This, to be sure, is not to suggest that assumptions about inferiority and superiority do not exist in the Netherlands (see the chapter by Uitermark, Duyvendak, and Rath in this volume and Rath 1999). But it does illustrate that these kinds of concepts do not travel easily. There is also the term "black," which in the United States refers to people of sub-Saharan African ancestry, but in the Netherlands can include Moroccans and Turks, among others. The latter is the case, for instance, when people in Amsterdam refer to "black schools" and "black neighborhoods" in areas with high numbers of immigrants, irrespective of the immigrants' skin color or phenotypic features (see Paulle 2007; Rath 1991; Vink 2010).

In the same vein, the process of incorporation of immigrants in the receiving society is described and analyzed in the Netherlands in terms of "integration," a term that in the United States is more often used in reference to the plight of African Americans. Integration in this context refers to the ending of systematic racial segregation. American social scientists tend to prefer to use the term "assimilation," a practice that Dutch scholars would rarely if ever adopt. In Dutch academic parlance, assimilation is almost a term of abuse implying the imposition of monolithic mainstream views and practices, not a term to describe and analyze the kind of social processes that happen continuously as immigrants become part of as well as remake mainstream society—what American sociologists Richard Alba and Victor Nee (2003) discuss in their influential book laying out a "new assimilation theory."

Theory suggests abstractions from everyday empirical realities, but this epistemological idea notwithstanding, theories are always built on particular empirical cases and emerge out of particular social, cultural, and political contexts. This holds true for social science in general and for public social sciences in particular. The same holds—*mutatis mutandis*—for notions about cities, about urban structures, about urban dynamics, and about the changing position of newcomers. While taking account of these intellectual challenges, this volume endeavors to describe and understand how immigrants have fared in the specific urban contexts of Amsterdam and New York, and how these cities have been transformed by massive recent immigration.

Central Questions

The book is organized around five main themes that are framed as questions about the impact of immigration. The questions probe the history of immigration, the integration of immigrants in the urban economy, the dynamics of political incorporation, the construction and effects of racial and religious differences, and the role of the children of immigrants in shaping the arts and public culture. Each chapter focuses on one city, drawing on the expertise of the author(s); each of the five sections is preceded by a short introduction (by the editors) that draws out the comparisons between the two cities.

We begin, in the first section, with history. The question posed is: *How has the immigrant past shaped the immigrant present in New York City and Amsterdam?* As one would expect, the chapter on New York by Nancy Foner demonstrates the power of the *longue durée*: immigrant inflows in one period shape the experiences of subsequent inflows. The creation of a welcoming city is strongly related to the institutions and the public culture and ethos that earlier waves of immigrants developed. Such a favorable social, cultural, political, and economic environment, that is, one that has been formed by subsequent inflows of immigrants, does not exist in Amsterdam. Amsterdam did experience mass immigration in earlier historical periods but, as the chapter by Leo Lucassen shows, these distant inflows are not appealed to or remembered in a way that has had any positive influence on the situation today. History matters in a different way, however. The institutionalization of religious and socioeconomic difference—as developed throughout the twentieth century, and unrelated to immigration—has had a far greater impact, particularly in the way the native Dutch deal with religious differences between groups in an increasingly secular society. Dutch politicians and opinion leaders do reflect on the Dutch past, but immigrants do not really have a presence in their take on history, something that interferes in the acceptance of immigrants as members of the Dutch nation.

The second section is about the economy, with a guiding question: *What difference does the urban economy make to immigrant incorporation?* In his chapter, David Dyssegaard Kallick demonstrates how racial and ethnic disparities and immigrant status influence labor market careers in New York City. In recent years, immigrants have displayed even lower unemployment rates than the native born. As Robert Kloosterman notes in his chapter, the reverse is true in Amsterdam: non-Western immigrants in particular have displayed higher unemployment rates than the native Dutch. Kloosterman explicitly addresses the regulatory environment in Amsterdam, including the restructuring of the welfare state, and argues that it has helped foster the booming of Amsterdam's economy and, indirectly, affected immigrants' labor market performance.

The third section is about the ideological representation of immigrants and the real and alleged boundaries between immigrants and the receiving society. Inspired by Aristide Zolberg and Long Litt Woon's paper "Why Islam Is Like Spanish" (1999), the third section poses yet another question: *Is Islam in Amsterdam like race in New York City?* In her chapter on New York, Mary Waters explores the social boundaries and barriers that people of African, Asian, and Latin American ancestry encounter. Racialization continues to structure everyday social relations and social opportunities, although in different ways than it did in the past. The white-black binary, which dominated racial relations in New York for much of the twentieth century, has not disappeared, but other terms are now needed to adequately describe New York's racial/ ethnic hierarchy, as the arrival of large numbers of immigrants from Asia and Latin America has changed the racial landscape. In Amsterdam, in contrast, social cleavages are not so strongly structured by "color," but by other features. As Uitermark, Duyvendak, and Rath note in their chapter on Amsterdam, religion—notably a specific version of Islam—in combination with lifestyle and class, are important today as social divides. Whereas Islam is often disparaged by many Dutch policymakers and opinion leaders as "backward" and "hindering integration," in Amsterdam in the past decade the local government and civic society institutions have actively influenced the formation of a particular—more liberal and "Western-oriented"—type of Islam that has the potential to facilitate the integration of Muslims into Dutch society.

Politics is the focus of the fourth section of this book, which revolves around the question: *How are immigrants entering the precincts of power in New York City and Amsterdam?* In both New York City and Amsterdam, immigrants and their children are making strides in electoral politics, although in neither city have they achieved elected office proportionate to their representation in the city population. In his chapter on New York City, John Mollenkopf demonstrates how politically active immigrants have benefitted from the gains won by earlier waves of immigrants as well as the civil rights movement of the 1950s and 1960s. On top of that, ethnic politics are viewed as legitimate in New York City. In Amsterdam, in contrast, there was no civil rights movement comparable to the one in the United States, there is not a huge native minority group, and ethnic politics are not seen as at all legitimate. As Floris Vermeulen, Laure Michon, and Jean Tillie show, immigrant ethnic groups that have been most successful in mobilizing ethnic loyalties—Turks for instance—have turned out to be the least successful in gaining access to appointed executive political positions. While they display "civic virtues" and constitute a politically interested group, ethnic politics are seen as problematic and undesirable. Immigrants are not expected to represent ethnic political constituencies in Amsterdam; in New York City, in contrast, these constituencies constitute a rich resource.

The final section looks at the second generation, and another domain. The guiding question is: *How are the children of immigrants shaped by, but also changing, New York City's and Amsterdam's cultural life?* The second generation seems to be a source of cultural creativity and innovation in all cities of immigration, but how and why they manage to do so varies considerably. In his chapter on New York City, Philip Kasinitz points to a "second-generation advantage," that is, the ability to combine elements of their parents' and receiving society's cultures in new ways, on the one hand, and being slightly outside the dominant culture, on the other hand. In New York City, the U.S.-born children of immigrants today, as in the mid-twentieth century, have established a strong presence in the American arts, including the visual arts, music, film, and theater. In Amsterdam, immigrants find it harder to gain access to and become accepted into the dominant cultural scene, as Christine Delhaye, Sawitri Saharso, and Victor van de Ven demonstrate. This situation reflects local particularities including the place of New York City and Amsterdam in the global art scene, the presence or absence of welcoming structures shaped by earlier inflows of immigrants, the celebration or marginalization of diversity, and—again—the specific role played by the government.

The five themes shed light on New York City and Amsterdam as global hubs of immigration. It is clear that more research remains to be done to produce a fuller picture of each of these themes. We believe that this collection of essays reveals telling patterns and represents a step forward in bringing a comparative—transatlantic—perspective to our understanding of two major world cities that have been reshaped in striking ways by the massive immigration of recent years.

NOTES

1. Many provisions, for example schools and other educational facilities, tax exemptions for house owners, subsidies for poor renters, and so forth are strictly speaking not provided by the city, but by other governmental or non-governmental entities, and are therefore not dependent on Amsterdam's tax base.

2. It should be noted that until the closing years of the twentieth century, only a few people in Amsterdam referred to particular categories of immigrants as "Muslim." In fact, it is since the late 1990s that the Dutch have become aware that many newcomers are followers of the Muslim faith. In governmental statistics, there are still few if any references to Muslims per se. See the chapter by Uitermark, Duyvendak, and Rath in this volume.

3. See http://statline.cbs.nl/StatWeb/publication/?VW=T&DM=SLNL&PA=37296 ned&D1=a&D2=0,10,20,30,40,50,(l-1)-l&HD=120426-2109&HDR=G1&STB=T, accessed April 26, 2012, for national statistics in the Netherlands, and http://www.os.amsterdam.nl/tabel/7221/, accessed May 15, 2012, for Amsterdam statistics.

4. Foner (2013).

5. See http://www.os.amsterdam.nl/tabel/8746/, accessed May 15, 2012.

6. Lobo and Salvo (2013).

7. For comparisons of immigrants in U.S. and Canadian cities, see Bloemraad (2006) and Reitz (2003).

8. Mercer Human Resource Consulting Worldwide Quality of Living Survey 2011, http://www.mercer.com/press-releases/quality-of-living-report-2011#City-Rankings, accessed April 23, 2012. In the same list, New York City ranked 47.

9. Go to http://www.iamsterdam.nl/.

10. See http://www.os.amsterdam.nl/tabel/7221/, accessed May 15, 2012.

11. Surinamese of Indian origin—the so-called Hindustani Surinamese—flocked to The Hague. See Van Niekerk (2000).

12. See http://www.os.amsterdam.nl/tabel/7221/, accessed May 15, 2012.

REFERENCES

Alba, Richard, and Victor Nee. 2003. *Remaking the American Mainstream: Assimilation and Contemporary Immigration*. Cambridge, MA: Harvard University Press.

Alba, Richard, and Mary Waters (eds.). 2011. *The Next Generation: Immigrant Youth in a Comparative Perspective*. New York: NYU Press.

Alexander, Michael. 2007. *Cities and Labour Immigration: Comparing Policy Responses in Amsterdam, Paris, Rome and Tel Aviv*. Aldershot: Ashgate.

Benton-Short, Lisa, Marie Price, and Samantha Friedman. 2005. "Globalization from Below: The Ranking of Global Immigrant Cities." *International Journal of Urban and Regional Research* 29 (4): 945–59.

Bertossi, Christophe, and Jan Willem Duyvendak. 2012. "National Models of Immigrant Integration: The Costs for Comparative Research." *Comparative European Politics* 10 (3): 237–47.

Bloemraad, Irene. 2006. *Becoming a Citizen: Incorporation of Immigrants and Refugees in the United States and Canada*. Berkeley: University of California Press.

Body-Gendrot, Sophie, and Marco Martiniello (eds.). 2000. *Minorities in European Cities: The Dynamics of Social Integration and Social Exclusion at the Neighborhood Level*. Basingstoke: Palgrave Macmillan.

Bovenkerk, Frank. 1984. "Rassen of klassen? De politieke economie van de gastarbeid." *Intermediair* 20 (47): 35–41.

Bovenkerk, Frank, Robert Miles, and Giles Verbunt. 1991. "Comparative Studies of Migration and Racism in Western Europe: A Critical Appraisal." *International Migration Review* 26 (3): 927–39.

Brettell, Caroline. 2003. "Bringing the City Back In: Cities as Contexts for Incorporation," in Nancy Foner (ed.), *American Arrivals: Anthropology Engages the New Immigration*. Santa Fe, NM: School for American Research Press.

Chua, Amy. 2007. *Day of Empire: How Hyperpowers Rise to Global Dominance—and Why They Fall*. New York: Anchor Books.

Crul, Maurice, and Jennifer Holdaway. 2009. "Children of Immigrants in Schools in New York and Amsterdam: The Factors Shaping Attainment." *Teachers College Record* 11: 1476–507.

Crul, Maurice, and John Mollenkopf (eds.). 2012. *The Changing Face of World Cities: Young Adult Children of Immigrants in Europe and the United States*. New York: Russell Sage Foundation.

Drennan, Matthew. 2010. "Economy," in Kenneth Jackson (ed.), *The Encyclopedia of New York City*. New Haven, CT: Yale University Press.

Favell, Adrian. 2001. "Integration Policy and Integration Research in Europe: A Review and Critique," in Alexander Aleinikoff and Douglas Klusmeyer (eds.), *Citizenship Today: Global Perspectives and Practices*. Washington, DC: Brookings Institute.

Foner, Nancy. 2000. *From Ellis Island to JFK: New York's Two Great Waves of Immigration*. New Haven, CT: Yale University Press.

———. 2005. *In a New Land: A Comparative View of Immigration*. New York: NYU Press.

———. 2007. "How Exceptional is New York? Migration and Multiculturalism in the Empire City." *Ethnic and Racial Studies* 30: 999–1023.

——— (ed.). 2013. *One Out of Three: Immigrant New York in the Twenty-First Century*. New York: Columbia University Press.

Foner, Nancy, and Roger Waldinger. 2013. "New York and Los Angeles as Immigrant Destinations: Contrasts and Convergence," in David Halle and Andrew Beveridge (eds.), *New York and Los Angeles: The Uncertain Future*. New York: Oxford University Press.

Garbaye, Romain. 2006. *Getting into Local Power: The Politics of Ethnic Minorities in British and French Cities*. Oxford: Blackwell.

Hochschild, Jennifer, and John Mollenkopf (eds.). 2009. *Bringing Outsiders In: Transatlantic Perspectives on Immigrant Political Incorporation.* Ithaca, NY: Cornell University Press.

Joppke, Christian. 2008. *Immigration and the Nation-State: The United States, Germany, and Great Britain.* Oxford: Oxford University Press.

Kasinitz, Philip, John Mollenkopf, Mary C. Waters, and Jennifer Holdaway. 2008. *Inheriting the City: The Children of Immigrants Come of Age.* Cambridge, MA: Harvard University Press.

Kloosterman, Robert C., and Jan Rath (eds.). 2003. *Immigrant Entrepreneurs: Venturing Abroad in the Age of Globalization.* Oxford/New York: Berg/NYU Press.

Lobo, Arun Peter, and Joseph Salvo. 2013. "A Portrait of New York's Immigrant Melange," in Nancy Foner (ed.), *One Out of Three: Immigrant New York in the Twenty-First Century.* New York: Columbia University Press.

Mollenkopf, John. 1999. "Urban Political Conflicts and Alliances: New York and Los Angeles Compared," in Charles Hirschman, Philip Kasinitz, and Josh DeWind (eds.), *The Handbook of International Migration.* New York: Russell Sage Foundation.

———. 2000. "Assimilating Immigrants in Amsterdam; A Perspective from New York." *Netherlands' Journal of Social Sciences* 36: 15–34.

Nell, Liza, and Jan Rath (eds.). 2009. *Ethnic Amsterdam: Immigrants and Urban Change in the Twentieth Century.* Amsterdam: Amsterdam University Press.

O+S (Onderzoek en Statistiek Amsterdam). 2010. *Amsterdam in Cijfers 2010.* Amsterdam: Dienst Onderzoek en Statistiek.

Paulle, Bowen. 2005. *Anxiety and Intimidation in the Bronx and the Bijlmer: An Ethnographic Comparison of Two Schools.* Amsterdam: Dutch University Press.

———. 2007. "Van kleur naar klasse: desegregatie in het onderwijs," in Lex Veldboer, Jan Willem Duyvendak, and Carolien Bouw (eds.), *De mixfactor: integratie en segregatie in Nederland.* Meppel: Boom Lemma.

Penninx, Rinus, Karen Kraal, Marco Martiniello, and Steven Vertovec (eds.) 2004. *Citizenship in European Cities: Immigrants, Local Politics and Integration Policies.* Aldershot: Ashgate.

Price, Maria, and Lisa Benton-Short (eds.). 2008. *Migrants to the Metropolis: The Rise of Immigrant Gateway Cities.* Syracuse, NY: Syracuse University Press.

Rath, Jan. 1991. *Minorisering: De Sociale Constructie van "Etnische Minderheden."* Amsterdam Sua.

———. 1999. "The Netherlands: A Dutch Treat for Anti-Social Families and Immigrant Ethnic Minorities," in Mike Cole and Gareth Dale (eds.), *The European Union and Migrant Labour.* Oxford: Berg.

———. 2011. "Debating Multiculturalism: Europe's Reaction in Context." *Harvard International Review*, January 6. http://hir.harvard.edu/debating-multiculturalism, accessed November 1, 2011.

——— (ed.). 2002. *Unraveling the Rag Trade: Immigrant Entrepreneurship in Seven World Cities.* New York: NYU Press.

Reitz, Jeffrey (ed.). 2003. *Host Societies and the Reception of Immigrants.* San Diego: Center for Comparative Immigration Studies.

Sabagh, Georges, and Mehdi Bozorgmehr. 2003. "From 'Give Me Your Poor' to 'Save Our State': New York and Los Angeles as Immigrant Cities and Regions," in David Halle (ed.), *New York and Los Angeles.* Chicago: University of Chicago Press.

Schain, Martin. 2008. *The Politics of Immigration in France, Britain, and the United States: A Comparative Study.* Basingstoke: Palgrave Macmillan.

Schuster, John. 1999. *Poortwachters over Immigranten. Het Debat over Immigratie in het Naoorlogse Groot-Brittanië en Nederland.* Amsterdam: Het Spinhuis.

Singer, Audrey, Susan Hardwick, and Caroline Brettell (eds.). 2008. *Twentieth-First Century Gateways: Immigrant Incorporation in Suburban America.* Washington, DC: Brookings Institution Press.

Van Niekerk, Mies. 2000. *De krekel en de mier. Fabels en feiten over maatschappelijke stijging van Creoolse en Hindoestaanse Surinamers in Nederland.* Amsterdam: Het Spinhuis.

Vink, Anja. 2010. *De Mythe Van De Zwarte School.* Amsterdam: Meulenhoff.

Waldinger, Roger. 1996. "From Ellis Island to LAX: Immigrant Prospects in the American City." *International Migration Review* 30: 1078–86.

———. 2001. "Strangers at the Gates," in Roger Waldinger (ed.), *Strangers at the Gates: New Immigrants in Urban America.* Berkeley: University of California Press.

Zolberg, Aristide, and Long Litt Woon. 1999. "Why Islam Is Like Spanish: Cultural Incorporation in Europe and the United States." *Politics & Society* 27: 5–38.

PART I

How Has the Immigrant Past Shaped the Immigrant Present in New York City and Amsterdam?

Historians have related the past to the present in numerous ways, the most familiar of which may be Hegel's vision that the present is a necessary outcome of the past. In *The Poverty of Historicism* (1957), Karl Popper attacked this teleological vision as the core of totalitarian ideologies that claim that the realization of their (communist or fascist) ideas is part of a grand historical plan. The Hegelian idea of the present as the inevitable outcome of an unfolding history has few adherents today. This of course does not mean that the present is unrelated to the past. Path-dependency is a key concept in numerous academic disciplines today: many historians, sociologists, and economists, among others, think in terms of historical continuity and causality, often under the banner of (neo)institutionalism. Nancy Foner has labeled this approach "then to now": an over-time perspective that examines the past to help account for the present (Foner 2006). She contrasts this with the "then and now" approach in which historical episodes are compared to the present in the search for similarities and differences—but not to explain the present by what happened in the past.

In her chapter, Foner's treatment of New York City's history of immigration embraces the "then to now" approach. She explains that this implies not just the idea that "history matters" (which few would disagree with) but a more specific dynamic: "The way migrant inflows in one period, in a dialectical process, change the very social, economic, political, and cultural context that greets—and affects the experiences and incorporation—of the next wave." The past here is more than just the background to contemporary developments: in one way or another the past *affects* the present. The mechanisms by which the past lives on are spelled out in Foner's chapter. First, institutions developed to deal with earlier waves of immigration continue to function in the integration of new waves of immigrants. Alongside this pivotal factor, New York's public culture and ethos—heavily influenced by earlier Italian and Jewish immigrants—continue to contribute to the city's openness to newcomers.

Foner's contribution shows us that both institutions and public culture matter. At the same time, she shows that a specific interpretation of the past gives the institutions and the immigrant-friendly public culture their content and legitimacy: the municipality as well as numerous immigrant organizations constantly mobilize the notion of New York City as the city of immigration *par excellence*, a story that celebrates the city's multicultural history and the ongoing contributions of immigrants to the city's wealth and cosmopolitan ambiance. In doing so, Foner shows that not only "objective" factors such as institutions but "subjective" evaluations of immigration have long contributed to making New York City a welcoming destination for new arrivals. This positive reading of past immigration is not set in stone or simply given by the fact of New York City's history, however. It is mobilized and remembered in specific ways. Though production of "collective memory" is not the focus of her chapter, Foner's discussion hints at how a public culture that values immigration can draw on positive collective memories of it, relating "then to now."

Leo Lucassen's contribution—"To Amsterdam: Migration Past and Present"—is a clear example of the contrasting "then and now" approach. As Amsterdam's history of immigration is not an unbroken one, Lucassen chooses to compare periods. He shows that the post–World War II wave of immigration can be compared—to a certain extent—to the seventeenth-century influx of immigrants into Amsterdam. Though this comparison can easily be misread as "nothing new under the sun," his argument is actually the opposite: "The long period of low immigration, well over a century, explains why the large-scale post-1960s immigration of guest workers from Southern Europe, Turkey, and North Africa as well as colonial migrants from Suriname was seen as unprecedented." In the public imagination in the immediate postwar years, neither the Netherlands nor the city of Amsterdam were notable as places of arrival, as magnets for immigration. The immigration waves of the 1960s were thus considered unprecedented, as not part of a longer history. Though this "then and now" approach can reveal similarities between Amsterdam's present and certain periods in its past—particularly its seventeenth-century heyday of immigration— Lucassen argues that the "time distance" is too great for this earlier history to have a real impact on current developments: "Migrations of centuries ago have had little direct effect on the institution or culture that have confronted the more recent postwar arrivals. Indeed, it is the very forgetting of the immigration in the far-off past [. . .] that have helped shape attitudes toward and the reaction to immigrants and their children in the contemporary period."

Whereas there is an "objective" argument, as Lucassen proposes, that immigrants who came to Amsterdam centuries ago have not created or influenced institutions available to contemporary arrivals, his "subjective" argument concerning the lack of collective memory due to the distance of time raises some questions. Lucassen of course observes that in Amsterdam "there is no shared memory, as in New York, where third-generation descendants of those who came in the great wave of the early twentieth century can literally shake hands with immigrants of the more recent wave." But what of the imagined past, the collective memory of the seventeenth century as a time when immigrants who made Amsterdam great and contributed to the so-called golden age of Dutch economic, political, and cultural power arrived—a memory "from Spinoza to the present" that repeatedly appears in contemporary public debates? Has there really been a "very forgetting of the immigration of the far-off past"? Indeed, Lucassen writes that the "collective memory of earlier migration is [. . . of] successful ('good') migrants then, like the Huguenots, rich Antwerp merchants, and Sephardic Jews, and of the 'bad' migrants now." By showing that episodes from the past—even the far-away past—are mobilized in contemporary debates, Lucassen suggests that the (imagined) past does affect the present. Though the comparison with New York City shows that an unbroken history of immigration strongly facilitates the mobilization of the immigrant past, a more episodic history does not necessarily hinder this dynamic.

In some cases, the boundary between a "then to now" and "then and now" approach becomes somewhat fluid. History can impact the present, even when there is no continuous "from then to now" line.

As for institutional mechanisms, as Lucassen notes, Amsterdam lacks an institutional infrastructure with roots in a not-too-distant immigrant past like that found in contemporary New York City. New York, as the chapter by Foner observes, is home to many institutions—from settlement houses to hospitals and ethnic politics and a lively ethnic press—that were developed or transformed by turn-of-the-twentieth-century Jewish and Italian immigrants and now provide services and opportunities for many newcomers and in some cases models for them to emulate and legitimacy for their own organizational efforts. The institutional weight of immigrant history in New York also strongly comes out in other chapters in this volume, especially in relation to politics (Mollenkopf) and the arts (Kasinitz). In Amsterdam, institutions based in the past—though not an immigrant past—have been important. It has been argued that the Dutch history of "pillarization"—the organization of society along denominational (Protestant, Catholic, humanist) lines in which each group had its own institutions, including schools, political parties, newspapers, and hospitals— played a somewhat comparable role to the immigrant-based infrastructure in New York by encouraging new immigrants to make use of public subsidies to create their own institutions and organizations (Rath 1991). In examining the institutional framework that serves to integrate immigrants into society, we thus need to keep in mind two caveats. First, there is the need to look beyond the (lack of continuity in) institutions specifically set up for immigrants and examine other relevant infrastructures established in the past. Second, institutions do not necessarily serve the roles for which they were intended. Muslim immigrants to the Netherlands, for example, have been unable to make much use of the remnants of the pillarized institutional framework theoretically available to them (Rath 1991) partly owing to the decline of the pillarized sytem itself but also to changed Dutch attitudes to pillarization. Muslim immigrants began to arrive in large numbers in the 1960s just as Dutch society was embarking on a radical course of secularization and depillarization.

Native Dutch became outspoken in their criticisms of the "pillarized" past and actively tried to discourage immigrants from using its legal framework (though they could not forbid immigrants from doing so as far as the legal framework remained in place, e.g., state subsidies for religious schools) (Duyvendak 2011).

This discussion of pillarization raises an additional issue. The two chapters in this section were written to focus specifically on how the immigrant past has affected the immigrant present in New York City and Amsterdam, but a broader question arises as to how history, more generally, has influenced attitudes toward and incorporation patterns of contemporary immigrants in the two cities. If the history of pillarization is relevant in Amsterdam, in New York, as Foner has considered elsewhere, the broader history of internal slavery in the United States and mid-twentieth-century civil rights reforms have clearly shaped the immigrant experience today (e.g., Foner and Alba 2010; Waters, this volume). In the Dutch case, immigration history may not play an important role in contemporary debates on immigrant integration but "history" more generally does. Numerous politicians and leaders of opinion have in fact argued that new immigrants should become well versed in Dutch history, the idea being that this would facilitate their integration in two ways: the native Dutch would become more welcoming with the knowledge that newcomers are eager to learn about the Netherlands and immigrants would be able to orient themselves in their new society more easily. While the importance of history is a recurrent theme in contemporary Dutch debates on national identity and integration, critics wonder just how a shared knowledge of a—very native—Dutch past would help immigrants integrate. In fact, Rogier van Reekum (2012) has argued that the version of the past currently being promoted by many Dutch politicians, in which immigrants are virtually invisible, seems to contribute to the exclusion of newcomers from mainstream Dutch society. As the chapters by Foner and Lucassen show, the mobilization of history can result in a positive climate for immigrants. But it all depends on what—and how—history is collectively remembered.

JAN WILLEM DUYVENDAK

REFERENCES

Duyvendak, Jan Willem. 2011. *The Politics of Home: Belonging and Nostalgia in Western Europe and the United States*. Basingstoke: Palgrave.

Foner, Nancy. 2006. "Then *and* Now or Then *to* Now: Immigration to New York in Contemporary and Historical Perspective." *Journal of American Ethnic History* 25: 33–47.

Foner, Nancy, and Richard Alba. 2010. "Immigration and the Legacies of the Past: The Impact of Slavery and the Holocaust on Contemporary Immigrants in the United States and Western Europe." *Comparative Studies in Society and History* 52 (4): 798–819.

Popper, Karl. 1957. *The Poverty of Historicism*. London: Routledge.

Rath, Jan. 1991. *Minorisering: de sociale constructie van "etnische minderheden."* Amsterdam: SUA.

Van Reekum, Rogier. 2012. "As Nation, People and Public Collide: Enacting Dutchness in Public Discourse." *Nations and Nationalism* 18: 583–602.

1

Immigration History and the Remaking of New York

NANCY FONER

New York is America's quintessential immigrant city. It has long been a major gateway for the nation's new arrivals and is a leading receiving center today. It is fitting that the two most powerful symbols of immigration in the United States—the Statue of Liberty and Ellis Island— stand in New York City's harbor. Millions of southern and eastern European immigrants passed through Ellis Island's halls a hundred years ago, and many remained in New York. In 1910, 41 percent of the city's residents were foreign born. In 2010, after more than four decades of heavy immigration, the proportion of foreign born—37 percent—was nearly as high, although the sheer size of the city's immigrant population, now slightly over three million, is larger than ever before.

Throughout its history, immigration has been a fundamental feature of New York City's population, institutions, and identity. From the very beginning in the seventeenth century, when New York City was a Dutch colonial outpost, it was a multicultural immigrant city—according to one account, 18 languages were then spoken in the streets of New Amsterdam at a time when its total population was perhaps 500 (Shorto 2005). In later eras, as Nathan Glazer and Daniel Moynihan (1970) note, immigrants came two by two—the Germans and Irish dominating the immigrant inflow in the mid-nineteenth century and Jews and Italians at the turn of the twentieth century. Since the late 1960s, New York has been in the midst of what, in absolute numbers, is the greatest wave in its immigration history. The newcomers now come from all over the world, with most arriving from Asia, Latin America, and the Caribbean.

How has New York's immigration history influenced the experiences of immigrants in the present period? My own earlier work applied a comparative perspective to get at aspects of this question. It compared contemporary immigrant New Yorkers and those a hundred years ago to dispel myths and nostalgic memories about immigrant folk heroes and heroines of an earlier era as well as to understand what is new—or the same—about immigration today (Foner 2000, 2005). In this chapter, I adopt a different approach to understanding the role of history: what I have called a then-to-now perspective that looks at changes that have taken place in New York City over time (Foner 2006). This is not just a question of path dependence in the sense that "history matters," or that earlier conditions affect the trajectory of subsequent paths. A then-to-now perspective, of the kind that I use here, points to a more specific dynamic: the way migrant inflows in one period, in a dialectical process, change the very social, economic, political, and cultural context that greets—and affects the experiences and incorporation of—the next wave. In the New York context, this approach involves examining how successive waves of migrants have transformed social and political institutions and cultural patterns in the city, remaking the New York mainstream, to adopt Richard Alba and Victor Nee's (2003) phrase.

In analyzing these processes, this chapter focuses on a period that stretches from the end of the nineteenth century, when the last great wave of immigration began, to the start of the twenty-first century, when the recent large wave is still going strong. I take up several related themes that reveal how an understanding of historical dynamics can explain or illuminate a variety of contemporary patterns involving and affecting present-day immigrants. I begin with a fundamental question: how the history of immigration to New York City has played a role in creating a relatively welcoming context of reception for today's immigrants. I then examine how institutions that were developed or transformed by Jewish and Italian immigrants and their children in an earlier era continue to serve, and sometimes provide a model for, current newcomers. There is also the role of longer-established groups—including African American and Puerto Rican internal migrants of the early and mid-twentieth century—as hosts for recent arrivals.

Next, I consider the public culture and cultural ethos that suffuse New York life and provide a backdrop for those becoming New Yorkers today. New York's public culture and what one might call its cultural ethos continue to reflect strong Italian and especially Jewish influences—at the same time as recent immigrants add their own distinctive elements. Most of the chapter is concerned with the impact of what, at least by New York standards, is a relatively distant past, yet historical changes in more recent times also need to be taken into account. Because the contemporary immigration now spans a nearly 50-year period, I conclude by considering how the immigration waves of the 1960s, 1970s, and 1980s—and replenishment of immigrant populations—have changed the context that the very newest arrivals face when they enter New York in the early twenty-first century.

New York City as a Long-Established Gateway

New York City has always been an immigrant mecca. To use Audrey Singer's (2004) term, it is a continuous gateway, or long-established destination for immigrants. Throughout the twentieth century, around a fifth or more of the city's population was foreign born; even at its lowest ebb, in 1970, after a several-decade lull in mass immigration, 18 percent of New Yorkers were born abroad.[1] Since then, the figure has been on the rise, standing at 37 percent in 2010 (see table 1.1).

These figures reflect a series of different inflows. At the beginning of the twentieth century, New York's foreign-born population was heavily Jewish and Italian. By 1920, Russian Jewish and Italian immigrants, who had been arriving in massive numbers since the 1880s, made up about 44 percent of the city's foreign-born population—one out of six of all city residents, or nearly 900,000 people. Altogether, immigrants and their U.S.-born children constituted a stunning 76 percent of New York City's population—a figure considerably higher than it is today, when the figure is an estimated 55 percent (Lobo and Salvo 2013).

Immigration from eastern and southern Europe was all but cut off by federal legislation in the early 1920s, but the city subsequently was on the receiving end of a massive internal migration—of African Americans from the South between World War I and the 1960s and Puerto Ricans after World War II. (As U.S. citizens by birth, island-born Puerto

Table 1.1. Foreign-Born Population of New York City, 1900–2010

Year	Total Population (in thousands)	Foreign-Born Population (in thousands)	Percentage of Foreign Born in New York City	Percentage of All U.S. Foreign Born in New York City
1900	3,437.2	1,270.1	37.0	12.2
1910	4,766.9	1,944.4	40.8	14.3
1920	5,620.0	2,028.2	36.1	14.5
1930	6,930.4	2,358.7	34.0	16.5
1940	7,455.0	2,138.7	28.7	18.3
1950	7,892.0	1,860.9	23.6	17.8
1960	7,783.3	1,558.7	20.0	16.0
1970	7,894.9	1,437.1	18.2	14.9
1980	7,071.6	1,670.2	23.6	11.9
1990	7,322.6	2,082.9	28.4	10.5
2000	8,008.3	2,871.0	35.9	9.2
2010	8,185.3	3.046.5	37.2	7.6

Source: Foner (2000); Lobo and Salvo (2013).

Table 1.2. Top Ten Source Countries of New York City Foreign Born, 2010

Country of Birth	Number	Percent
Dominican Republic	378,199	12.4
China	351,314	11.5
Mexico	187,086	6.1
Jamaica	169,863	5.6
Guyana	138,549	4.5
Ecuador	138,097	4.5
Haiti	97,516	3.2
Trinidad and Tobago	84,347	2.8
India	72,803	2.4
Russia	70,123	2.3
Total Foreign Born	3,046,451	100.0

Source: Lobo and Salvo (2013).

Ricans are not considered immigrants.) In 1960, the city was more than one-fifth black and Hispanic, a dramatic change from 1920 when the figure was only around 3 percent. Large-scale immigration from abroad began again in the late 1960s, in large part owing to the passage of the Immigration and Nationality Act of 1965. At the beginning of the twenty-first century, immigrants from the Dominican Republic, China, Mexico, and Jamaica were the top four groups, but there were substantial numbers from other Latin American, Asian, and Caribbean countries as well as from Europe and, in recent years, from Africa, too. In fact, in 2010, the four largest groups were only a little over a third of all the foreign born, and no other country accounted for more than 5 percent (table 1.2).

This continuous inflow is one of the factors that makes New York a relatively welcoming place for contemporary immigrants in contrast to many other cities and towns in the United States, which have less experience with immigration. I say one factor because others also are involved. These include the remarkable ethnic diversity of the contemporary foreign-born population—and that every major ethnoracial group in the city (blacks, Hispanics, whites, and Asians) has a sizable proportion of immigrants;[2] the substantial number of high-skilled immigrants (in 2010, slightly more than a quarter of the foreign born had a college degree or more); a segmented political system, "organized for mobilization around ethnic group lines, and a political culture that sanctions, indeed encourages, newcomers to engage in ethnic politics" (Waldinger 1996: 1084); and a broad range of institutions, from the public educational system to strong labor unions, that provide a range of services and programs that assist immigrants and their children (Foner 2005, 2007). This said, the long history of immigration in the twentieth century is of great significance in explaining why New York is an immigrant-friendly city. In New York, the post-1965 immigration started from a fairly high level. Or to put it another way, immigration to the city represents a gradual increase, not a sudden and jarring growth spurt.

It is not just that New Yorkers are used to immigration and ethnic succession. Because of the continued inflows—as well as the huge size of the present foreign-born population—the vast majority of New Yorkers have a close immigrant connection. If they are not immigrants themselves, they have a parent, grandparent, or great-grandparent who is. Many of the nearly 1.1 million Jewish New Yorkers have grandparents or great-grandparents who arrived at the turn of the twentieth century from eastern Europe; hundreds of thousands have roots in Italy and Ireland. Indeed, New York's white population is dominated by first-, second-, and third-generation Catholics (Irish and Italians) and Jews (Mollenkopf 1999: 419). Although Puerto Ricans are not considered immigrants—those born on the island are U.S. citizens at birth—the more than 700,000 Puerto Rican New Yorkers have their origins outside the mainland United States. Moreover, many black New Yorkers are descended from immigrants who arrived in the early twentieth century from what was then the British Caribbean.

Institutions

Today's immigrants may not be aware of it, but they live in a city containing a wide array of mainstream institutions that owe their existence, or many of their features, to earlier European immigrants and their children. In their modern guise, these institutions provide services and opportunities for many new arrivals and, in some cases, give legitimacy to their own organizational efforts and offer models which some seek to emulate.

New York, it has been said, is a union town, a feature which owes much to the legacy of earlier European immigration. A high percentage of New Yorkers are union members—higher than the share in any other major U.S. city—and unions are an influential force on the city's political scene.[3] Some of the most powerful labor unions in New York City, with large numbers of immigrant members, were founded by European immigrants in the early twentieth century, with the lead often taken by those steeped in American Jewish radicalism. Many Chinese immigrants in the city, for example, belong to a national labor union (Workers United) that incorporated earlier unions, among them the International Ladies Garment Workers' Union (ILGWU), whose roots go back to the turn-of-the-twentieth-century organizing of Jewish and Italian workers to improve conditions in New York City's garment industry; the ILGWU's long-time Russian-born Jewish president, David Dubinsky (who held office from 1932 to 1966), was an influential figure in New

York's labor and political circles. Another Russian-born Jewish immigrant, Leon J. Davis, founded a small (heavily Jewish) pharmacists' union in New York City in the 1930s that—after an organizing drive of black and Puerto Rican hospital workers in the late 1950s—eventually turned into a large and powerful healthcare workers union, whose members now include substantial numbers of West Indian immigrants (Fink and Greenberg 1989; Foner 2002). Davis served as president of the union for half a century; his successors include a Puerto Rican and the current African American leader.

The hospitals immigrants go to and the congregations where they worship also often date back to the immigrant past. New Yorkers of all class and ethnic backgrounds seek care at major nonprofit hospitals whose names indicate their Jewish origins.[4] Maimonides Medical Center in Borough Park, Brooklyn, to mention one of many with roots in the eastern European immigration, now takes care of patients from nearby Pakistani, Chinese, Indian, Polish, Russian Jewish, and Latino immigrant communities; the hospital was founded by a Jewish immigrant from Minsk at the beginning of the twentieth century.[5] Elsewhere in Brooklyn, in the heart of the West Indian community, Interfaith Medical Center was created by a merger that included Brooklyn Jewish Hospital, which was founded at the turn of the twentieth century by Jewish doctors barred from other hospitals to meet the needs of the growing Jewish immigrant population. Beth Israel Medical Center, which now serves large swathes of lower Manhattan, was incorporated in 1890 by a group of Orthodox eastern European Jewish immigrants on the Lower East Side because hospitals, at the time, would not treat patients who had been in the city less than a year.

Synagogues established by earlier Russian Jewish immigrants or their children have attracted recent Jewish immigrants from the former Soviet Union in some neighborhoods. (In at least one case, the Flushing Jewish Center in Queens, a synagogue was sold to a Korean church; in another instance, a synagogue, Temple Israel of Jamaica, Queens, was turned over to a Muslim mosque [Avins 2008].) An increasing number of Catholic churches, built for Irish or Italian congregations, conduct masses in Spanish as well as other languages. In the mid-1990s, 14 churches in Brooklyn and Queens celebrated masses in French or Haitian Creole, and Catholic churches in Washington Heights have turned into Dominican congregations, holding mass in Spanish and inviting religious officials from the Dominican Republic to participate in church activities. With the miniscule number of Italians left in East Harlem, the Church of Our Lady of Mount Carmel stopped holding Italian-language masses in 2004; it is now the site of a Haitian celebration of Our Lady of Mount Carmel every July, in which Haitians make a pilgrimage from their neighborhoods in the city and metropolitan area for the feast day of the Madonna (McAlister 1998; Garland 2006).

It has been many years since New York City's public schools were dominated by the children of Italian and Jewish immigrants, or the teaching staff was a Jewish stronghold. Today, only 14 percent of the students are non-Hispanic whites of any kind. Nonetheless, Jewish influence lingers on in the closure of the public schools (and the City University of New York) on the Jewish fall holidays of Rosh Hashanah and Yom Kippur, a practice instituted in 1960 when Jewish pupils constituted a third of the public school system's enrollment, Jewish teachers 45 percent of the total, and Jews were the great majority among the school principals (Lederhendler 2001: 14). The immigrant past also continues to have an impact on the City University of New York, where the majority of the 239,000 undergraduate students in 2011 were first- or second- generation immigrants. CUNY was not established by immigrants, though it was a stepping stone to upward mobility for thousands of second- and third-generation Jews and Italians. Today, many faculty members and administrators are descendants of the earlier wave (myself among them). Moreover, successful second-generation Jewish alumni, in particular, have been generous donors, and, as a result, important CUNY institutions bear their names, among them, the Weissman School of Arts and Sciences (at Baruch College) and the Sophie Davis School of Biomedical Education (at City College).

One of the most direct links to Jewish immigrant history is the settlement houses on the Lower East Side developed in the late nineteenth century to provide various services, such as classes, off-the-street playgrounds, and visiting nurses. Several of these settlement houses—including the Educational Alliance, University Settlement, and Henry Street Settlement—are alive and well, offering an array of social services, arts programs, and health services to current Lower East Side residents, including Chinese and Dominican immigrants and their children. Another organization, the Hebrew Immigrant Aid Society (HIAS), which was founded to help earlier Russian Jewish immigrants at Ellis Island, played a large role in assisting and resettling post-1970 Jewish immigrants from the former Soviet Union. Now that the population of Jewish refugees has diminished, HIAS has directed its resources to assisting other refugees as well.

Interestingly, the developer planning the controversial Muslim community center near Ground Zero, Sharif El-Gamal, consciously modeled it after Jewish community centers in New York—the 92nd Street Y (Young Men's and Young Women's Hebrew Association) on Manhattan's Upper East Side and Jewish Community Center (JCC) on the Upper West Side—that have their roots in organizations founded by German Jewish immigrants in the late 1800s and that now provide educational, cultural, and recreational programs for the broader New York community. Indeed, his daughters learned to swim at the JCC, where he was a member (Barnard and Haughney 2010).

"Institutions" often refers to organizations founded for specific purposes, but the term can have other meanings as well. The ethnic press and ethnic politics in New York City may be considered institutions in the sense that they involve practices and customs that are significant in the life of the city. Although both have seen numerous changes in the recent period, at the same time they represent, in many ways, a continuation of practices that were institutionalized and played a key role in earlier immigrant eras. In this way, the immigrant past has contributed to New Yorkers' comfort with—and serves to legitimize—practices in the immigrant present that have come to be seen as part of longstanding New York traditions.

Much has been written about the lively Yiddish press in turn-of-the-twentieth-century New York City; the combined circulation of Yiddish dailies in New York was over 500,000 in 1916, the most popular among them the socialist *Forverts* (Forward). Founded in 1897, and edited for many years by the legendary Abraham Cahan, the *Forward* became "the pacemaker of Yiddish journalism"; its peak circulation, in the 1920s, hovered around a quarter million (Michels 2005; Rischin 1962). New York's most popular Italian-language newspaper was *Il Progresso*, founded in 1880; it sold around 100,000 copies a day in the early twentieth century (Mangione and Morreale 1992). The *Forward* still exists, with biweekly Yiddish and weekly English-language editions, but *Il Progresso* shut down in the 1980s.

Despite competition from television, the ethnic press has experienced a boom in the wake of the massive recent immigration, and the city now has the largest number of ethnic publications in its history (Scher 2001). In 2001, at least 198 magazines and newspapers were publishing in 36 languages, including seven New York daily newspapers in Chinese with a combined circulation of half a million (Scher 2001). A free weekly publication for the West Indian community, *Caribbean Life*, has a circulation of 97,000, and the *Gleaner* newspaper in Jamaica has followed its readers to New York with a weekly North American edition to serve them. Like Jewish and Italian newspapers of an earlier era, many ethnic publications today "interpret American life for their readers, chronicle the struggles of the immigrants here—and take an active role in helping their readers think of themselves as political actors and as a political constituency" (Scher 2001).

Ethnic politics has long been a central element of New York City politics, and no group "finds challenge unexpected or outrageous" (Glazer and Moynihan 1970: xxx; see Mollenkopf, this volume). The Irish, of course, were masters of the art; under Celtic tutelage, as Steven Erie (1988: 4) puts it, Tammany Hall, a once-powerful but now-defunct New York City political organization, ran the city (with minor exceptions) from 1874 to 1933. By the 1880s, Tammany Hall had consolidated its control over the Democratic Party in the city so completely that the two organizations were indistinguishable (McNickle 1993: 7). In the early twentieth century, Tammany adapted to, benefited from, and reinforced ethnic political identities as it moved to install and promote friendly leaders from rising constituencies, especially the substantial Jewish voting population that threatened to swell the vote of socialists (Mollenkopf 1992: 81).[6]

Tammany politician and Manhattan borough president John F. Ahearn, who built his career on the heavily Jewish Lower East Side, was said to eat corned beef and kosher meat "with equal nonchalance . . . and it's all the same to him whether he takes his hat off in church or pulls it down over his ears in the synagogue" (quoted in Barrett 2012: 192–93). (Italians at this time were much less of a threat to Tammany Hall; as late as 1911, only 15,000 Italians were registered voters in the city [McNickle 1993: 48].) Whether the priorities of the immigrants were patronage and prestige, as in the case of the late-nine-teenth- and early-twentieth-century Irish, or protection from discrimi-nation and reforms to provide more equal access to jobs and power, in the case of mid-twentieth-century Jews, ethnicity was a way for aspir-ing leaders to mobilize their base, attain political representation, and contend to be part of the governing coalition, all the while shifting old alliances and creating new coalitions (McNickle 1993: 2; Mollenkopf and Sonenshein 2009: 77).

Political machines are certainly no longer what they used to be, and much else has changed about the structure of urban politics facing new ethnic minorities today. Yet ethnic politics is still very much part of the New York political scene and is shaping patterns of political incorpora-tion among the newer immigrants (Mollenkopf and Sonenshein 2009: 78). That long-established white groups, the Irish, Italians, and Jews, used "ethnic arithmetic" to pursue their goals and entry into the politi-cal system gives legitimacy to similar efforts by politicians of recent immigrant origin today as they seek to rally voters, build coalitions, and gain influence in the halls of power. Indeed, politicians descended from the earlier European waves also continue to make blatant ethnic appeals in a timeworn way. Mayor Michael Bloomberg, whose grandparents were Jews from eastern Europe, not only has made trips to Israel to woo the Jewish vote but, after two years in office in 2003, had already visited the Dominican Republic three times. In May 2005, he rolled out the first of his television campaign spots in Spanish.

New York's Public Culture and Cultural Ethos

New York City's public culture and cultural ethos bear the stamp of ear-lier European immigrants—and shape the context in which present-day immigrants are leaving their own mark.

I have already mentioned the Jewish holidays in the public schools as well as the ethnic flavor of New York City politics, with its Jewish and Italian influences. Indeed, the impact of the enormous Jewish commu-nity throughout the twentieth century in New York is no doubt a factor in the long-time liberal bent to New York City politics.

Admittedly, there has been a conservative swing in the so-called "Jewish vote" in recent years as Jews have moved in large number into the city's higher economic ranks, as many Jews, especially in the outer boroughs, have felt threatened by the increasing power of racial minorities (Mollenkopf 1992), and as the Orthodox Jewish population has grown. Yet, overall, in the twentieth century the Jewish influence on politics was markedly liberal. The left-wing political culture born a hundred years ago on the Lower East Side in Jewish socialism and the labor movement continued to hold a strong attraction to many children and grandchildren of Yiddish-speaking Jews into the 1960s (Michels 2005). In general, the Jewish labor movement took the lead, according to historian Joshua Freeman, in forging what he calls New York's "social democratic polity": "a diverse, working class, political community committed to affordable housing, health care, education, access to the arts, and civil rights" (quoted in Michels 2005: 256). Even today, when Jews are no longer as reliably liberal as they used to be—and other groups, most notably African Americans, are more reliably Democratic—Jews continue to make up a significant portion of the "white liberal" vote in affluent areas of the city like Manhattan's Upper West Side and Brooklyn's Park Slope and of spokespeople for liberal causes.

The large size and relative prosperity of New York City's Jewish population and the fading of prejudice against Jews have made the city a place where it is comfortable to be Jewish—where many Jews take Jewishness for granted (Lederhendler 2001). For the better part of the twentieth century, Jews (the overwhelming majority from eastern Europe) made up a quarter or more of the population of the city—a number and proportion far larger than any other major American city. Although as many Jews left for the suburbs their numbers have shrunk in recent years—from two million in the late 1950s to nearly 1.1 million in 2011—they are still a significant presence (Berger 2003; Cohen, Ukeles, and Miller 2012). This is relevant not only for third- and fourth-generation descendants of the earlier arrivals, but also for the not insignificant number of recent Jewish immigrants from the former Soviet Union and Israel and the small contingent from Latin America. (In 2006, there were a little under 200,000 immigrants from the former Soviet Union living in the city, most of them Jewish, and in 2000, around 22,000 Israelis.)

Indeed, Jews may feel more comfortable in New York than ever before (Glazer 1993). Until the 1950s, and often beyond, Jews faced harsh discrimination in and exclusion from elite occupations, work-places, and social clubs in New York City; they felt "at home in America" (Moore 1981) in their own, heavily Jewish, neighborhoods, in sectors of the economy they dominated, and in flourishing Jewish organizations. Now that Jews have entered, and been accepted in, virtually all main-stream elite institutions, this comfort level is true in most of them as well. For well-off and well-educated Jews—and there are high propor-tions of them today—this includes places like the New York Yacht Club and the University Club, two of the city's most prestigious private clubs, which as late as 1963 each told the *New York Times* that they had "at least one Jewish member" (Gray 2003). In the Upper East Side private girls' school my daughter attended, to give another example, there were hardly any Jews before World War II; today, in an environment where many of the girls are Jewish (or "half-Jewish," with one Jewish parent), *bar mitzvahs* and *bat mitzvahs* (Jewish coming-of-age rituals) have become part of the social calendar, as they have throughout New York City's elite private-school world.

The legacy of the Jewish as well as Italian immigration has affected other aspects of New York's culture. Cultural patterns from southern Italy and eastern Europe, to be sure, typically underwent significant change in the New York context and some customs, such as the *bat mitzvah* for Jewish daughters, are invented traditions that were created in the United States (Joselit 1994). Whether Old World cultural patterns were invented, transformed, or, in some cases preserved in traditional forms in New York, many have become part of New York's public cul-ture. Certainly this is the case with food. Pizza and bagels, to mention just two foods, have become dietary mainstays in New York, includ-ing among the children of contemporary immigrants and many of their parents as well. In a new ethnic twist, many Korean Americans and Chinese Americans now own bagel stores, and Ecuadorians and Ban-gladeshis (among others) pizza parlors (Gardner 2005). It is nothing unusual during Passover week for supermarkets to have special sections with food, including matzo and gefilte fish, displayed for the holiday. Even though many immigrants live in areas where this is not the case, they often work in neighborhoods where it is, and as part of their jobs (for example, as domestic workers) they may even have to prepare or serve the special dishes for their employers or those in their care.

Established Hosts

Another way that immigrant history lives on in the present is that earlier immigrants and their descendants often play the role of "hosts" to the new arrivals, passing on lessons about New York and the United States and shaping the newcomers' thinking and actions.

David Roediger and James Barrett argue that when Italians came to New York at the turn of the twentieth century, it was Irish American faces they often saw. As neighbors, coworkers, policemen, schoolteachers, priests, bartenders, union bosses, and landlords, Irish Americans introduced Italian immigrants to new values and taught them about U.S. racism and "the perils of being on the wrong side of the color line" (2004: 183; see also Barrett 2012). When Russian Jews, for their part, started to arrive on the Lower East Side, they came to a heavily German immigrant community—which served, in Tony Michels's words, as their gateway to America (2005: 42). German American socialist neighbors exerted a strong influence on Russian Jewish intellectuals, providing practical assistance and organizational models as well as exposing them to new ideologies.

The entrenched hosts in post-1965 New York often have been African Americans and Puerto Ricans who, as noted, were themselves migrants, or descendants of migrants, who came to the city in the mid-twentieth century from the South and the Caribbean. Mittelberg and Waters's (1992) term "proximal hosts" best describes them. Following their analysis, African Americans and Puerto Ricans are the groups that many newcomers have been assigned by native-born Americans on the basis of color or ethnicity—West Indians and Africans placed with African Americans, Hispanic immigrants with Puerto Ricans.

Grappling with how to relate to their proximal hosts is a complicated process. On the one hand, black and Latino immigrants often seek to distinguish and separate themselves from native minorities as a way to avoid the stigma associated with these groups. On the other hand, West Indian immigrants often identify with African Americans on the basis of the shared experience of being black in America and members of the two groups join together, on occasion, in political alliances. For second-generation West Indian New Yorkers, becoming American has meant becoming black American even if, at the same time, they embrace

in New York for many decades or, in some cases, members of the second generation who were born and grew up in the city.

All of the present-day arrivals enter a city that has created new programs and services in response to the post-1965 influx, including special immigrant schools, language programs, and translating services in hospitals that were either not available, or less available, to those who came several decades ago. New York City's public schools are increasingly a second-generation world; at the beginning of the twenty-first century, nearly two-thirds of New Yorkers under eighteen were second- or 1.5-generation immigrants (Kasinitz, Mollenkopf, and Waters 2004: 2).

Also contributing to the comfort factor today are changes in New York City's public culture as a result of several decades of Latino, black, and Asian immigration. There are new flavors and foods in the city's restaurants and food stands, and, as Philip Kasinitz points out (this volume), new immigrant and second-generation art forms in concert venues, theaters, and museums. Practically every group now has its own festival or parade, the largest being the West Indian American Day Parade, which attracts between one and two million people every Labor Day on Brooklyn's Eastern Parkway and has become a mandatory campaign stop for politicians seeking citywide office. Since 2004 the city has sponsored an annual Immigrant Heritage Week, honoring "the vibrant immigrant cultures, heritages and communities found in every corner of the City" through film screenings, art exhibits, walking tours, and other programs. Many post-1965 groups' holidays are now officially recognized through the city's parking rules, which suspend alternate side parking on Muslim, Hindu, and Chinese—as well as Protestant, Catholic, and Jewish—holidays.

New museums have sprouted up to spotlight the history or arts of Asian and Latino groups. Two notable additions are the Museum of the Chinese in America in lower Manhattan, founded in 1980 and moved in 2009 to a building designed by architect Maya Lin, and El Museo del Barrio in East Harlem, created in 1969 to focus on the Puerto Rican diaspora in the United States, but recently changed—with considerable conflict—to include all Latin Americans and Puerto Ricans in the United States. Older museums dedicated to Ellis Island–era immigrants are taking steps to include the post-1965 arrivals; the Tenement

Museum has added walking tours on the contemporary Lower East Side and the Ellis Island Immigration Museum will soon open a Peopling of America Center that will include the post–Ellis Island era.

Conclusion

Today's immigrants, it is clear, are remaking New York. This is nothing new. What is new is that they bring their own cultures and customs to the city—and, of relevance here, that they come to a New York that has been influenced by particular immigrant communities of the past and the people who came of age in them. This is not just ethnic succession, in which one group follows or replaces another. As immigrants plant their roots in New York City, they create and change institutions and add new cultural elements that alter the urban environment, which, in turn, provides the context for the next set of arrivals. I have mainly focused on the imprint of Jewish and Italian immigrants and their descendants on New York's institutions and culture, but African American and Puerto Rican newcomers to the city in the mid-twentieth century also left their mark, transforming, among other things, the racial and ethnic order—and ending up in the position of proximal hosts for many of the latest arrivals from abroad.[7] We are currently witnessing another variation on a time-worn theme, as the very latest Asian, Latin American, and Caribbean immigrants enter a New York that has changed in response to their pioneering compatriots who settled in the city in the early stages of the post-1965 inflow.

This continuous remaking of the city by immigrant groups is a distinctive feature of New York's history and one way it stands out not just from Amsterdam and other European urban centers but from many other gateway cities in the United States as well (Foner 2007). It plays a role in making New York City a relatively friendly place for immigrants today—and a city that likes to celebrate its immigrant heritage.

To be sure, there is plenty of racial and ethnic prejudice in New York City. As Mary Waters notes (this volume), nativism—opposition to minority groups on the grounds of foreignness—is not strong in New York City, but inequalities based on race are deeply entrenched. People of color continue to experience prejudice and discrimination, and residential segregation between blacks and whites persists at extraordinarily high levels. Then, too, some long-term residents make invidious distinctions between today's arrivals and their own grandparents and great-grandparents who came in the past, looking back with rose-colored glasses to idealized immigrant heroes and heroines a hundred years ago, against whom real live newcomers today inevitably fall short (Foner 2000). Moreover as I have noted, other factors shape how New York City has greeted immigrants in the current period, including the remarkable ethnoracial diversity of and relatively good skill mix among the contemporary immigrant flows (Foner 2005, 2007).

Yet, at least in part because of its immigrant history, New York is a city that feels comfortable with immigration. Today's New York City is a remarkable amalgam and mix of cultures that bear the stamp of the Irish, Italians, and Jews of earlier eras as well as immigrants from a welter of Asian, Latin American, and Caribbean countries today. If you go to one of the many street fairs on Manhattan's major avenues, you can eat knishes and pizza alongside tacos, egg rolls, and West Indian patties. That, some would say, is the essence of immigrant New York.

NOTES

1. This lull in immigration, it should be emphasized, had nothing to do with policies in New York, but rather with immigrant restrictions enacted at the federal level in the 1920s. Indeed, as Claudia Goldin (1994) has shown, in the first two decades of the twentieth century congressmen from big cities in the Northeast with high proportions of immigrants, including New York, generally opposed immigration restrictions, as the ever-increasing foreign-born constituency gained the vote or influenced elections in other ways (see also Jou 2011).

2. According to pooled 2006–10 American Community Survey data, more than a quarter of New York City's non-Hispanic whites, about a third of non-Hispanic blacks, about half of Hispanics, and nearly three-quarters of Asians were foreign born (see Waters, this volume).

3. In 2011–12, 22 percent of all wage and salary workers in New York City were union members, higher than the share in any other major U.S. city and about double the national average rate. Among the foreign born in New York City, the unionization rates of those who had become U.S. citizens and those who entered the country before 1990 were comparable to or higher than those of U.S.-born workers (Milkman and Braslow 2012).

4. In New York City, every private hospital is constituted as a nonprofit organization, subject to federal and state regulations that require them to provide care to low-income and indigent residents. In addition to many nonprofit hospitals,

New York City also has 11 city-run hospitals, part of the largest municipal healthcare system in the United States (Levine 2010: 30).

5. Maimonides's emergency room is the fifth busiest in the nation, seeing nearly 110,000 patients in 2009 (Alvarez 2010).

6. Between 1914 and 1920, New York's predominantly Jewish voting districts elected ten state assemblymen, seven city councilmen, one municipal judge, and one congressman on the Socialist Party ticket (Michels 2005: 3).

7. For an account of how Irish immigrants remade the institutions and culture of New York, and other U.S. cities, that served as the context for Jewish and Italian arrivals in the early twentieth century, see Barrett (2012).

REFERENCES

Alba, Richard, and Victor Nee. 2003. *Remaking the American Mainstream.* Cambridge, MA: Harvard University Press.

Alvarez, Lizette. 2010. "Life and Death, Stat." *New York Times*, October 3.

Avins, Jenni. 2008. "Holliswood Temple Rededicated as a Mosque." *Queens Courier*, October 15.

Barnard, Anne, and Christine Haughney. 2010. "Islamic Center Also Challenges a Young Builder." *New York Times*, August 26.

Barrett, James R. 2012. *The Irish Way: Becoming American in the Multiethnic City.* New York: Penguin.

Bashi Bobb, Vilna, and Averil Clarke. 2001. "Experiencing Success: Structuring the Perception of Opportunities for West Indians," in Nancy Foner (ed.), *Islands in the City: West Indian Migration to New York.* Berkeley: University of California Press.

Berger, Joseph. 2003. "City Milestone, Number of Jews is Below Million." *New York Times,* June 16.

Butterfield, Sherri-Ann. 2004. "'We're Just Black': The Racial and Ethnic Identities of Second Generation West Indians in New York," in Philip Kasinitz, John Mollenkopf, and Mary Waters (eds.), *Becoming New Yorkers: Ethnographies of the New Second Generation.* New York: Russell Sage Foundation.

Cohen, Steven, Jacob Ukeles, and Ron Miller. 2012. *Jewish Community Study of New York: 2011 Comprehensive Report.* New York: UJA Federation of New York.

Erie, Stephen. 1988. *Rainbow's End: Irish-Americans and the Dilemmas of Urban Machine Politics, 1840–1985.* Berkeley: University of California Press.

Fink, Leon, and Brian Greenberg. 1989. *Upheaval in the Quiet Zone: A History of Hospital Workers' Union, Local 1199.* Urbana: University of Illinois Press.

Foner, Moe. 2002. *Not for Bread Alone: A Memoir by Moe Foner.* Ithaca, NY: Cornell University Press.

Foner, Nancy. 2000. *From Ellis Island to JFK: New York's Two Great Waves of Immigration.* New Haven, CT: Yale University Press.

———. 2005. *In a New Land: A Comparative View of Immigration.* New York: New York University Press.

———. 2006. "Then *and* Now or Then *to* Now: Immigration to New York in Contemporary and Historical Perspective." *Journal of American Ethnic History* 25: 33–47.

———. 2007. "How Exceptional is New York?: Migration and Multiculturalism in the Empire City." *Ethnic and Racial Studies* 30: 999–1023.

———. 2011. "Black Identities and the Second Generation: Afro-Caribbeans in Britain and the United States," in Richard Alba and Mary C. Waters (eds.), *The Next Generation: Immigrant Youth in a Comparative Perspective.* New York: NYU Press.

Gardiner, Jill. 2005. "Asians are Making Their Mark in City's Bagel Business." *New York Sun,* January 4.

Garland, Sarah. 2006. "A Reunion of Little Italy in East Harlem." *New York Times,* September 5.

Glazer, Nathan. 1993. "The National Influence of Jewish New York," in Martin Shefter (ed.), *Capital of the American Century: The National and International Influence of New York City.* New York: Russell Sage Foundation.

Glazer, Nathan, and Daniel Moynihan. 1970. *Beyond the Melting Pot.* 2d ed. Cambridge, MA: MIT Press.

Goldin, Claudia. 1994. "The Political Economy of Immigration Restriction in the United States, 1890 to 1921," in Claudia Goldin and Gary Libecap (eds.), *The Regulated Economy.* Chicago: University of Chicago Press.

Gray, Christopher. 2003. "Streetscapes/50 West 54th Street, Former Home of the City Athletic Club; 1909 Jewish Response to Exclusion Based on Bias." *New York Times,* June 22.

Jiménez, Tomás R. 2010. *Replenished Ethnicity: Mexican Americans, Immigration, and Identity.* Berkeley: University of California Press.

Joselit, Jenna Weissman. 1994. *The Wonders of America: Reinventing Jewish Culture, 1880–1950.* New York: Hill and Wang.

Jou, Chin. 2011. "Contesting Nativism: The New York Congressional Delegation's Case Against the Immigration Act of 1924." *Federal History.* shfg.org/shfg/wp-content/uploads/2010/07/5-jou_Layout-11-final-2.pdf.

Kasinitz, Philip. 2008. "Becoming American, Becoming Minority, Getting Ahead: The Role of Racial and Ethnic Status in the Upward Mobility of the Children of Immigrants." *Annals of the American Academy of Political and Social Science* 620: 253–69.

Kasinitz, Philip, Juan Battle, and Ines Miyares. 2001. "Fade to Black? The Children of West Indian Immigrants in Southern Florida," in Rubén Rumbaut and Alejandro Portes (eds.), *Ethnicities: Children of Immigrants in America.* Berkeley: University of California Press.

Kasinitz, Philip, John Mollenkopf, and Mary C. Waters (eds.). 2004. *Becoming New Yorkers: Ethnographies of the New Second Generation.* New York: Russell Sage Foundation.

Kasinitz, Philip, John Mollenkopf, Mary C. Waters, and Jennifer Holdaway. 2008. *Inheriting the City: The Children of Immigrants Come of Age.* Cambridge, MA: Harvard University Press.

Lederhendler, Eli. 2001. *New York Jews and the Decline of Urban Ethnicity, 1950–1970.* Syracuse, NY: Syracuse University Press.

Levine, Mark. 2010. "St. Vincent's Is the Lehman Brothers of Hospitals," *New York Magazine* (October 25): 24–31.

Lobo, Arun Peter, and Joseph Salvo. 2013. "A Portrait of New York's Immigrant Melange," in Nancy Foner (ed.), *One Out of Three: Immigrant New York in the Twenty-First Century.* New York: Columbia University Press.

Mangione, Jerre, and Ben Morreale. 1992. *La Storia: Five Centuries of the Italian American Experience.* New York: Harper Collins.

McNickle, Chris. 1993. *To Be Mayor of New York: Ethnic Politics in the City.* New York: Columbia University Press.

Michels, Tony. 2005. *A Fire in Their Hearts: Yiddish Socialists in New York.* Cambridge, MA: Harvard University Press.

Milkman, Ruth, and Laura Braslow. 2012. *The State of the Unions 2012: A Profile of Organized Labor in New York City, New York State, and the United States.* New York: Joseph Murphy Institute for Worker Education and Labor Studies and the Center for Urban Research, City University of New York.

Mittlelberg, David, and Mary C. Waters. 1992. "The Process of Ethnogenesis among Haitian and Israeli Immigrants in the United States." *Ethnic and Racial Studies* 15: 312–35.

Mollenkopf, John. 1992. *A Phoenix in the Ashes: The Rise and Fall of the Koch Coalition in New York City Politics.* Princeton, NJ: Princeton University Press.

———. 1999. "Urban Political Conflicts and Alliances: New York and Los Angeles Compared," in Charles Hirschman, Philip Kasinitz, and Josh DeWind (eds.), *The Handbook of International Migration.* New York: Russell Sage Foundation.

Mollenkopf, John, and Raphael Sonenshein. 2009. "The New Urban Politics of Integration: A View from the Gateway Cities," in Jennifer Hochschild and John Mollenkopf (eds.), *Bringing Outsiders In: Transatlantic Perspectives on Immigrant Political Incorporation.* Ithaca, NY: Cornell University Press.

Moore, Deborah Dash. 1981. *At Home in America: Second Generation New York Jews.* New York: Columbia University Press.

Rischin, Moses. 1962. *The Promised City: New York's Jews, 1870–1914.* Cambridge, MA: Harvard University Press.

Roediger, David, and James Barrett. 2004. "Making New Immigrants 'Inbetween': Irish Hosts and White Panethnicity, 1890 to 1930," in Nancy Foner and George Fredrickson (eds.), *Not Just Black and White: Historical and Contemporary Perspectives on Immigration, Race, and Ethnicity in the United States.* New York: Russell Sage Foundation.

Scher, Abby. 2001. "NYC's Ethnic Press." *Gotham Gazette.* www.gothamgazette.com/commentary/80.scher.shtml.

Shorto, Russell. 2005. "All Political Ideas Are Local." *New York Times Magazine*, October 2.

Singer, Audrey. 2004. "The Rise of New Immigrant Gateways." *The Living Cities Census Series* (February). Washington, DC: Brookings Institution.

Vickerman, Milton. 2001. "Tweaking a Monolith: The West Indian Immigrant Encounter with 'Blackness,'" in Nancy Foner (ed.), *Islands in the City: West Indian Migration to New York*. Berkeley: University of California Press.

Waldinger, Roger. 1996. "From Ellis Island to LAX: Immigrant Prospects in the American City." *International Migration Review* 30: 1078–86.

2

To Amsterdam

Migrations Past and Present

LEO LUCASSEN

Introduction

One of the classic pitfalls of the historical discipline is the temptation to see the present as the inevitable outcome of developments in the past.[1] Professional historians are often highly critical of such a simplistic teleological path dependency reasoning, but in practice it is not so easy to avoid—not in the least because there *are* real path dependencies and the past therefore *does* matter for the present. The question is how does the past matter, to what extent, and under what conditions. As I will argue in this chapter, these issues are fundamental when reflecting on the influence of past migrations on the present in Amsterdam.

Instead of seeing the present, or the recent past, as the culmination point of past experiences, or looking for easy similarities, I focus on a specific period in Amsterdam's past and make structured comparisons in order to see what is constant and what is new. Using a temporal comparison ("then and now") in order to ascertain the similarities and differences in the migration and settlement process in various historical periods provides a way to understand how migration in the past has affected the present. This comparative historical method has been applied by, among others, Nancy Foner in analyzing New York's two great waves of immigration in the past 120 years (Foner 2000) and myself for Western Europe (Lucassen 2005; Foner and Lucassen 2012). In the case of Amsterdam we need to go back further in time, because the first great wave took place in the seventeenth century, leading to an all-time high in the share of foreign born in the urban population. I then look at the nineteenth century, when the situation seems to be completely reversed, with very low percentages of foreigners. The third part of the chapter is devoted to the second great wave, which started with the decolonization of Indonesia after World War II, and gathered speed in the 1970s with the concurrent mass immigration of colonial migrants from Suriname and family reunification among Turkish and Moroccan former guest workers (Vermeulen 2006).

In all three cases I consider characteristics of the migrants (their human capital, for example, religious background, numbers, and networks), the dynamics of the migration process, and the institutional reaction to the influx of newcomers at the city and national level. A central question is the extent to which the most recent immigrations are similar to *and* different from past ones and why this is so. The answer to this question can help us to better assess the impact of the past on the present.

The Big Picture

An overview of immigration to Amsterdam in the last four centuries, measured by the relative share of foreign born in the total urban population, makes clear that large-scale immigration has a long history. As figure 2.1 shows, the absolute number of foreign born in the current period is exceptionally high, but the second quarter of the seventeenth century stands out in terms of the relative share of foreign born, almost 40 percent.

Figure 2.2 provides another view of long term developments and indicates that after very high immigration in the seventeenth and eighteenth centuries Amsterdam's population became more and more native born. Only after World War II did the share of foreign born grow again significantly, although still not reaching the height of the 1630s.

The Golden Age

In the seventeenth-century, the Dutch Republic reached the apogee of its economic, political and cultural power, with Amsterdam as its epicenter.

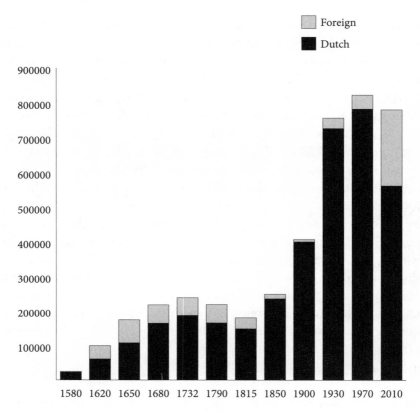

Figure 2.1. Foreign Born and Natives in Amsterdam, 1580–2010
Source: Kuijpers and Prak (2004: 191); O+S (2010).

The city grew from 25,000 in 1580 at the beginning of the revolt against the Spanish king Philip II to almost a quarter of a million 150 years later. Moreover, it became the center of global trade routes and developed a sophisticated financial system; the Amsterdam (stock) Exchange (established in 1609), a revolutionary development, guaranteed an impartial and correct proceeding of the transactions of the many traders and merchants who had chosen the "Venice of the North" as their business seat (Prak 2005; Lesger 2006). Linked by extensive networks with merchants in other cities, both in and outside Europe, Amsterdam became one of the richest and most well-organized emporia in the world. Grain, wood,

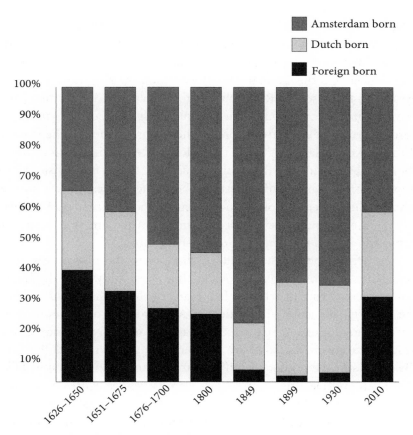

Figure 2.2. Origin of the Population of Amsterdam, 1626–2010
Source: Lucassen (2012).

textiles, sugar, coffee, and tea, as well as spices from the New World and southeast India were stored and partly processed in the city, which not by coincidence was also home of the fleet of the Dutch East India Company (VOC). Finally, Amsterdam became an important sector of what are now known as "creative industries," especially painting and publishing (Deinema and Kloosterman 2012).

The bustling economic activities, which only gradually decreased in the course of the eighteenth century when the city was outpaced by London in many respects (Van Lottum 2007), attracted numerous migrants. First of all, there were those who wanted to be enlisted as sailors by the VOC. Although mortality among sailors to Asia was high—almost one-third died because of tropical diseases—there were enough men without options in the poorer parts of Europe (especially Scandinavia and the German states) who took the risk of what to our eyes looks like a sort of Russian roulette. In total, the Dutch merchant fleet and navy recruited a million people in the period 1600–1800, 50 percent of whom came from abroad, the majority entering the system through Amsterdam. Although the sailors stayed in the city for only a short while, waiting for their ships to set sail, they left a considerable imprint through numerous guest and boarding houses, pubs, and the like. Furthermore, of those who did return and had managed to save enough money, quite a few settled down in Amsterdam, often married native women, and became part of the social fabric.

Apart from the transient sailors, there were the newcomers who decided to stay for longer periods of time. Best known are the high-skilled merchants and artisans, like many of the Sephardic Jews from the Iberian Peninsula who settled in Amsterdam around 1600, fleeing the persecutions in Spain and Portugal. A second, more numerous group came from the southern Netherlands, Antwerp, and the textile centers in the border region of Flanders and France, around Lille (Lucassen and De Vries 2001). They were largely categorized as refugees, escaping the Spanish armies who repressed Protestant heretics. At least as important for their decision to move to Amsterdam, however, was the closure of the Antwerp harbor by the Dutch Republic in 1585, which further strengthened Amsterdam's position.

Foreign merchants, artisans, and scholars enriched the Dutch Republic and stimulated innovation by providing intensive cross-cultural contacts. Their arrival helped to establish new merchant networks, extending the traditional Dutch-Baltic-Mediterranean trade system with new networks in the Middle East, Asia, and South America (Roitman 2011), and to develop new financial, banking, and trading techniques, which contributed to a highly successful economic institutional structure (Gelderblom and Jonker 2005). Antwerp merchants like Balthasar Coymans, Guillaume Bartolotti, Jan Calandrini, Jaspar Quingetti, Isaac le Maire, Dirck van Os, and Pieter van Pulle made Amsterdam into *the* money and capital market of Europe (Gelderblom 2003). Together with other refugees, like the Huguenots after 1685, these relatively high-skilled migrants made up some 25 percent of the total inflow in the early modern period. An estimated 35,000 to 50,000 French Huguenots came to the Netherlands (including the Cape Colony in South Africa), of whom at least 5,000 settled in Amsterdam. As skilled—and Protestant—refugees they were granted economic concessions, such as the free acquisition of urban citizenship, free entry into the guilds, and loans with low interest for craftsmen. It was not long, however, before the guilds started to complain and in 1690 the Amsterdam city government was forced to withdraw a number of concessions, such as free citizenship, after which many Huguenots left for Germany, England, and other Dutch cities. Those who stayed would soon play an important role in sectors like publishing and silk production; some would serve as skilled professional soldiers in the army of the Dutch Republic (Asche 2011; Kuijpers 2005: 16, 87).

We are much less well informed about the remaining 75 percent in this span from the late sixteenth century to the mid-eighteenth century, most of whom were low-skilled labor migrants, who were constantly needed in a time when more people died than were born in European cities (De Vries 1984; Lucassen and Lucassen 2009). Ongoing immigration was vital to compensate for this "urban graveyard" effect, and many of the newcomers came from abroad. The bulk of the low-skilled migrants from Scandinavian countries and German states ended up in the Amsterdam proletariat. Women worked in the textile industry, as domestics, and as prostitutes, whereas male foreign journeymen were overrepresented in the building trades and in occupations such as bakers, butchers, and tailors. Most journeymen never made it to become "masters" who set up their own businesses, and instead remained dependent wage workers (Kuijpers 2005).

This was certainly the destiny of most migrants from Scandinavia— especially from southern Norway—and northwest Germany. As Lutherans, they experienced some legal discrimination, but, unlike many of their children, the first generation held on to their own churches, language, and networks, often marrying among themselves and living in close proximity to one another. In contrast to Jews, who were clearly second-class inhabitants and excluded from the guilds and public office, over time those from Scandinavia and northwest Germany lost their ethnic traits, often within two or three generations, many of them ending up in the Amsterdam proletariat. This formation of an underclass without ethnic markers is an often neglected, because it is a largely invisible, outcome of long-term settlement processes.

The only exception to this process of de-ethnicization of the many foreign immigrants in Amsterdam were the poverty-stricken Jewish migrants from German states and Poland who migrated in large numbers to Amsterdam and soon outnumbered their Iberian co-religionists. These Ashkenazim were not only poorer, but also much more orthodox than Sephardic Jews and could easily be recognized by their clothes, beards, and headwear. They lived highly concentrated in the "Jewish corner," close to what is now known as the Waterlooplein and until the emancipation of the Jews in 1796 were second-class citizens. The majority earned a meager living by petty trade and all sorts of odd and irregular jobs (Cohen 1982; Sonnenberg-Stern 2000). The institutional and social discrimination they faced affirmed their position as ultimate outsiders.

Harassment of Jews by Christians in public spaces in Amsterdam was not uncommon, but there was no outright violence, let alone official persecution. The urban politics of toleration was explicitly aimed at preventing violence between religious groups. That all denominations except the Dutch Reformed (Calvinist) Church, such as Catholics, Baptists, Lutherans, and Jews, were discriminated against was accepted and formed a firm basis of the remarkable tradition of interreligious peace in Amsterdam and the Dutch Republic in general. This tradition of toleration was quite exceptional in Europe at the time, where religious cleansing was normal. Only in the Ottoman Empire, with its pillarized millet system in which separate religious communities had their own legal courts, was a similar balance kept (Parker 2006).

Regulating Entrance and Settlement

When the economic tide turned at the end of the seventeenth century, almost all Dutch cities decided to prevent the immigration of people who were most likely to become a financial burden for the poor relief system. Amsterdam was the only city in the Dutch Republic that resisted the temptation to be selective at its gates. The city council of Amsterdam argued that immigration restrictions would damage its economic position. It depended on a continuous inflow of low-skilled migrants, not only for the urban economy, but also to satisfy the ongoing demand for sailors and soldiers on the ships of the VOC. The authorities realized that this open-door policy put a strain on poor relief funds, however.

In the heyday of the Golden Age earlier in the seventeenth century, the large majority of relief recipients in Amsterdam were already foreign born. In 1614, 90 percent of the 2,500 families receiving alms from the new institution of almoners (*aalmoezeniers*), came from outside the Republic. The main purpose of this institution was to provide second-rate poor relief, at a much lower level than that to which "locals" were entitled. It was a safety net for immigrants, but one that became available only after three years of residence and which—given its paltry quality—had a clear deterrent nature. Most migrants had to look for help from their religious communities; the Lutherans and Jews had great trouble amassing enough funds and often tried to push their co-religionists onto other denominations (Roitman 2011; Cohen 1982). From the end of the seventeenth century onward, Amsterdam developed measures to limit demands on poor relief funds without deterring labor migrants. District wardens were asked to check the necessary minimal residence requirements to be eligible for poor relief, and conditions for support were tightened.

It is interesting to note that local welfare arrangements, both in the sending and receiving localities, exerted some influence on migration patterns, which shows that this phenomenon is not limited to twentieth-century welfare states. Small cities and villages in the northwest of Germany often provided poor inhabitants with travel money to leave for Amsterdam to avoid a drain on their own poor relief funds. We are particularly well informed about the policies of Husum, a small town in East Friesland in northwest Germany that was hit by floods (1634) and warfare. In an attempt to restrict local relief expenses, the urban authorities provided hundreds of poor inhabitants with the money to travel to Holland, where work was abundant and wages high. Between 1618 and 1682, at least 320 Husum residents received assistance for their journey to the Dutch coastal provinces, most of them ending up in Amsterdam (Kuijpers 2005: 63). While many found employment, single women with children became dependent on poor relief provided by the city and the Lutheran church. Thus, the availability of poor relief in

Amsterdam, modest as it may have been, constituted an important pull (Kuijpers 2005: 66; Van de Pol and Kuijpers 2005).

Amsterdam's open-door policy did not prevent tensions between established residents and outsiders. Already in the second half of the seventeenth century, Amsterdam-born building workers and carpenters complained about foreign competition, while in some instances textile workers refused to work together with journeymen from Hamburg (Knotter and Van Zanden 1987: 411–12; Nederveen Meerkerk 2012). As a result, the position of migrant workers deteriorated and most found themselves locked in the secondary segment of a dual urban labor market, with less job security and lower wages—a pattern that we also see in other Dutch cities and which resembles the position of many low-skilled immigrants today.

Migration Dynamics and Integration in Early Modern Amsterdam

In sum, in the period from 1600 to 1800 Amsterdam was a vibrant city of constant immigration. Most newcomers, even the Calvinists among them, were initially stereotyped and discriminated against, but—apart from the Jews—this did not lead to long-term exclusion and ethnic-minority formation. Ethnic boundaries were easily crossed and within a few generations boundaries blurred and shifted as most foreign immigrants quickly assimilated, even as many experienced downward social mobility. Most children and grandchildren of foreign immigrants married natives and many, especially Lutherans, also converted to the Dutch Reformed Church to avoid discrimination. At the same time, as a result of ongoing immigration, especially from German states and Scandinavia, a vibrant ethnic infrastructure remained intact. Immigrants from these areas often lived in specific parts of Amsterdam where they had their own churches, pubs, shops, and workshops.

The migration was channeled through ethnic networks, but many migrants were well aware of the opportunities that Amsterdam offered as a global nodal point, so that personal information networks were not always decisive. Amsterdam was part of the German urban guild-network that inspired traveling journeymen to change jobs every few years, and most potential migrants knew that there were enough "masters" in Amsterdam they could turn to. Organizational or nonpersonal network migration therefore was at least as important as classical chain migration involving close family and other relatives (Lesger, Lucassen, and Schrover 2002). Some extra-economic attractions notwithstanding, especially relatively generous poor relief, it was the Amsterdam labor market, including the maritime opportunity structure, that dictated the rhythm of migration in this period.

The Slack Season (1800–1960)

After the Napoleonic era, the Netherlands became a kingdom (1813) and the former southern Netherlands, present-day Belgium, was added to its territory. Already in 1830, however, the new provinces rebelled and demanded independence, which was soon realized (1839). This geopolitical defeat coincided with a more general atmosphere of economic and cultural decline, much lamented by contemporaries. Although these complaints were exaggerated, it was clear that the heyday of Dutch global power was over. The Netherlands retained its colonies in the East (present-day Indonesia) and the West (Suriname), but lost South Africa to the British and lagged behind industrializing neighbors like England, Belgium, France, and Germany.

This shift in the geopolitical and economic balance had repercussions for migration dynamics. The Dutch highly specialized agricultural sector remained important, as well as international trade, but the demand for migrants dropped significantly. This is reflected not only in a dramatic decrease of the share of foreign born in the Dutch population as a whole in the nineteenth century, but also in the declining proportion of immigrants in Amsterdam's population (see table 2.1). The declining demand for migrant labor in Amsterdam was partly a result of the shift from sail to steamships in the maritime sector. Also, the very modest level of industrialization meant that there was not much demand for migrants from abroad in the industrial sector. Instead, endogenous population growth and internal migration to cities like Amsterdam and Rotterdam became the sources of urban population growth in the nineteenth century.

Although migration from abroad decreased markedly in this period, Scandinavians and Germans, especially sailors, still found their way to Amsterdam. As a result, the center of Amsterdam retained a strong German flavor. The census of 1849 shows that the concentration of German

Table 2.1. Foreigners, Jews, and the Amsterdam Population, 1800–1940

	Total Population	Foreigners	Percentage	Jews	Percentage
1800	220,000	51,000	23	22,000	10
1849	224,000	9,630	4.2	25,000	11
1869	265,000	6,695	2.5	30,000	11
1899	510,000	7,126	1.4	60,000	12
1930	760,000	23,260	3	65,000	8
1940	800,000	NA	NA	77,000	10

Note: "Foreigners" refers to inhabitants who are of non-Dutch nationality.

born in the heart of Amsterdam (roughly between the Oude Zijds and Nieuwe Zijdsvoorburgwal) was high throughout the nineteenth century, ranging from 10 to 20 percent of the population. Germans owned cafés and inns and were active as shopkeepers, tailors, shoemakers, and bakers. They remained influential in the building trades, especially plastering, albeit on a seasonal basis, and owned department stores that often specialized in textiles (like C&A). Less well-known were German market gardeners who set up small farms in the nineteenth century at the outskirts of the city such as the Watergraafsmeer, profiting from the great demand for fresh vegetables (Kaal and Van Lottum 2003). Much less numerous but eye catching were Italian and Swiss chimney sweeps and Belgian straw hat makers. Many of the migrant entrepreneurs made use of personnel from their regions of origin, thus creating new ethnic networks (Cottaar and Lucassen 2001; Chotkowski 2006).

The Jewish Minority

To understand the multicultural dynamics of the time, it would be misleading to concentrate only on Amsterdam's foreign migrants. Jewish inhabitants of the capital must also be considered, most of them the offspring of immigrants who arrived in the seventeenth and eighteenth centuries. Although their position as second-class citizens was officially lifted with the Emancipation Act of 1796, Jews remained de facto a despised minority, especially the poor Yiddish-speaking Ashkenazim, who were segregated in their own neighborhoods, schools, and occupations. With a population of some 22,000 at the end of the eighteenth century, they made up almost 10 percent of the total population in Amsterdam, a share that did not change much until the forced transportations to the Nazi death camps from 1942 onward (see table 2.1).

During the first half of the nineteenth century, Jewish religious leaders tried to hold onto their erstwhile semiautonomous position with power delegated by the city authorities. Nonetheless, gradually more and more Jews freed themselves from the restrictions of their own religious community and slowly the spatial and social segregation diminished in the course of the nineteenth century (Sonnenberg-Stern 2000; Lucassen 1994). Some Jews assimilated by converting to Christianity, while others developed a more liberal version of Judaism and out-married with non-Jewish partners.

After a period of Jewish outmigration to the provinces in the east and north of the country in the first half of the nineteenth century, a reverse (internal) migration started from the 1860s onward, adding to the endogenous growth of the Amsterdam (Ashkenazim) community. Whereas in cities like Paris and London native Jewish communities received large numbers of Eastern European refugees in the 1880s and 1890s, the bulk of the Jewish newcomers in Amsterdam were internal migrants. Between 1880 and 1914 only about 1,500 foreign (mostly Russian) Jews settled permanently in the capital (Hofmeester 1990). The appeal of Amsterdam to Dutch Jews in the second half of the nineteenth century was mainly economic; the new diamond industry in particular offered ample opportunities to Jewish workers.

Social anti-Semitism notwithstanding, assimilation continued to progress in the twentieth century. As in most Western European countries, strict religious observance declined among Jews, and in Amsterdam the number of interreligious marriages among them increased from 5 percent in 1910 to 10 percent in 1920 and almost 17 percent in 1934 (Lucassen 1994: 35). If it had not been for the Nazi occupation and the ensuing Holocaust, most probably assimilation would have run its course. Ethnic boundaries were already shifting, so that Jews in the end would have been fully included in the Amsterdam and Dutch populations. Instead, almost all Amsterdam Jews were rounded up, deported, and murdered, leaving a traumatic black hole in a city that had been a center of Jewish life since the early seventeenth century.

Some of the deported Jews were recent immigrants, refugees who had crossed the Dutch border after Hitler seized power in Germany in January 1933. Most of the Jewish refugees settled in Amsterdam, especially in the southern, wealthier part (Van Kolfschooten 1998). They created a vibrant exile community of well-to-do Germans, some of whom had moved their textile and fur businesses and factories, thus adding to the development of Amsterdam's industries (Deinema and Kloosterman 2012). Others were active in the business of publishing so-called Exile authors, like Joseph Roth, Bertolt Brecht, and Stefan Zweig (Dittrich and Würzner 1982).

Other Migrants

During the 1920s, when Amsterdam's economy flourished, immigration picked up again and many labor migrants flocked there and to other areas in the western—urbanized—part of the Netherlands (Lucassen 2002). Germany remained the main supplier, but for the first time small numbers of non-Europeans made their presence felt. One group of newcomers were from the Dutch East Indies, who came to study or were servants accompanying Dutch colonial migrants on leave. From the colony in the west, Suriname, small numbers found their way to port cities like Rotterdam and Amsterdam. They were predominantly African Surinamese ("Creole") men, descendants of former African slaves. Some were musicians, active in Amsterdam's emerging jazz scene; others were models for sculpture and painting students of the Academy of Arts. Their presence attracted considerable attention, both from young Dutch women as well as from the local police who portrayed them as voracious sexual predators (Cottaar 2003).

A third conspicuous group of non-European immigrants in Amsterdam were Chinese sailors and restaurant owners. There is a long tradition of Asian sailors working on Dutch ships, but until the late nineteenth century they remained within the Indian Ocean region. Shortly before World War I, steamship companies began to recruit Chinese boilermen, who accepted low wages and were not organized in unions. From that time onward Chinese boarding houses and small restaurants appeared in the dock areas of Rotterdam and Amsterdam (Binnen Bantammerstraat). In the 1920s the first Chinese restaurants opened their doors, catering not only to Chinese workers but also to the Dutch public in Rotterdam, Amsterdam, and The Hague, the center for Dutch colonials on leave from expatriate jobs in the Dutch East Indies. Thus, a combination of colonial connections and globalization of world trade confronted the population of Amsterdam with small numbers of Asian and African migrants and added an extra exotic flavor to the reputation of the capital as a cosmopolitan center (Van Rossum 2009).

The Asian presence in Amsterdam was strengthened after World War II by the settlement of refugees from Indonesia, which became independent in 1949 after a short but brutal colonial war that cost the life of more than 100,000 Indonesians and 5,000 Dutch colonials and soldiers. The result was an exodus of some 300,000 Eurasians between 1945 and 1965, most of them offspring of mixed Dutch-Indonesian relations (Willems 2001, 2003). Thousands of them settled in Amsterdam. At the time most were perceived as different because of their skin color and Indonesian accent, or their identity as ex-colonials. There was also resentment among the native population because of special housing arrangements that were made for this group. Within a few decades, however, the Eurasians became almost invisible. For one thing, the conscious decision of the Dutch government not to label "repatriates" from Indonesia "immigrants" stressed that they belonged to the Dutch nation. Second, these Eurasians had, on average, high human capital and a mastery of Dutch. Finally, their arrival coincided with the onset of a long economic boom period.

While the Eurasians blended in rapidly, other immigrants from Asia, especially Chinese from Hong Kong who set up thousands of Chinese restaurants as well as small shops ("tokos") in the Netherlands, remained highly visible. In cities with a large clientele, like Amsterdam, small "Chinatowns" developed, which in the past decade have grown into institutionalized, highly commercial tourist attractions (Rath 2007; Willems et al. 2010).

The Second Wave of Immigration: A Fundamental Change in Migration Dynamics

By 1960, despite the modest globalization of the Amsterdam population, it was marked by increasing "autochthonization"—with the vast majority of residents having deep roots, for many generations, in the Netherlands—in a city where only fading traces of its migration past remained. In 1960 only 1 percent of the total population were foreigners. Given the long downward slide of foreign immigration since the 1830s, with only a brief uptick in the interwar years, it is not surprising that immigration in the past left only a vague (and selective) imprint on the collective memory of the population. This was reinforced by the nationalistic framing of Dutch history in which the role of migrants, including in the early modern period, had largely been erased. Thus the idea took root that the Dutch belonged to an ethnically homogenous nation in which migration had made only few inroads.

This was also largely true in Amsterdam, but at the same time the sensitivity (and tolerance) for ethnic differences in the postwar period was more pronounced than in other Dutch cities because of the strong Jewish presence (descendants of immigrations between 1600 and 1900) until the deportations of Jews to the death camps in 1942. Until that time a moderate social anti-Semitism was part of daily life in the capital, but at the same time assimilation (in terms of mixed interreligious marriages [Tammes 2010]) had increased significantly since the formal Emancipation Decree in 1796. After the war, especially since the 1960s, the feelings of guilt for having done so little to stop the deportations and debates about the dubious role of the Amsterdam municipal police and civil servants increased. These feelings of guilt were heightened because of the very high percentage of Jews who were deported from the Netherlands in comparison with other occupied countries (Tammes 2007). Moreover, memories of the Holocaust—and Nazi racial laws concerning the "superior" Aryan "race" and "inferior" Jewish "race"—have contributed to a discomfort with the term "race" (as well as "racism") in discussions of present-day immigrants and their children.

The memory of the Jewish minority thus became part of Amsterdam's collective identity, even if, sometimes, in twisted and complicated ways, as indicated by the recent identification of Ajax hooligans and other supporters with Jews (Spaaij 2006: 197). Before World War II, Ajax was known as a Jewish soccer club. It did not have significantly more Jewish members than other Amsterdam clubs, but it nonetheless acquired a Jewish image by the 1930s. Beginning in the 1970s supporters of rival clubs in Rotterdam and The Hague started to insult Ajax supporters with anti-Semitic slogans. In reaction, Ajax supporters took "Jews" as an honorary nickname and began using Jewish and Israeli symbols and flags.

The history of Jews in Amsterdam in World War II aside, the long period of low immigration, well over a century, explains why the large-scale post-1960s immigration of guest workers from Southern Europe, Turkey, and North Africa as well as colonial migrants from Suriname was seen as unprecedented in Amsterdam as it was in the rest of the Netherlands. At first the attitude to the new immigration was neutral and at times positive. Influenced by the cultural revolution of the 1960s, many people, especially the young, stressed the importance of tolerance and antiracism, and the new immigrants were often viewed with curiosity and sympathy. That they initially arrived in a period of almost zero unemployment and remarkable economic growth also shaped the warm or neutral welcome they received.

This changed in the early 1970s when economic growth leveled off, and the oil crisis put an end to the recruitment of guest workers. But, unexpectedly, the migration did not cease or taper off. Although the economy slipped into a recession, the number of immigrants increased and within a decade multiplied by five or six times as a consequence of family reunification. The human capital of these newcomers was on average quite low, as guest workers had been specifically recruited for low-skilled jobs in the labor market. The result was a massive immigration while male migrants themselves lost their jobs in huge numbers. As figure 2.3 shows, unemployment was at remarkably high rates among Moroccans in the Netherlands in the 1980s, rising to about 50 percent in 1990, a year in which immigration from Morocco was at near-peak numbers.

The reversal of the normal migration dynamics—heavily determined by labor market needs in the receiving area—is explained by a curious mix of unintended and unexpected effects of Dutch welfare state arrangements, political decisions, and restrictive aliens policies (Lucassen and Lucassen 2011: ch. 3). The initial idea behind the guest worker program was that workers would rotate, staying in the Netherlands only two years, and then being replaced by other guest workers. Thus permanent settlement would be prevented. However, already in the early 1960s, employers, supported by right-wing parties in Parliament, successfully lobbied to have this "two-year work stay" provision dropped with the argument that it would be too costly. The result was that guest

Figure 2.3. Migration to and from Morocco Compared to Unemployment among Moroccans in the Netherlands, 1970–2007
Source: Lucassen and Lucassen (2011: 66).

workers were allowed to stay much longer, and thus, without much notice, gained access to both social rights (through the social welfare system) and legal rights (because the longer a migrant stayed, the stronger his or her residence rights). Another political decision in the early 1960s—concerning the right of women to join their spouses in the Netherlands—also had unanticipated long-term effects. The rules of the Ministry of Justice, responsible for immigration policies, did not allow this family migration, but Christian Democratic parties successfully forced the immigration authorities to reverse the policy, arguing that the unity of the family had to prevail under all circumstances (Bonjour 2009, 2011).

Initially, neither of the two political decisions, embedded in a new welfare state and residence regime, had many visible effects. Most guest workers still assumed that they would return to their home countries after a couple of years and few made use of the right to bring spouses to the Netherlands. This changed, however, in the mid-1970s when the Dutch government decided to stop the guest-worker recruitment scheme and imposed a restrictive aliens policy. At this point, guest workers from non–European Union (EU) countries realized that by returning to their countries of origin, where unemployment was very high, they would give up both their social and their residence rights in the Netherlands. Many decided to stay put and send for family members to join them. Paradoxically, the early restrictive aliens policies limiting the time allowed to work in the Netherlands and ability to bring over wives and children ended up leading to exactly the opposite of what the policies intended. The late 1970s and 1980s saw a mass immigration from Turkey and Morocco, which coincided with an economic recession in which sectors in which most guest workers were employed—the old and now vanishing manufacturing industries—were hit especially hard.

The same fundamental change in migration dynamics, which occurred all over Western Europe, is an element of what James Hollifield has dubbed the "liberal paradox" (1992). Although economically speaking the timing of the large in-flows to Europe in the 1970s was unfortunate, coming as they did in the midst of a long recession following the oil crisis of the early 1970s, liberal European democracies continued to keep the door open in this period. This began to change, however. Particularly since the turn of the twenty-first century, the Netherlands, as well as other European countries, have actively sought to restrict immigration from non-EU nations by making it much harder to bring spouses and, in general, raising the barriers for potential immigrants from "non-Western countries" (largely a codeword for poor Muslims) unless they qualify as skilled or "knowledge" migrants.

In addition to guest-worker migration, the decolonization of Suriname in 1975 led to an equally large migration stream of African and Hindustani Surinamese migrants, most of whom settled in the big cities in the western part of the country (Amsterdam, Rotterdam, and The

Hague). By the end of 1976, roughly a third of Suriname's population was living in the Netherlands. The introduction of visa requirements for Surinamese migrants in 1980 to curb the inflow initially produced the opposite effect: many tried to beat the ban, whereas those already present stayed on for fear of finding the door closed next time if they left. The immigration from Suriname tapered off after 1982, but until the end of the twentieth century there was a steady flow of around 5,000 per year (Lucassen and Lucassen 2011: 76).

Between 1975 and 1990 the large-scale migrations of guest workers and their families and Surinamese changed the composition of Amsterdam's population dramatically, particularly in low-income neighborhoods where the bulk of the newcomers settled. With the benefit of hindsight it is not difficult to understand that the unfortunate timing of the migration, occurring in a difficult economic period, was bound to produce social problems and tensions with the Dutch population in neighborhoods where new migrants with low human capital lived in large numbers. (The Surinamese, for example, became heavily concentrated in the Bijlmermeer neighborhood while former guest workers clustered in sections of the eastern and western parts of the city.) Parents, especially those from Turkey and Morocco, often spoke little Dutch; the men lost their jobs and could not function as role models for their children; and schools were badly prepared for the sudden arrival of students with different linguistic, social, and cultural backgrounds. These handicaps were less evident for the Surinamese, who profited from a "colonial bonus": most had already learned Dutch in the colony, had adopted Christian religions (at least among the African Surinamese), could more easily identify with Dutch culture, and on average were better schooled. This premigration assimilation explains why, as compared to Turks and Moroccans, their children did better in school, experienced more upward social mobility, and (among African Surinamese) out-married with Dutch partners at higher rates (Lucassen and Laarman 2009).

Invisible Migrants

If high-skilled migrants of the remote past (Sephardic Jews, Huguenots, Antwerp merchants) are firmly embedded in the collective memory, and low-skilled Germans and Scandinavians largely forgotten, today it is low-skilled migrants who stand out in public discourse—while the highly skilled are overlooked or ignored, and indeed are largely invisible.

In current political discussions the term "migrants" is mainly reserved for those who (allegedly) cause problems, are lower class and welfare dependent, and are seen as culturally very different from long-established Dutch, or to put it bluntly, low-skilled Muslims. Yet to understand the economic and cultural impact of immigration on Amsterdam in the postwar period, we should also pay attention to the medium- and high-skilled migrants, who are active as students or professionals in the financial district, cultural industries, the arts, trade, and multinational businesses. Apart from Europeans, this includes many Japanese, Indians, Chinese, Americans, and high-skilled newcomers from all over the world. In 2011 some 174 nationalities were present in the city, which is considerably more than just the Turks and Moroccans who are the focus of so much public attention. Altogether in Amsterdam in 2010, the share of foreigners—defined here as those without Dutch citizenship—was 12 percent of a total population of about 780,000 inhabitants. Table 2.2 provides figures on the top 20 groups, who represented 80 percent of all foreigners in the capital in 2010.

What is striking is the large number of Europeans and Americans, presumably most of them highly skilled and well educated. These migrants, however, seldom play a role in the highly politicized discussions of migration, and many Dutch would not even consider them to be proper immigrants, as this term has become so strongly associated with groups seen to be problematic.

The Myopic View of Immigration

When we look at another overview of Amsterdam's demographics, produced by the municipal statistics bureau, that categorizes the population along ethnic lines, a very different picture emerges (see table 2.3). It illustrates the national shift in categorization from "foreigners" to "allochthones," that is, "people born abroad, or of whom at least one parent was born abroad"; within the allochthone category, the principal distinction is between groups characterized as "Western" (including

Table 2.2. Country of Origin of Top 20 Groups of Non-Dutch Citizens in Amsterdam, 2010

Morocco	15,241		Poland	1,968
Turkey	10,190		Bulgaria	1,810
U.K.	7,087		BD	1,636
Germany	5,601		India	1,614
U.S.	3,905		Suriname	1,599
Italy	3,662		Belgium	1,469
France	3,195		China	1,437
Ghana	3,045		Indonesia	1,373
Spain	2,666		Japan	1,190
Portugal	2,560		Romania	1,170

Note: People with double nationality are not included. BD: British Dominions (Canada, Australia, New Zealand)
Source: O+S (2010: ch. 2).

those from Oceania, Japan, and Indonesia) and "non-Western" (including those from the Dutch Antilles and Suriname). Those categorized as allochthones can be foreigners, but not necessarily so and given relatively liberal Dutch naturalization policies (at least until the end of the twentieth century), most children of immigrants, as well as many immigrants themselves, have by now been naturalized and therefore have Dutch passports.[2] This highly specific Dutch way of categorizing not only has consequences for the social sciences—making it impossible, for example, to distinguish between the first (foreign-born) and second (Dutch-born) generation in government statistics—but also for perceptions of immigrant groups (Foner and Lucassen 2012).

The breakdown of the Amsterdam's population this way, as set out in table 2.3, is the result of the myopic political discussion at the national level about immigration that developed since the large-scale settlement of guest workers and Surinamese from the 1970s onward (Scholten 2011). Policy makers and politicians decided, for good reasons, that underclass and minority formation of the low-skilled migrants who arrived during the recession of the 1980s had to be prevented as much as possible and they devised an integration policy that targeted specific

Table 2.3. Allochthones and Autochthones in Amsterdam, 2011

	Total number	Percentage
Moroccans	*70,646*	*9*
Surinamese	*68,971*	*9*
Turks	*41,075*	*5*
Antilleans	*11,777*	*1*
Other non-Western allochthones	*80,682*	*10*
Total non-Western allochthones	273,151	35
Western allochthones	119,373	15
Autochthones	388,035	50
Total population	780,559	100

Source: O+S (2011).

problematic immigrant groups and even included the indigenous group of Travelers (caravan dwellers). Although this policy, with the slogan "integration with the retention of one's identity," became known as the (once) famous Dutch multicultural model, the bulk of the money went into programs to alleviate socioeconomic deprivation (education, labor market, and housing) and prevent long-term minority-group formation. Subsidies for establishing ethnic organizations or education in one's mother language were only a minor component of the policy, and of a temporary nature, but were highly symbolic of the recognition and acceptance of different ethnic cultures (Lucassen and Lucassen 2011; Duyvendak and Scholten 2010).

The unintentional effect of categorizing groups as "ethnic minorities" and later on as "allochthones" was that these categories soon became fixed social entities that acquired what Everett C. Hughes once called a "master status," eclipsing all other characteristics (Hughes 1945). This was further buttressed by the subdivision of allochthones into generations (Foner and Lucassen 2012). Children of Moroccans, for example, born in the Netherlands and with Dutch citizenship remained "Moroccan," but with the prefix "second-generation." The consequence is that ethnic origin is portrayed as the dominant feature of a person's social position and identity.

There is another critical element involved in present-day perceptions of immigrant-origin groups. The current polarized discussion about immigration and integration in the Netherlands, as I emphasized, can be partly explained by the badly timed low human capital immigration, which underlies the worrying statistics about unemployment, low school performance, and criminality. At least as important in recent public discourse is the cultural turn at the end of the 1980s, which shifted the debate from "minorities" to "Muslims" as a threat to the core values of Western democratic societies, such as free speech, gender equality, and gay rights. The main turning point was the reaction of Muslims in Western European countries to Salman Rushdie's book *The Satanic Verses* in the beginning of 1989, which can be considered the Berlin Wall of the multicultural debate.

When Muslims took to the streets of London, Rotterdam, The Hague, Brussels, Berlin, and Paris to support Ayatollah Khomeini's fatwa on Rushdie, in some cases burning copies of the book, many Dutch were shocked and interpreted these actions as an attack on the progressive, liberal achievements of the cultural revolution of the 1960s in the Netherlands (Lucassen and Lucassen 2011: 21–24). Soon, however, the anti-Muslim sentiment was annexed by the right (Frits Bolkestein), and by left-wing converts like Pim Fortuyn and Ayaan Hirsi Ali. Fortuyn, in particular, was successful in introducing the idea that the left was to blame, because it had introduced and embraced a cultural relativist multicultural model that undermined the core values of Western democracies. Not surprisingly, this "frame" and anti-Muslim sentiment were strengthened by the terrorist attacks on New York and Washington on September 11, 2001, the murder of Pim Fortuyn in 2002, and the brutal murder of Theo van Gogh in 2004 in broad daylight in the streets of Amsterdam by an Amsterdam-born Muslim fundamentalist of Moroccan origin (Buruma 2007).

The position of Amsterdam in this national debate is ambiguous. On the one hand, in comparison with other Dutch cities it is home to the largest number of Moroccans and Turks, both in relative and absolute terms. Furthermore, their concentrations in certain neighborhoods has led to visible street criminality and antisocial behavior, as well as harassment of indigenous Jews and gays, especially by young men of Moroccan descent. Amsterdam is also known as a center of small groups of Muslim extremists (think of the assassin of Theo van Gogh), including jihadist Salafi Muslims (Roex et al. 2010). On the other hand, anti-immigrant populist parties, like Fortuyn's eponymous Lijst Pim Fortuyn (LPF) and more recently Geert Wilders's Freedom Party (PVV), have been much less successful in Amsterdam than in Rotterdam and The Hague. In the June 2010 national elections, populist anti-immigrant parties received about 10 percent of the votes in Amsterdam as compared to 17 percent in The Hague and 20 percent in Rotterdam. It is likely that Amsterdam's more favorable economic opportunity structure, with a strong cosmopolitan cultural industry sector and large proportion of highly educated inhabitants, has something to do with these results (see Kloosterman, this volume). Indeed, it has been a municipal strategy to revamp Amsterdam into a highly diverse, culturally exciting hub for white-collar creative professionals, a strategy that has insulated Amsterdam somewhat from national trends.[3] Another factor may be involved, as well. In contrast to Rotterdam, a substantial part of the Amsterdam working class has moved to the nearby satellite municipality of Almere, where the populist anti-immigrant parties gained 26 percent of the vote in the 2010 elections. It seems that these factors are more important than Amsterdam's long tradition as a major immigrant city in accounting for why anti-immigrant political parties have not done as well there as in other major Dutch urban centers.

Conclusion

Compared to the case of "New Amsterdam" (Foner 2000), the juxtaposition of old and new immigration in "Old Amsterdam" produces a slightly different picture. Amsterdam's immigrant past is much more remote than New York City's and, given the long time lag, has failed to engage collective memories to the same degree. Although the myopic thinking in "good" (then) and "bad" (now) migrants has also framed discussions in New York (Foner 2000), in Amsterdam, the collective memory of earlier migration is even more selective, with a very one-sided focus on successful ("good") migrants then, like the

Huguenots, rich Antwerp merchants, and Sephardic Jews, and on the
"bad" migrants now. That the bulk of the migrants in the early modern period ended up at the bottom of the labor market and a considerable portion of today's newcomers are highly skilled is largely ignored.
Furthermore, there is no personal or institutional continuity or shared
memory, as in New York, where third-generation descendants of those
who came in the great wave of the early twentieth century can literally
shake hands with immigrants in the most recent wave. Nor is it just a
matter of memory. It is highly relevant in New York City to examine
how immigrants a hundred years ago influenced institutions affecting
contemporary newcomers (see Foner, this volume) whereas in Amsterdam, the last great wave of migration three centuries ago has had a negligible impact on the present and occurred at a time when, among other
things, a completely different political system and economic institutions existed.

What stands out in Amsterdam, in looking at immigration in the
past and present, are the contrasts between the distant then and the
immediate now. One difference has to do with migration dynamics that
developed beginning in the 1950s. As I have explained, the unintended
effects of generous welfare state policies, combined with the equally
unintended effects of restrictive aliens policies in the 1970s, led to a
mass settlement of low-skilled newcomers at a bad moment in the business cycle. The consequence was not only that the demographic and
cultural composition of neighborhoods in the capital (and other cities)
was transformed, but also that a range of social and cultural problems
developed. These problems seriously eroded the acceptance of immigrants and contributed to the widespread view that immigration was
economically, socially, and culturally detrimental. Although immigration has always provoked negative reactions in the Netherlands,
the configuration in Amsterdam in the 1970–2010 period stands out
because of the very different migration dynamics. During the Golden
Age, the pull of the labor market played a much more important role in
determining the ups and downs of migration and produced a better fit
between labor market needs and migration flows.

Another difference between Amsterdam's past and present can be
captured in the term democracy. During the seventeenth and eighteenth centuries, when Amsterdam pursued its open door policy as

the only Dutch city, the merchant elite determined migration policies and democracy was an alien idea; protest and discomfort among native Amsterdammers (a problematic concept given the high rates of immigration at the time) could not be channeled and mobilized by political entrepreneurs. Current populist policies may be detrimental to the economic and social fabric of societies, but they are still an integral part and expression of the contemporary democratic regime.

Finally, the current discomfort with immigration in Amsterdam (and beyond) is the product of the ideal of equality, first formulated on a mass scale by the French Revolution, but systematically elaborated by European welfare states after World War II. One of the effects was that by diminishing social and economic differences states increasingly problematized segments of the population regarded as social misfits and labeled with terms like "antisocials" and "underclass." Social engineering programs that were developed since the early twentieth century sometimes gave way to eugenic measures (as in Scandinavia) and after World War II were also applied to immigrants with a weak social position (Lucassen 2010). Thus, fighting discrimination and inequality has given way to a wide range of social programs and policies, of which the Dutch minorities or integration policy since the late 1970s is one. As I have argued, these have had beneficial and cushioning effects, as they prevented widespread underclass formation, but at the same time an unintended consequence is that they contributed to problematizing and essentializing immigrants and their descendants. Categorizations like "allochthones" are not just statistical notions meant for policy use, but have been transformed into social facts that are difficult to eradicate, with use of the term "third-generation Moroccans" (or Turks) the most recent telling example.

In short, fundamental ideological and institutional shifts have created very different migration and integration dynamics in the present than existed in earlier eras of mass migration in Amsterdam. Migrations of centuries ago have had little direct effect on the institutions or culture that have confronted the more recent postwar arrivals. Indeed, it is the very forgetting of the role of migration in the far-off past—and common belief in a relatively ethnically homogenous city before the postwar waves—that have helped shape attitudes toward and the reaction to immigrants and their children in the contemporary period.

NOTES

1. I thank the editors of this volume, Jan Rath, Jan Willem Duyvendak, Rogier van Reekum, and Nancy Foner, for their constructive criticism on an earlier version.
2. It should be noted that Turks and Moroccans, who cannot give up their original nationality, often have two passports and thus double nationality.
3. I thank Rogier van Reekum for this suggestion.

REFERENCES

Asche, Matthias. 2011. "Huguenots in Europe Since the 16th Century," in Klaus J. Bade, Pieter C. Emmer, Leo Lucassen, and Jochen Oltmer (eds.), *The Encyclopedia of Migration and Minorities in Europe: From the 17th Century to the Present*. New York: Cambridge University Press.

Bonjour, Saskia. 2009. *Grens En Gezin: Beleidsvorming Inzake Gezinsmigratie in Nederland, 1955–2005*. Amsterdam: Aksant.

———. 2011. "The Power and Morals of Policy Makers: Reassessing the Control Gap Debate." *International Migration Review* 45 (1): 89–122.

Buruma, Ian. 2007. *Murder in Amsterdam: The Death of Theo van Gogh and the Limits of Tolerance*. London: Atlantic Books.

Chotkowski, Margaret. 2006. *Vijftien ladders en een dambord. Contacten van Italiaanse migranten in Nederland 1860–1940*. Amsterdam: Aksant.

Cohen, Robert. 1982. "Passage to a New World: The Sephardi Poor of Eighteenth-Century Amsterdam," in Lea Dasberg and Jonathan N. Cohen (eds.), *Neveh Ya'kov. Jubilee Volume Presented to Dr. Jaap Meijer*. Assen: Van Gorcum.

Cottaar, Annemarie. 2003. "Onzedelijk of Preuts? Surinaamse Modellen in De Hoofdstad." *Optima* 4: 125–35.

Cottaar, Annemarie, and Leo Lucassen. 2001. "Naar de Laatste Parijse Mode: Strohoedenmakers uit het Jekerdal in Nederland 1750–1900." *Studies over de sociaal-economische geschiedenis van Limburg/ Jaarboek van het Sociaal Historisch Centrum voor Limburg* 46: 45–82.

Deinema, Michael, and Robert Kloosterman. 2012. "The City and the Art of Earning: Cultural Industries in the Twentieth-Century Netherlands," in Leo Lucassen and Wim Willems (eds.), *Living in the City. Urban Institutions in the Low Countries, 1200–2010*. New York: Routledge.

De Vries, Jan. 1984. *European Urbanization 1500–1800*. London: Methuen.

Dittrich, Kathinka and Hans Würzner, eds. 1982. *Nederland En Het Duitse Exil 1933–1940*. Amsterdam: Van Gennep.

Duyvendak, Jan Willem, and Peter W. A. Scholten. 2010. "Beyond the Dutch 'Multicultural Model': The Coproduction of Integration Policy Frames in the Netherlands." *Journal of International Migration and Integration* 12: 331–48.

Foner, Nancy. 2000. *From Ellis Island to JFK: New York's Two Great Waves of Immigration*. New Haven, CT: Yale University Press.

Foner, Nancy, and Leo Lucassen. 2012. "Legacies of the Past," in Maurice Crul and John Mollenkopf (eds.), *The Changing Face of World Cities*. New York: Russell Sage Foundation.

Gelderblom, Oscar. 2003. "From Antwerp to Amsterdam: The Contribution of Merchants from the Southern Netherlands to the Commercial Expansion of Amsterdam (c. 1540–1609)." *Review* 26 (3): 247–82.

Gelderblom, Oscar, and Joost Jonker. 2005. "Amsterdam as the Cradle of Modern Futures Trading and Options Trading, 1550–1650," in William N. Goetzmann and K. Geert Rouwenhorst (eds.), *The Origins of Value: The Financial Innovations That Created Modern Capital Markets*. Oxford: Oxford University Press.

Hofmeester, Karin. 1990. *Van Talmoed Tot Statuut. Joodse Arbeiders En Arbeidersbewegingen in Amsterdam: Londen En Parijs, 1880–1914*. Amsterdam: Stichting Beheer IISG.

Hollifield, James F. 1992. *Immigrants, Markets, and States: The Political Economy of Postwar Europe*. Cambridge, MA: Harvard University Press.

Hughes, Everett C. 1945. "Dilemmas and Contradictions of Status." *American Journal of Sociology* 50 (March): 353–59.

Kaal, Harm, and Jelle van Lottum. 2003. "Duitse Warmoezeniers in Watergraafsmeer in de 18e en 19e Eeuw." *Holland* 35 (4): 263–76.

Knotter, Ad, and Jan Luiten van Zanden. 1987. "Immigratie En Arbeidsmarkt in Amsterdam in De 17e Eeuw." *Tijdschrift voor Sociale Geschiedenis* 13: 403–31.

Kuijpers, Erika. 2005. *Migrantenstad: Immigratie En Sociale Verhoudingen in Zeventiende-Eeuws Amsterdam*. Hilversum: Verloren.

Kuijpers, Erika, and Maarten Prak. 2004. "Gevestigden En Buitenstaanders," in Willem Frijhoff (ed.), *Geschiedenis Van Amsterdam*. Amsterdam: SUN.

Lesger, Clé. 2006. *The Rise of the Amsterdam Market and Information Exchange: Merchants, Commercial Expansion and Change in the Spatial Economy of the Low Countries, c.1550–1630* Aldershot: Ashgate.

Lesger, Clé, Leo Lucassen, and Marlou Schrover. 2002. "Is There Life Outside the Migrant Network? German Immigrants in XIXth Century Netherlands and the Need for a More Balanced Migration Typology." *Annales de Démographie Historique* 2: 29–50.

Lucassen, Jan. 1994. "Joodse Nederlanders 1796–1940: Een Proces Van Omgekeerde Minderheidsvorming," in Hetty Berg, Thera Wijsenbeek, and Eric Fischer (eds.), *Venter, Fabriqueur, Fabrikant: Joodse Ondernemers En Ondernemingen in Nederland, 1796–1940*. Amsterdam: Joods Historisch Museum and NEHA.

Lucassen, Jan, and Leo Lucassen. 2009. "The Mobility Transition Revisited, 1500–1900: What the Case of Europe Can Offer to Global History." *Journal of Global History* 4 (4): 347–77.

Lucassen, Leo. 2002. "Bringing Structure Back In: Economic and Political Determinants of Immigration in Dutch Cities, 1920–1940." *Social Science History* 26 (3): 503–29.

———. 2005. *The Immigrant Threat: The Integration of Old and New Migrants in Western Europe since 1850*. Urbana and Chicago: University of Illinois Press.

Lucassen, Leo. 2010. "A Brave New World: The Left, Social Engineering, and Eugenics in Twentieth-Century Europe." *International Review of Social History* 55 (2): 265–396.

———. 2012. "Cities, States and Migration Control in Western Europe: Comparing Then and Now," in Bert de Munck and Anne Winter (eds.), *Gated Communities? Regulating Migration in Early Modern Cities*. Aldershot: Ashgate.

Lucassen, Leo, and Jan Lucassen. 2011. *Winnaars En Verliezers: Een Nuchtere Balans Van Vijf Eeuwen Immigratie*. Amsterdam: Bert Bakker.

Lucassen, Leo, and Boudien de Vries. 2001. "The Rise and Fall of a Western European Textile-Worker Migration System: Leiden, 1586–1700." *Revue du Nord* 15 (Hors serie): 23–42.

Nederveen Meerkerk, Elise. 2012. "Employment, Education and Social Assistance: The Economic Attraction of Early Modern Cities," in Leo Lucassen and Wim Winders (eds.), *Living in the City. Urban Institutions in the Low Countries, 1200–2010*. New York and London, Routledge.

O+S (Onderzoek en Statistiek Amsterdam). 2010. *2010 Jaarboek*. Amsterdam: Dienst Onderzoek en Statistiek.

———. 2011. *Kerncijfers Amsterdam 2011*. Amsterdam: Dienst Onderzoek en Statistiek.

Parker, Charles H. 2006. "Paying for the Privilege: The Management of Public Order and Religious Pluralism in Two Early Modern Societies." *Journal of World History* 17: 267–96.

Prak, Maarten. 2005. *The Dutch Republic in the Seventeenth Century: A Golden Age*. Cambridge: Cambridge University Press.

Rath, Jan (ed.) 2007. *Tourism, Ethnic Diversity, and the City*. New York: Routledge.

Roex, Ineke, and Sjef van Stiphout, et al. 2010. *Salafisme in Nederland. Aard, omvang en dreiging*. Amsterdam: IMES.

Roitman, Jessica. 2011. *The Same but Different? Inter-Cultural Trade and the Sephardim 1595–1640*. Leiden and Boston: Brill.

Scholten, Peter. 2011. *Framing Immigrant Integration: Dutch Research-Policy Dialogues in Comparative Perspective*. Amsterdam: Amsterdam University Press.

Schrover, Marlou. 2006. "Whenever a Dozen Germans Meet: German Organisations in the Netherlands in the Nineteenth Century." *Journal of Ethnic and Migration Studies* 32 (5): 847–64.

Sonnenberg-Stern, Katrina. 2000. *Emancipation and Poverty: The Ashkenazi Jews of Amsterdam, 1796–1850*. Basingstoke: Macmillan.

Spaaij, Ramón. 2006. *Understanding Football Hooliganism: A Comparison of Six Western European Football Clubs*. Amsterdam: Amsterdam University Press.

Tammes, Peter. 2007. "Jewish Immigrants in the Netherlands During the Nazi Occupation." *Journal of Interdisciplinary History* 37: 543–62.

———. 2010. "Jewish–Gentile Intermarriage in Pre-war Amsterdam." *History of the Family* 15: 298–315.

Van de Pol, Lotte, and Erika Kuijpers. 2005. "Poor Women's Migration to the City: The Attraction of Amsterdam Health Care and Social Assistance in Early Modern Times." *Journal of Urban History* 32 (1): 44–60.

Van Kolfschooten, Frank. 1998. *De koningin van Plan Zuid: Geschiedenissen uit de Beethovenstraat*. Amsterdam: Veen.

Van Lottum, Jelle. 2007. *Across the North Sea: The Impact of the Dutch Republic on International Labour Migration, C. 1550–1850*. Amsterdam: Aksant.

Van Rossum, Matthias. 2009. *Hand Aan Hand (Blank En Bruin). Solidariteit En De Werking Van Globalisering, Etniciteit En Klasse Onder Zeelieden Op De Nederlandse Koopvaardij, 1900–1945*. Amsterdam: Aksant.

Van Zanden, Jan Luiten, and Maarten Prak. 2006. "Towards an Economic Interpretation of Citizenship: The Dutch Republic between Medieval Communes and Modern Nation States." *European Review of Economic History* 10: 111–45.

Vermeulen, Floris. 2006. *The Immigrant Organising Process: The Emergence and Persistence of Turkish Immigrant Organisations in Amsterdam and Berlin and Surinamese Organisations in Amsterdam, 1960–2000*. Amsterdam: Amsterdam University Press.

Willems, Wim. 2001. *De Uittocht Uit Indië, 1945–1995*. Amsterdam: Bert Bakker.

———. 2003. "No Sheltering Sky: Migrant Identities of Dutch Nationals from Indonesia," in Andrea L. Smith (ed.), *Europe's Invisible Migrants*. Amsterdam: Amsterdam University Press.

Willems, Wim, Annemarie Cottaar, et al. 2010. *Een Draak Met Vele Gezichten: Chinatown Den Haag 1920–2010*. The Hague: De Nieuwe Haagsche.

PART II

What Difference Does the Urban Economy Make to Immigrant Incorporation?

The spatial concentration of economic activities and the concomitant proliferation of economic opportunities have always encouraged individuals to gravitate to urban environments. The development of Amsterdam and New York as diverse and economically powerful world cities and immigrant meccas is evidently no exception. Both cities emerged at sites where (international) water ways and country roads meet. And both have become catchment areas for individuals looking for new opportunities. These individuals have indeed propelled further developments, economic and otherwise. Savvy entrepreneurship, hard—often unremitting—labor, and confidence strengthened the strategic exploitation of their favorable geographical locations. Amsterdam and New York started as trading posts, and both soon found themselves at the crossroads of different, but interconnected population flows and economic systems. It is no coincidence that Amsterdam (in the seventeenth century) and New York (in the twentieth century) were able to rise to become vibrant hearts of globally dominant empires (Chua 2009).

Patterns that developed in times of yore created path dependencies that make themselves felt even today. Within their own countries, but also at a global level, Amsterdam and New York are still thriving economic centers, providing jobs and other economic opportunities to hundreds of thousands of immigrants—documented and undocumented alike—as well as international businesspersons, among others.

In considering the following two chapters on the economy in New York and in Amsterdam it is useful to situate them in the context of the two different, but complementary, approaches that have shaped much of the work on immigrants and urban economies. While some social scientists approach the interrelationship of economy and migration from an immigration perspective, others take the political economy as a starting point. Those in the first category typically focus on the arrival of immigrants in the host city and subsequent processes of incorporation into the labor market. Among the topics of research interest are the formation and mobilization of economically relevant ethnic networks, the creation of ethnic occupational niches, the role of ethnic businesses in helping or hindering incorporation and mobility, and the persistence or disappearance of economically relevant ethnic boundaries. The economy-immigration nexus is usually seen as a field of immigrant assimilation, or integration, with the units of analysis being individual immigrants or the ethnic groups they constitute. Some scholars look at the role of the government and other regulatory institutions: how and to what purpose do politicians and policy makers seek to influence post-migratory processes? Common research topics are the nature of employment or self-employment of group X compared to group Y—and the reasons for the patterns. Do immigrants from Turkey fare better in the labor market than immigrants from Suriname? Are Korean immigrants more entrepreneurial than Dominicans? It is obviously interesting—and important—to explore how particular immigrant groups find their way into the labor market and how they compare to each other, although in some cases "ethnic dynamics" may seem to be more relevant than "economic dynamics" and the nature of the economies in which immigrants operate.

Those in the second category, who take the political economy as their starting point, focus on different questions having to with what are often called local accumulation regimes. Their research revolves around such themes as the embeddedness of the urban economy in wider (regional or global) structures, the industries that dominate a particular urban setting, the job or entrepreneurial opportunities these industries create, the skills, competences, qualifications, and networks needed to successfully contribute to those economies, and the transformation of urban economies from being based on manufacturing industries to being based on the production, circulation, and consumption of knowledge and of goods and services with a high symbolic value. Some also pay attention to the regulatory regimes that foster or thwart such economic developments. Typical units of analyses are industries or urban economic systems. These are the institutions that provide opportunities to urbanites, immigrants and natives alike, although—given particular economic or regulatory conditions—some individuals profit more from these opportunities than others.

The two chapters in this section of the volume address the question as to what difference the urban economy makes to immigrant incorporation, with the authors taking different epistemological positions and speaking to, and drawing on, different literatures. David Dyssegaard Kallick explores how foreign-born and U.S.-born New Yorkers are faring in the New York labor market, thus focusing to a large extent on issues that fit in with the first category of approaches laid out above. He examines racial and ethnic disparities and immigrant status and explores how important they are in shaping success in New York City's labor market for immigrants and native born alike. Robert Kloosterman, taking a political economy approach, discusses the urban economic transformations that Amsterdam has undergone in the past few decades, from being in deep economic crisis to having a thriving and strong urban economy, and how these structural changes have affected immigrants' labor market performance.

The chapters point to a number of similarities between New York and Amsterdam, one of them being that the labor markets in each city are profoundly different from those that existed in the mid-twentieth century. At that time, both economies had much stronger manufacturing-industry sectors, offering numerous jobs to blue-collar workers under a Fordist accumulation regime. Globalization, more particularly the introduction of a new international division of labor, fostered the downgrading of such industries and the concomitant relocation of relatively well-paid manufacturing jobs to regions with cheaper labor. By the end of the twentieth century, both New York and Amsterdam had managed to carve out a niche in the new global economy as postindustrial, service-oriented cities, although both the scale and impact in

New York City are much greater than in Amsterdam (cf. Sassen 1991; Hamnett 1994, 1996). In both cities, these developments have seriously impacted the labor market position of newcomers.

In his chapter, Kloosterman argues that policies of the national and local governments are critical in explaining the turnaround in Amsterdam's economy in recent decades— and economic opportunities for immigrants and natives alike—as the policies reshaped Dutch institutional frameworks. In various ways and by developing a wide array of instruments, the Dutch government stimulated growth at the lower end of the service sector, for example. It managed to make fundamental changes in the welfare system (for instance, dramatically reducing the rights to unemployment and disability benefits) and what had been a relatively static corporatist organization of the economy. This restructuring boiled down to a liberalization of the economy. At the same time, the government policies have led to a cultural shift in the way people in the Netherlands think about their economic activities and the institutional makeup of such activities—including what Kloosterman calls an entrenched subculture of unemployment—a cultural shift that admittedly would not have been possible without various bottom-up initiatives as well. In the end, the economic recovery documented by Kloosterman resulted in much better labor market prospects, even though many low-skilled immigrants are still lagging behind.

In Kallick's chapter, in contrast, immigrant experiences are at the heart of the analysis. Taken as a whole, as he shows, immigrants in New York City do almost as well as U.S.-born workers in terms of wages, benefits, and occupational status, but because so many family members work in immigrant households, the foreign born are actually more likely to live in families in the middle-income brackets than the U.S. born. There is, however, a lot of difference in how different immigrant groups are faring in the economy, with a large proportion in some groups, such as Mexicans, struggling to make ends meet in low-level jobs, while a substantial proportion in other groups, such as Asian Indians, are doing quite well. Race and ethnicity also continue to play a determining role among the U.S. as well as foreign born, leading Kallick to conclude that they may be more important than nativity in predicting success in New York City's labor market.

A striking difference between the two cities that comes out in the two chapters has to do with unemployment. In New York, immigrants have had lower unemployment rates than the native born in recent years, while in Amsterdam the reverse is true, especially when it comes to non-Western immigrants. The labor market–welfare state nexus is key, with Amsterdam still offering a much broader array of social welfare benefits to immigrants (as well as the native born). In the absence of the more generous state protections available in Amsterdam, immigrant New Yorkers often have no alternative but to take whatever jobs are on offer, including low-end, low-wage jobs that may still leave them in poverty. A full consideration of the urban economy's impact on immigrants thus needs to consider not only labor market issues but also the social welfare benefits, or safety net, made available by local and national governments.

JAN RATH

REFERENCES

Hamnett, Chris. 1994. "Social Polarisation in Global Cities: Theory and Evidence." *Urban Studies* 31 (44): 401–25.

———. 1996. "Why Sassen Is Wrong: A Response to Burgers." *Urban Studies* 33 (1): 107–11.

Sassen, Saskia. 1991. *The Global City: New York, London, Tokyo.* Princeton, NJ: Princeton University Press.

3

Immigrants in New York City's Economy

A Portrait in Full Living Color

DAVID DYSSEGAARD KALLICK

New York is in a period of immigration as extensive as at any time in its long history as a hub of international migration. As of 2009, three million immigrants lived in New York City, comprising 36 percent of the population—making immigration comparable to the twentieth-century peak in 1910, when two million immigrants made up 41 percent of the city's population.[1] Today, immigrants are central to every aspect of city life, certainly including the economy: immigrants' share of total economic output is nearly exactly equivalent to their share of the population (Fiscal Policy Institute 2007).

Over the last few decades, the city has seen moderate economic growth, punctuated by serious recessions. There has been a big expansion in the finance sector, and an increased number of low-wage service jobs. Median wages have been flat or falling, while earnings at the top have been climbing fast.

Perhaps the most striking feature of the city's economy in recent decades has been the extraordinary degree of income polarization. A chart developed by economists Thomas Piketty and Emmanuel Saez (Saez 2010) tracking the share of income going to the top 1 percent of tax filers in the United States as a whole in the last hundred years shows that income concentration has returned to a level not seen since before the stock market crash of 1929, with the top 1 percent receiving 24 percent of all income in 2007. This national trend pales, however, in comparison to the degree of polarization in New York City, where the top 1 percent of taxpayers received 44 percent of all income in 2007 (figure 3.1). That is both staggering and new: as recently as 1980 just 12 percent of income accrued to the top 1 percent in New York City. It is into this context that immigrants are entering the New York City economy today—one in which all workers in low- and middle-wage jobs face substantial challenges.

How, then, are immigrants faring in New York City's economy? Considering this question is a bit like looking through a kaleidoscope: the picture changes depending on how you turn the various parts. In answering this question, I will present several important twists of the dial.

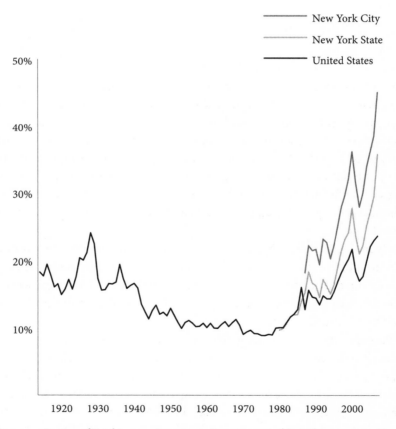

Figure 3.1. Portion of Total Income Accruing to Top 1 Percent of Tax Filers, 1914 to 2007
Sources: Saez (2010); Fiscal Policy Institute (2010).

First, I will compare immigrants to U.S.-born New Yorkers—the broadest gauge of how well immigrants are fitting into the city's economy. I will show the extent to which immigrants are employed and concentrated in certain jobs, how income in immigrant families compares to that of U.S.-born families, and whether immigrants are as likely as U.S.-born families to be union members or to own homes.

Then, I will look into the most salient racial and ethnic categories in New York: white, black, Latino, and Asian. Both U.S.-born and foreign-born groups are highly diverse, with the differences among ethnoracial groups often as significant as the differences based on nativity. The kaleidoscope is twisted a bit further by looking at different countries of origin for immigrants. While immigrants overall are spread fairly well across a broad occupational spectrum, some groups are strongly clustered—so that Mexican immigrants, for example, are highly concentrated among low-wage workers and immigrants from India among high-wage workers.

While other studies have looked at how immigrants are faring in the New York City economy,[2] here I will provide a full-color portrait, considering how immigrants compare to U.S.-born workers, as well as how subsets of each group compare across and within the lines of nativity. In the analysis that follows, the terms "immigrants" and "foreign born" are used interchangeably. All people born in another country and living in the United States are counted as immigrants, whether or not they have become naturalized citizens and regardless of legal status. The figures on immigrants include both legal and undocumented immigrants, except where otherwise noted. People born in the United States, including in U.S. territories such as Puerto Rico and the Virgin Islands, and children born abroad to U.S.-citizen parents, are defined as U.S. born, as are U.S.-born children of immigrants (the second generation).

The Overall Picture: How Immigrants Compare to U.S.-Born Workers

Taken as a group, immigrants in New York City are not as dramatically different from their U.S.-born counterparts on various economic measures as is often assumed, even when including the estimated half-million or so undocumented immigrants.

Not that there are no differences. Immigrant wages are lower than wages for U.S.-born workers—by about 15 to 25 percent after adjusting for level of educational attainment. Among those at the most modest level of educational attainment—people over 25 years old who have not finished high school—the median annual wage for full-time workers was $24,000 for immigrants and $30,000 for U.S.-born workers in 2009. The median annual wage for those who had completed college was $52,000 for immigrants and $64,000 for the U.S. born, and for those with advanced degrees, $70,000 for immigrants and $85,000 for the U.S. born (table 3.1).

While there are concentrations of immigrants in some occupations, and many low-wage immigrant workers, there are also a substantial number of immigrants working in generally higher-paid white-collar jobs. About half of immigrants work in white-collar jobs—belying a common impression that a "typical" immigrant works in one of a few low-skill, low-wage jobs. The other half work in blue-collar and service jobs—as do about a quarter of U.S.-born New Yorkers.

The difference between the occupations of U.S.-born and foreign-born workers is hardly trivial, yet there are enough immigrants in higher-wage positions that generalizations about low-wage immigrants often land wide of the mark. Immigrants, who are 46 percent of the New York City resident labor force, are spread significantly across the economic spectrum: they make up between 20 and 85 percent of nearly

Table 3.1. Immigrant and U.S.-Born Median Annual Wages in New York City, 2009

	Foreign born	U.S. born	Difference between the two
Less than high school	$24,000	$30,000	-20%
High school	$30,000	$40,000	-25%
Some college	$38,000	$45,000	-16%
College completion	$52,000	$64,000	-19%
Advanced degree	$70,000	$85,000	-18%
All	$37,000	$55,000	-33%

Note: New York City residents 25 years of age and older, working year-round (50 or more weeks per year) and full-time (35 or more hours per week), employed in the civilian labor force with at least $100 in annual wages.

Source: Fiscal Policy Institute analysis of 2009 American Community Survey.

all detailed occupations (that is, occupations at the level of specificity of cooks, designers, or bus drivers). Of the 58 detailed occupations with more than 7,500 immigrants, there is only one in which immigrants make up less than 20 percent of workers—lawyers and judges, an occupational category with 12 percent foreign-born workers, a very low share for New York, though hardly a trivial share in general. To anyone familiar with New York City it will not be a surprise to learn that immigrants make up three-quarters of the city's construction laborers and nursing aides, as well as half of the building cleaners. It may come as a surprise, however, to find that immigrants are 52 percent of computer programmers, 50 percent of accountants, 40 percent of physicians and surgeons, 54 percent of registered nurses, and 32 percent of college professors, to pick just a few examples.

Unions play an important role in the city's economy, helping to raise wages for low-wage workers and to keep wages for workers with the same level of experience roughly comparable. Unionization rates are somewhat lower for immigrants than for U.S.-born workers, but the difference is relatively modest—in 2009–10, 23 percent of immigrants in New York City were union members, compared to 26 percent of U.S.-born workers (Milkman and Braslow 2010). The fact that these rates are so much higher than for the nation as a whole—where the unionization rate was just 13 percent during the same period—makes it clear that the degree of unionization in a local area or industry is a far more important factor than nativity in determining labor union membership (Fiscal Policy Institute 2007; 2001–2006 data for both New York and the U.S.).

In the United States, most people get family health insurance through their employer (usually paid in part by the employer and in part by the employee). A small number purchase insurance directly from insurance companies, usually at a high premium. Those with very low incomes can get health insurance through Medicaid (government health insurance for low-income individuals); low-income families in New York can get care through the state's Child Health Plus and Family Health Plus programs; and senior citizens are eligible for Medicare (a federal program that pays for certain health care expenses for those 65 and older). In addition, a significant number of people are simply uninsured, risking potentially huge health costs. The quality of health care for those with insurance is generally good and often excellent. For those without insurance, however, the risk of getting sick and incurring a devastating debt is very real, and even people with insurance can wind up with debilitating debts if a procedure winds up being only partially covered. One indication of the extent of the risk is revealed by a recent study, which found that in 2008, unanticipated health care costs were the reason for 49 percent of home foreclosures in the country (Robinson, Egelhof, and Hoke 2008).

In New York City, health-care coverage for people under 65 years old follows the same pattern as for wages—immigrants are moderately less likely to have employer-provided coverage than U.S.-born residents. A little under half of U.S.-born New Yorkers get health insurance through their employer, as do 41 percent of their foreign-born counterparts. U.S.-born workers are also somewhat more likely to have public insurance (Child Health Plus, Medicaid, or Family Health Plus)—35 percent of U.S.-born New Yorkers have public insurance, as do 27 percent of foreign born. Similarly small numbers (4 percent) of the U.S. and foreign born have insurance they purchased themselves. The big difference between immigrants and the native born is among those with no insurance at all: 29 percent of foreign-born New York City residents are uninsured, compared with 13 percent of U.S. born (author's calculations based on figures in United Hospital Fund 2010: 63.)

That 43 percent of immigrants in New York City are of prime working age, from 16 to 64 years old, accounts for most, though not all, of the difference between immigrants' 36 percent share of the population and 46 percent share of the labor force. The other significant factor is that immigrants—or, more exactly, immigrant men—have a higher labor force participation rate than their U.S.-born counterparts. Labor force participation rates for U.S.- and foreign-born women are in fact identical, at 58 percent. Yet immigrant men are considerably more likely to be in the labor force than U.S.-born men—76 percent compared to 66 percent. Whether this is by choice, by necessity, or because some low-wage employers may be more likely to hire immigrants than U.S.-born workers, it means that immigrants on average are more likely to be working.

Looking at unemployment, immigrants in New York are also faring comparatively well. Although the Great Recession of 2008–2009 has pushed up unemployment rates for both U.S.- and foreign-born workers, the unemployment rate for immigrant workers was slightly lower than for U.S-born workers both in the second half of 2009, at the low point of the recession, and in the six months from October 2010 to March 2011, one year into the still very weak recovery. The unemployment rate for immigrants went from 8.6 percent at the recession's low point to 8.2 percent a year into the recovery, while the unemployment rate for U.S.-born workers went from 11.1 percent to 9.4 percent over the same period (Fiscal Policy Institute 2011: 18).

Immigrants may be less likely to be unemployed than U.S.-born workers, but when they are, they often face harsher conditions. Some categories of immigrants are excluded from eligibility for unemployment insurance (although so are significant numbers of U.S.-born workers). For example, substantial numbers of both immigrants and U.S.-born workers—but a bigger share of immigrants— are either paid off the books, or are misclassified as independent contractors when they are actually employees, making it difficult for them to receive unemployment benefits unless they can retroactively prove their eligibility. In addition, to receive unemployment benefits, immigrants must be authorized to work in the U.S. even if they do not have a current job. This policy excludes all undocumented immigrants—about one out of six immigrants in New York City. It also excludes immigrants who are in the United States on work-dependent visas, such as H1B visas, which are frequently used for finance and technology jobs. Unemployment insurance, in any case, is not a very soft cushion against unemployment for any workers, U.S. or foreign born. In 2008, the maximum unemployment insurance payment was just $405 per week, and the average payment, at only $296 per week, was less than 30 percent of the average weekly wage in New York State (Fiscal Policy Institute 2008).

One important point of difference with U.S.-born New Yorkers is that immigrants tend to have more workers per family. Immigrant families (those with at least one immigrant adult) are more likely to have two people working than those of their U.S.-born counterparts—37 percent of immigrants live in two-worker families, compared to 31 percent of U.S.-born New Yorkers. An even more noticeable difference is the number of immigrants living in families with three or more family members working—17 percent, compared to 8 percent for U.S.-born families.

The consequence of having more family members working is that, despite their lower overall wages, immigrants are more likely to live in families in middle-income brackets, as table 3.2 shows. The share of people living in immigrant families with less than $20,000 per year in income (14 percent) is two percentage points lower than the U.S.-born share (17 percent—a difference that registers as two percentage points due to independent rounding). By contrast, the share of people living in immigrant families in the middle three income brackets—ranging from $20,000 to $80,000—is from three to five percentage points higher than for U.S.-born families. As at the bottom of the income distribution, the share at the top of the income distribution is also lower for immigrant families, with a difference of three points for people earning from $80,000 to $200,000, and six percentage points for people earning over $200,000 per year.

Living in families with more working adults may have other advantages. For example, having more workers per family may help explain how immigrants manage to have similar rates of home ownership to U.S.-born New Yorkers. In New York City, 31 percent of first-generation immigrants live in owner-occupied housing, the same as for New Yorkers who have lived in the U.S. for three generations or more. The study from which these data are drawn separates second-generation immigrants from the first generation and third generation or higher—and reveals, interestingly, that home ownership is highest among second-generation immigrants. At 44 percent, the home-ownership rate for the second generation is considerably higher than for either first-generation

Table 3.2. Family Income Distribution in New York City, U.S. and Foreign Born, 2009

Share of individuals in families with incomes	Foreign born	U.S. born	Percentage point difference
Under $20,000	14%	17%	-2%
$20,000 to $39,999	21%	16%	5%
$40,000 to $59,999	16%	14%	3%
$60,000 to $79,999	14%	11%	3%
$80,000 to $199,999	29%	32%	-3%
$200,000 plus	6%	11%	-6%
Median family income	$56,500	$67,200	–

Note: Families are considered "foreign born" if they include at least one foreign-born adult. Differences may not sum due to rounding.
Source: Fiscal Policy Institute analysis of 2009 American Community Survey.

immigrants or third-or-higher-generation Americans (Waters and Bach 2011). These levels of home ownership, it should be noted, are far below the U.S. norm; in the country as a whole, families generally own their own homes. In New York City, however, there is a large stock of rental apartments, and two-thirds of New Yorkers—including many high-income residents—live in rental apartments. As with labor union membership, local conditions are far more important than nativity in determining how likely people are to own their homes.

There is also a downside in the housing picture for New York City immigrants: immigrants are considerably more likely than the U.S. born to live in overcrowded housing. A recent study found that 15 percent of immigrants live in overcrowded housing, compared to 9 percent of New Yorkers overall. The study used a definition of crowding that was moderate, defining overcrowding as more than one person per room—four or more people, for example, in a three-room apartment (Waters and Bach 2011).

Recognizing Diversity: How Immigrants and U.S.-Born Worke~ Differ by National Origin and Race and Ethnicity

presented so far, based on medians and averages, is impor-
~e, after all, the most comprehensive measures we have
are faring in the city's economy. Yet, in New York, both
U.S.-born residents are extremely diverse groups. As a
~ures can mask a very wide range of experiences.
~eveloped literature, for example, documenting the
~s of a wide variety of immigrant groups, from Indian
~wners to Mexican restaurant workers to Chinese garment
~ers and software engineers (e.g., Chin 2005; Foner 2000; Smith 2006; Waldinger 1996). Immigrants *on average* are spread broadly across the occupational spectrum. But this composite picture is made up of many different immigrant groups. As figure 3.2 shows, about half of all immigrant workers in New York City are in white-collar jobs, but the same is true of just 17 percent of Mexican immigrants, 24 percent of Ecuadorians, 27 percent of Hondurans, and 34 percent of Dominicans and Peruvians. As against these low percentages, about half of workers from Jamaica, Guyana, and Bangladesh are in white-collar jobs, as are about three-quarters of workers from India, Russia, and Hong Kong.

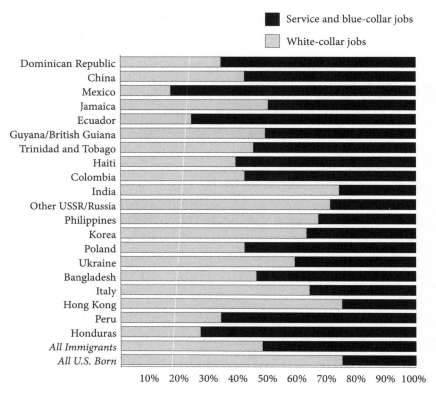

Figure 3.2. Immigrant Share of White-Collar Jobs in New York City, 2009
Source: Fiscal Policy Institute analysis of 2009 American Community Survey, based on broad occupations as defined in *Immigrants and the Economy,* Fiscal Policy Institute, 2009. Universe is New York City residents 16 years and older, employed in the civilian labor force. The service and blue-collar category also includes a very small number of farm, fishing, and forestry jobs. Order of groups in the chart is determined by share of labor force. Thus, the largest immigrant group in the labor force is immigrants born in the Dominican Republic, second is those born in China, third in Mexico, and so on.

Or consider home ownership. We saw that overall U.S.- and foreign-born levels of home ownership are quite similar in New York City. Yet, the overall figures hide a great deal of variation among different national origin groups. Just 8 percent of Mexican immigrants live in owner-occupied housing, at the low end of the range, while at the high end 47 percent of Europeans do (not including those from the former Soviet Union). To some extent this difference may reflect the fact that a higher proportion of Mexicans are very recent arrivals as compared to Europeans, who include many long-time New York residents. Yet, that is clearly not the whole explanation. Dominicans, for example, one of the earliest groups in the post-1965 "new immigration," have only a 10 percent rate of home ownership. New Yorkers born in China, Taiwan, and Korea have a 41 percent home-ownership rate, people from the Indian subcontinent have a 29 percent rate, and those from the Caribbean excluding the Dominican Republic have a 37 percent rate of home ownership—a range that seems independent of when the group first came to the United States (Waters and Bach 2011). No doubt other factors, including the availability of economic resources to purchase homes and cultural preferences for home ownership, as well as access to rent-stabilized apartments (whose rents are protected from sharp increases), are involved.[3] Indeed, the fact that Dominicans are concentrated in neighborhoods with substantial amounts of rent-stabilized apartments is no doubt an important reason why they have such low rates of home ownership (ibid.).

In addition to country of origin, legal status obviously makes a difference for immigrants. Of the half-million undocumented immigrant men, women, and children living in New York City, about 375,000 are in the labor force. Unlike immigrants overall, undocumented immigrants are clearly concentrated at the bottom of the economic ladder, and likely held there in part by their lack of working papers. There are some 21,000 undocumented immigrants working as cooks, 19,000 as janitors and building cleaners, 12,000 as sewing machine operators, and 11,000 as dishwashers in New York City. Bear in mind that undocumented workers are included in the statistics already presented for immigrant workers, suggesting that the economic gap between legal immigrants and U.S.-born workers is more modest than these overall data reflect (Pew Hispanic Center estimates for Fiscal Policy Institute 2007).

Although there is certainly some connection between country of origin and immigrants' legal status, in New York, undocumented immigrants are rather diverse. About a quarter of undocumented immigrants in New York City are from Mexico and Central America (27 percent), a quarter from South and East Asia (23 percent), and another quarter from the Caribbean (22 percent). About one in ten come from South America or Europe, one in twenty from Africa, and a tiny share from the Middle East, including Turkey (Pew Hispanic Center estimates for Fiscal Policy Institute 2007). This stands in stark contrast to the United States as a whole, where the clear majority of undocumented immigrants are from Mexico.

Undocumented immigrants, it should be noted, are particularly vulnerable to being mistreated by employers—to receiving reduced wages and enduring severely trying, sometimes dangerous, working conditions in the low-wage labor market where there is little enforcement of basic labor rights. A recent study of labor law violations in New York City found that undocumented immigrants were the most likely to be victimized. When it came to minimum wage violations, for example, the survey found that among men, 17 percent of low-wage workers experienced violations—for U.S.-born workers, the figure was 10 percent, for legal immigrants, 15 percent, and for undocumented immigrants,

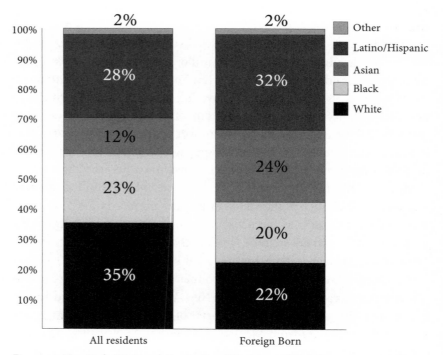

Figure 3.3. New York City Population by Race/Ethnicity and Nativity, 2009
Source: Fiscal Policy Institute analysis of 2009 American Community Survey. White, black, and Asian are non-Hispanic portions of each group.

29 percent. Among women, 24 percent of all low-wage workers experienced minimum-wage violations—13 percent for U.S.-born women, 24 percent for legal immigrants, and 40 percent for undocumented immigrants (Bernhardt, Polson, and DeFilippis 2010).

If immigrants are a varied group, so, too, are U.S.-born New Yorkers. Race and ethnicity make a real difference, the four major ethnoracial categories so often used in data on New York City—white, black, Latino, and Asian—being especially pertinent. (In the data used in this chapter, "white" refers to non-Hispanic white, "black" to non-Hispanic black, and "Asian" to non-Hispanic Asian.) Among all New Yorkers, figure 3.3 shows that about a third (35 percent) are white, about a quarter each Latino (28 percent) and black (23 percent), and the smallest share (12 percent) are Asian. Among immigrants, Latinos make up about a third (32 percent), Asians and whites about a quarter each (24 and 22 percent), and blacks make up a fifth (20 percent).

In considering the U.S. born, when we look at wages, table 3.3 shows that U.S.-born blacks and Latinos earn just 60 and 57 percent of the wages of U.S.-born whites, respectively, while Asians earn 83 percent of the amount whites do. Even *after* accounting for level of educational attainment, there is a substantial difference in wages by race and ethnicity. This ethnoracial disparity among U.S.-born workers, in fact, is in many cases greater than the disparity between U.S.- and foreign-born workers. At every educational level, white U.S.-born workers have the highest wages. U.S.-born blacks earn between 69 and 78 percent of what U.S.-born whites earn. U.S.-born Latinos follow roughly the same pattern, with a slightly higher top of 82 percent of U.S.-born white wages (among those with a high school diploma). U.S.-born Asians show the least differential with U.S.-born whites, earning between 83 and 94 percent of what whites earn, but there is still a notable gap. (U.S.-born Asians with less than high school fall outside of this range, but the results here do not have robust statistical significance since the sample size is small.)

U.S. racial and ethnic categories are also relevant in understanding economic incorporation among immigrants, even if in many cases (especially among "Asians" and "Latinos"), immigrants may not think of themselves in terms of these labels. Particularly notable is the premium on being white: at nearly every level of educational attainment,

Table 3.3. Median Annual Wages by Race/Ethnicity

New York City, 2009			Earnings compared to U.S.-born white earnings	
	Foreign born	U.S. born	Foreign born	U.S. born
Less than high school				
White	$32,000	$40,000	80%	100%
Black	$30,000	$28,000	75%	70%
Latino/Hispanic	$20,800	$30,000	52%	75%
Asian	$22,000	$20,000	55%	50%
High school				
White	$37,000	$45,000	82%	100%
Black	$31,000	$35,000	69%	78%
Latino/Hispanic	$29,000	$37,000	64%	82%
Asian	$28,100	$39,000	62%	87%
Some college				
White	$45,000	$55,000	82%	100%
Black	$40,000	$40,000	73%	73%
Latino/Hispanic	$32,000	$41,100	58%	75%
Asian	$36,000	$49,000	65%	89%
College degree				
White	$63,000	$72,000	88%	100%
Black	$51,000	$50,000	71%	69%
Latino/Hispanic	$42,000	$51,000	58%	71%
Asian	$53,000	$60,000	74%	83%
Advanced degree				
White	$85,000	$90,000	94%	100%
Black	$59,000	$65,000	66%	72%
Latino/Hispanic	$52,000	$68,000	58%	76%
Asian	$71,000	$85,000	79%	94%
All				
White	$52,000	$70,000	74%	100%
Black	$38,000	$42,000	54%	60%
Latino/Hispanic	$28,000	$40,000	40%	57%
Asian	$40,000	$58,000	57%	83%

Note: New York City residents 25 years of age and older, working year-round (50 or more weeks per year) and full-time (35 or more hours per week), employed in the civilian labor force with at least $100 in annual wages.

Source: Fiscal Policy Institute analysis of 2009 American Community Survey.

white immigrants earn more—often considerably more—than black, Latino, or Asian immigrants. (The one exception is among immigrants with some college but no college degree. For this group, black immigrants earn 73 percent of the level of U.S.-born whites, while white immigrants earn just 82 percent of the U.S.-born white level.)

An analysis of poverty rates also highlights the significance of race and ethnicity in immigrant economic incorporation. Poverty rates are about the same for U.S.- and foreign-born New York City residents—19 percent for U.S. born and 18 percent for foreign born, as can be seen in figure 3.4. But there is a great deal of variation within both groups, and nativity is not the most important dividing line. U.S.-born poverty rates range from 10 to 31 percent, and foreign-born rates from 13 to 23 percent. Latinos are the most likely to live in poverty, and whites are the least likely to be in poverty. Indeed, the groups for which nativity make the biggest differences—blacks and Latinos—both have considerably *lower* poverty rates for immigrants than for U.S. born.

Home ownership rates also reveal substantial differences among ethnoracial groups for both U.S. and foreign born. Among New Yorkers whose parents were born in the United States (the "third generation or higher" group of U.S. born), a 31 percent overall home ownership level can be disaggregated to show that among Latinos the level is 15 percent, among blacks 22 percent, and among whites 43 percent. Again, the differences among those in U.S.-born racial and ethnic groups are considerably larger than the difference between U.S. born and foreign born overall.

Conclusion

The New York City economy is hugely profitable for a small number of people, yet low- and middle-wage workers, regardless of nativity, face substantial challenges in the early twenty-first century, not only because of the Great Recession and subsequent slow recovery, but also because of deep polarization of the city's economy. In this context, immigrants today are playing such a large and varied role that there is no black-and-white answer to the question of how immigrants are faring in the city's economy. What is needed is a full-color portrait.

Overall, immigrants are doing somewhat less well than U.S.-born New Yorkers on a number of individual measures such as wages,

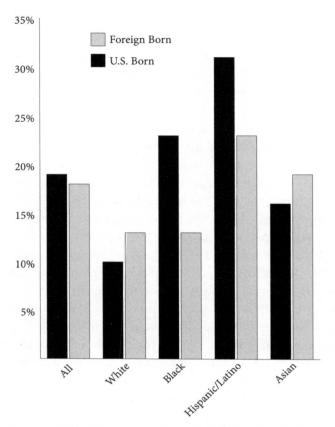

Figure 3.4. U.S. and Foreign Born Poverty Rates in New York City, by Race and Ethnicity, 2009
Source: Fiscal Policy Institute analysis of 2009 American Community Survey. White, black, and Asian are non-Hispanic portions of that group.

benefits (whether employer-based or public), and occupational status. To a significant extent, immigrants make up for these differences by having more family members working. This can be both positive and negative—it can provide a base for a better standard of living and home ownership, on the one hand, but can also be associated with overcrowded housing and a struggle to eke out a living on two or more low-wage jobs, on the other.

Within both U.S.-born and foreign-born groups there is very substantial variation. Among immigrants there is a great deal of difference in how groups from different countries of origin are faring in the economy, with a large proportion in some groups struggling to make ends meet while in other groups, a very substantial fraction are doing rather well. By the same token, U.S.-born New Yorkers are also an extremely varied group, with the ethnoracial disparities in wages among U.S.-born New Yorkers often bigger, for example, than the difference between immigrants and the U.S. born. Among immigrants, too, racial and ethnic differences are crucial. In the end, though immigrant status certainly is of great consequence, race and ethnicity may well be more important than nativity in predicting success in New York City's labor market for immigrants and native born alike.

NOTES

1. Unless otherwise noted, all current data are from the Fiscal Policy Institute's analysis of the 2009 American Community Survey and relate to New York City residents. When I use the present tense, I am referring to 2009. Historical data are from the decennial Census. Thanks to Jonathan DeBusk for his work on the data analysis, and to James Parrott for his frequent input on the analysis.
2. See, for example, Waldinger (1996, 2001) and Wright and Ellis (2001).
3. New York City has about one million rent-stabilized apartments. Each year, the Rent Guidelines Board sets the allowable increase for the renewal of leases for these apartments. About half of rental apartments in New York City are subject to some form of rent control or rent stabilization. Rent stabilization is not the norm in the United States, though it is also a factor in a number of other localities.

REFERENCES

Bernhardt, Annette, Diana Polson, and James DeFilippis. 2010. *Working Without Laws: A Survey of Employment and Labor Law Violations in New York City.* New York: National Employment Law Project.
Chin, Margaret M. 2005. *Sewing Women: Immigrants and the New York City Garment Industry.* New York: Columbia University Press.
Fiscal Policy Institute. 2007. *Working for a Better Life: A Profile of Immigrants in the New York State Economy.* New York: Fiscal Policy Institute.

Fiscal Policy Institute. 2008. "New York's Unemployment Insurance System: A Vital Safety Net for New York Workers and Their Families during Economic Downturns" (March 12). New York: Fiscal Policy Institute.

———. 2009. *Immigrants and the Economy: Contribution of Immigrant Workers to the Country's 25 Largest Metropolitan Areas* (December). New York: Fiscal Policy Institute.

———. 2010. "Grow Together or Pull Further Apart?: Income Concentration Trends in New York" (December 13). New York: Fiscal Policy Institute.

———. 2011. *The State of Working New York City 2011: Scant Recovery for Workers— Some See Gains but Recession Conditions Persist for Most* (July 20). New York: Fiscal Policy Institute.

Foner, Nancy. 2000. *From Ellis Island to JFK: New York's Two Great Waves of Immigration.* New Haven, CT: Yale University Press.

Milkman, Ruth, and Laura Braslow. 2010. "The State of the Unions: A Profile of 2009–2010 Union Membership in New York City, New York State, and the USA." New York: Joseph S. Murphy Institute for Worker Education and Labor Studies, Center for Urban Research, and NYC Labor Market Information Service, City University of New York.

Robinson, Christopher T., Richard Egelhof, and Michael Hoke. 2008. "Get Sick, Get Out: The Medical Causes of Home Mortgage Foreclosures." *Health Matrix: Journal of Law-Medicine* 18: 65–104.

Saez, Emmanuel, 2010. "Striking It Richer: The Evolution of Top Incomes in the United States," July 17. Available at http://www.econ.berkeley.edu/%7Esaez/.

Smith, Robert C. 2006 . *Mexican New York.* Berkeley: University of California Press.

United Hospital Fund. 2010. "Health Insurance Coverage in New York, 2008" (June). New York: United Hospital Fund.

Waldinger, Roger. 1996. *Still the Promised City?* Cambridge, MA: Harvard University Press.

——— (ed.). 2001. *Strangers at the Gate: New Immigrants in Urban America.* Berkeley: University of California Press.

Waters, Tom, and Victor Bach. 2011. "Many Immigrant Communities are Vulnerable to Unaffordable Rents and other Housing Stresses." New York: Community Service Society.

Wright, Richard, and Mark Ellis. 2001. "Immigrants, the Native-Born, and the Changing Division of Labor in New York City," in Nancy Foner (ed.), *New Immigrants in New York.* 2d ed. New York: Columbia University Press.

4

From Amsterdamned to I Amsterdam

The Amsterdam Economy and Its Impact on the
Labor Market Position of Migrants, 1980–2010

ROBERT C. KLOOSTERMAN

Introduction

Only a little more than two decades ago, Amsterdam was a "city in crisis" (Terhorst and Van de Ven 2003: 95). Economic prospects looked bleak, parts of the infrastructure were deteriorating, crime was rising, and middle-class families left the city in droves for the green suburbs. These middle-class families were partly replaced by people from non-Western countries such as Turkey, Morocco, and Suriname but this inflow could not stem the tide and the city's population declined from 869,000 inhabitants in 1960 to 676,000 in 1984 (Bosscher 2007c: 541). Overall unemployment was very high, much higher than the national average and also higher than in other large cities in the Netherlands. Among the migrant population, unemployment rates were considerably higher than among the native population. A postindustrial dystopia located within a seventeenth-century décor with high structural unemployment, increasing poverty and social polarization (partly along ethnic lines), political radicalization, and endemic (squatter) rioting looked just around the corner (Mak 1995).[1]

Things, however, turned out rather differently. Instead of an outlier in a negative sense, Amsterdam has been more of a winner in the first decade of the twenty-first century, reversing the collective doom of

Amsterdamned to the individualistic optimism of *I Amsterdam*, the current slogan of the city. Its population grew steadily and stood at 780,000 at the end of 2010 (Tomesen 2011); its economy grew rapidly and so did employment. Native Dutch clearly benefited from this turnaround and for them a full-employment situation arrived after 2000, but migrants were also able to improve their labor market position albeit to a (much) lesser extent. Notably, young migrants are doing better in labor market terms than the generation of their parents some 20 years ago. Though their rates of unemployment are still higher compared to the native population, the improvement is undeniable with employment rates having gone up and a marked increase in average household income. Of course, the arrival of a prosperous and, apparently resilient, economy based on "cognitive-cultural" activities such as producer, consumer, and public services as well as a whole array of creative industries (Scott 2008, 2011) did not bring about an urban utopia. Instead, we see the emergence of a *digital city* with new social fault lines, partly overlapping with ethnicity or origin, in which educational qualifications seem much more important than in its predecessor, the industrial city.

How did these changes come about? Below, I will provide a brief, multilevel analysis of this remarkable turnaround and its consequences for the labor market, in particular those regarding migrants from non-Western backgrounds. Most of the data used are labor market statistics gathered by the statistics department of the city of Amsterdam (O+S).[2] I start with the grim Amsterdam labor market situation in the 1980s and explain why migrants were relatively hard hit. After that, I turn to the current state of the Amsterdam economy and address how the changes have come about not only by looking at the structural shifts in the Amsterdam economy but also taking into account the changes at the national level. Finally, I aim at putting the Amsterdam trajectory in a broader context.

The data point in the direction of a very strong urban resurgence in Amsterdam. This small, albeit cosmopolitan capital city, with its strong tradition in both producer services (with a long-standing international orientation) and (increasingly internationally oriented) cultural industries, was able to benefit from structural changes in the national and the global economy and has become an attractive place to live and work for young, highly educated people. The turnaround of Amsterdam was, however, also made possible by a significant overhaul of the national institutional framework that changed the way the Dutch labor market functioned.

Amsterdamned: Amsterdam's Labor Market in the 1980s

In 1988, some 72,300 people were officially without work in Amsterdam, which amounted to 24 percent of the city's workforce (Kloosterman 1994a). This postwar high was about twice as high as the national rate. Before 1980, the unemployment rate in Amsterdam was low and, in addition, in line with national average. After 1980, however, Amsterdam became the frontrunner in terms of the relative increase in unemployment, with more than a doubling of the number of unemployed in the 1980s (see figure 4.1). With this increase, Amsterdam did not just beat the national average but also the other large Dutch cities—The Hague, Rotterdam, and Utrecht (ibid.: 1327). The incidence of unemployment also changed. At the start of the 1980s, migrants were underrepresented among the unemployed, but at the end of the decade, the rate of unemployment among migrants was even higher than the already very high city average. Ethnic minorities were not only overrepresented, but they also showed a rise in absolute numbers of unemployed, whereas the absolute number of unemployed Dutch already showed a decline in the second half of the 1980s.

What can account for these trends in unemployment rates and, in particular, the change in the fate of migrants on the Amsterdam labor market in the 1980s? I start with looking at the national level and explain how the institutional framework impacted on the first phases of the transition from an industrial to a postindustrial economy in the Netherlands. I then focus on how Amsterdam fits in this more general framework.

The Golden Age of high economic growth and full employment ended with the first oil crisis in 1973. The exogenous shock of the oil price hike in combination with a strong rise in wage costs (including taxes and payments for social benefits) and the introduction of environmental protection laws eroded overall profitability of Dutch firms (Van Zanden 1997). Manufacturing activities—notably the textile industry, car making, shoemaking, shipbuilding, and furniture making—were

Figure 4.1. Job Seekers without Work as a Percentage of the Total Population Age 15–64 in Amsterdam, 1980–2006
Source: O+S (2010).

especially hard hit. The share of manufacturing in total employment in the Netherlands fell from 26.0 percent in 1973 to 18.8 in 1987 (Van Zanden 1997: 218). Growth of employment, then, had to come from the expansion of service activities. Service activities, however, tend to differ from manufacturing as they typically require face-to-face contact, cannot usually be stocked, and therefore have to be produced on the spot when demand is there. Service activities are also prone to suffer from Baumol's cost disease. This refers to the phenomenon in which wage costs in the service sector tend to rise faster than gains in labor productivity and, hence, erode profitability. The reason is that wages in services are generally linked to those in manufacturing, where labor productivity is relatively easy to raise and wage increases are possible without a rise in costs. The institutionally determined coupling of the legal minimum wage with the overall trend in manufacturing was thus undermining the employment growth potential of low-value-added services in Dutch society. It gradually became clear that an institutional framework geared toward a society dominated by manufacturing was not necessarily very well suited to a service economy.

Gøsta Esping-Andersen (1990, 1999) has made this point very convincingly in his comparison of three types of institutional labor market regimes and their impact on postindustrial employment trajectories. According to him, the *liberal welfare state* (as represented by the United States) with its relative lack of regulations allows for strong growth in low-paid service jobs as workers are, on the one hand, not protected by high minimum wages, and, on the other, unemployment benefits are both low and temporary. The *socialist welfare state* (represented by Sweden) has a high minimum wage and high unemployment benefits or what Esping-Andersen calls a high level of "decommodification"—that is, the protection of workers against the vagaries of the labor market such as losing one's job and, hence, one's income. This high level of decommodification dampens growth of low-wage service jobs in the private sector, but job creation by the state compensates for that. The third type, the *corporatist welfare state*, found in the Federal Republic of Germany and the Netherlands (Kloosterman 1994b, 1996), has a relatively high level of decommodification with high unemployment benefits as well as a high minimum wage thwarting the creation of low-wage service jobs in the private sector. In contrast, to the socialist model, however, the state does not step in with an active labor market policy and also refrains from the large-scale creation of low-wage jobs. In addition, in order to protect the "traditional family," its fiscal regime and the lack of child care discourage women from participating in the labor market. The social consequences of a corporatist welfare state, then, provide strong protection for insiders (those who have a job), a relatively low rate of active labor participation, and a large pool of outsiders, partly on welfare (unemployment or disability benefits) and partly outside the labor market altogether (housewives). The postindustrial employment trajectory of a corporatist welfare state, consequently, is characterized by high unemployment rates as flexible, low-wage service jobs are neither created on a sufficiently large scale by the private nor the public sector. In addition, newcomers on the labor market tend to remain outsiders as job creation falls behind the growth of the labor supply. Notably in the Netherlands migrants were hard hit with registered unemployment rates of 42 percent among Turks and 31 percent among Moroccans in 1989 (Kloosterman 1998).

For a long time, the postindustrial employment trajectory of the Netherlands indeed was very bleak. Although unemployment rose only modestly in the 1970s (partly because of the sharp rise in the number of people living on disability benefits), the first half of the 1980s proved to be an outright disaster with very high (national) unemployment rates (see figure 4.1). According to Göran Therborn (1986: 86) the Netherlands was "perhaps the most spectacular failure in the world." Within the Netherlands, the city of Amsterdam stood out as the worst case. Why, then, was the labor market situation in Amsterdam even worse than the national average and what were the consequences for its migrant population?

In the 1970s and up to 1983, unemployment in the capital city moved very much in line with the national trend, but after that a widening gap occurred. While the national rate started to go down from a peak of 17 percent of the workforce, the unemployment rate in Amsterdam kept on rising to its peak of 24 percent in the second half of the 1980s (Kloosterman 1994: 1327). At the end of that decade, moreover, it became clear that ethnic minorities were strongly overrepresented among the unemployed. In 1990, about a third of the unemployed in Amsterdam belonged to an ethnic minority, which was almost three times as high as their share in the total Amsterdam labor force at that time (Kloosterman 1994: 1328). The data also showed that when unemployment went down among the native Dutch population after 1985, unemployment among migrants kept rising.

A closer look at shifts in the demand and supply side of the Amsterdam labor market helps to explain this pattern. Amsterdam, like many other larger European cities in the 1970s and early 1980s (Hohenberg and Hollen Lees 1995; Clark 2009), was a shrinking city not just with respect to its population, but also in terms of employment. After reaching a record high of 393,500 jobs in 1969, decline set in and in the first half of the 1980s the bottom was reached (see figure 4.2). The decrease was in large part caused by the loss of jobs in manufacturing—notably the closing of the Ford plant in 1981 and of the Nederlandsche Dok

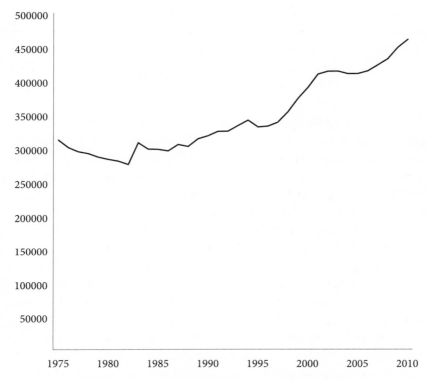

Figure 4.2. Total Employment in Amsterdam, 1975–2010 (Number of Workers)
Source: O+S (2010).

en Scheepsbouw Maatschappij (NDSM) ship builders in 1985, but other activities such as wholesale were also shedding jobs as businesses moved out of Amsterdam to escape congestion. The overall demand for labor in Amsterdam, then, shrank until about 1985. Due to deindustrialization, demand for low-skilled industrial labor fell considerably and the so-called guest workers were especially hard hit. In 1979, about 68 percent of Moroccan and about 71 percent of Turkish workers in the Netherlands were in manufacturing (Roosblad 2002: 34). We do not have data specifically for Amsterdam for that year, but it seems plausible that a large share of Moroccans and Turks in Amsterdam were also working in manufacturing. We do have data on the ethnic employment distribution for Amsterdam in 1991. They show that only 26 percent of Moroccans and about 25 percent of Turks in Amsterdam were still working in manufacturing as against 9 percent of the native Dutch (*Etnische groepen in Amsterdam; Jaarbericht 1994* 1994). Apparently, a shakeout had occurred with dire consequences for the guest workers from Turkey and Morocco.

Demand for labor picked up again after 1984. The growth of employment in Amsterdam, about 46,000 jobs from 1984 to 1990, even exceeded the growth of the labor force in the city, which increased by about only 12,600 in that same period (Kloosterman 1994: 1328). This time, however, services were driving the job growth. The demand coming from services was bifurcated. On the one hand, mainly producer services generated demand for high-skilled workers, while, on the other, consumer services were looking for lower skilled, part-time workers who are not only more flexible but also cheaper as they as do not have the same rights regarding job protection and employer contributions as full-time workers. These shifts in the demand for labor reflected the transition to an urban economy dominated by services activities away from one in which manufacturing was a mainstay.

The supply side of the Amsterdam labor market did not adjust easily or in a timely manner to these structural changes in the 1980s. On the contrary, the composition of the Amsterdam labor force seemed to be moving away from what was needed to suit the local demand in the 1980s. The loss of population—which started in 1960 and lasted until 1985—was mainly caused by the exodus to the suburbs of the middle classes, not just those with middle incomes but also those with a relatively high level of job security. The less-educated, less-skilled—and therefore mostly low-paid—workers tended to remain, thereby making the city less prosperous in relative terms and also more vulnerable to economic shocks, which resulted in an upgrading of the demand for labor.

Amsterdam, much more than the other large cities in the Netherlands, was also home to a rich palette of alternative subcultures. The legacy of the 1960s with Amsterdam as the psychedelic capital of Europe lingered on and attracted (partly self-professed) artists, drug users, squatters, and other representatives of partly overlapping fringe cultures (Bosscher 2007a, 2007b; Jobse and Musterd 1992: 40). High unemployment benefits (about as high as the minimum wage), a tolerant social climate, and the availability of cheap living spaces owing to the exodus of the middle classes made Amsterdam a magnet for those who had a rather weak attachment to the formal labor market. Persistent cultures of unemployment developed, not just among older workers laid off in the shakeout in manufacturing and whose chances of finding work were rather slim anyway, but also among youngsters who had just finished school (Engbersen et al. 1993).

When job growth picked up again in the second half of the 1980s, in Amsterdam itself and in the larger metropolitan area including Schiphol, the consequences of the composition of the Amsterdam population became manifest. Job growth did not result in a decline of the unemployment rate in Amsterdam, which actually kept on rising. There was a clear spatial mismatch on the Amsterdam labor market. The jobs created in the services sector went to higher-educated youngsters in general and, in the case of the rapidly increasing number of part-time jobs, in particular to young women. The rise in the number of commuters to Amsterdam in the second half of the 1980s suggests that a significant share of the newcomers came from outside Amsterdam. The pool of unemployed in Amsterdam remained to a large extent untouched by the return to a growth path. Given the high rate of unemployment, not just in Amsterdam but elsewhere as well, employers could afford to be selective. Older former industrial workers, low-skilled migrants, and members of alternative subcultures (in the not very likely case that they bothered to apply) were at the far back of the labor queue as seen by employers. Meanwhile, manufacturing kept on shedding jobs and the entry of low-skilled youngsters—both from native and migrant backgrounds—in Amsterdam continued to fill the pool of unemployed. Increasingly, the burden of unemployment came to fall on migrants as higher-educated native applicants were gradually finding jobs.

The capital city of the Netherlands thus became Amsterdamned, doing worse than most other cities, and within Amsterdam, migrants were overrepresented among the many unemployed. In retrospect, however, we can see that around 1985 a turning point was reached. It was not just that there was a revival of job and population growth, but also the city became in vogue again for certain groups of people with higher incomes, which constituted a significant break with the past. Highly educated young singles and members of two-income households (still without children) preferred the center of the city of Amsterdam with its vast range of cultural

and other facilities instead of the suburbs. A much broader urban renaissance was around the corner, but few people were aware of that when
about a quarter of the city's labor force was unemployed.

I Amsterdam: Labor Market Patterns in the Digital City

Now, more than 20 years later, Amsterdam has been transformed from a
laggard into a strong urban economy. In all but one year (1995), employment growth has been continuous (see figure 4.2), with total employment increasing from 302,000 in 1988 to 461,000 in 2010. Unemployment, meanwhile, has gone down considerably, notwithstanding the
growth of the Amsterdam labor force from about 290,000 in 1989 to
383,000 ten years later. In 2009, only 25,000 people were registered as
unemployed, which amounted to 6.5 percent of the total labor force.
This was only slightly higher than the national average of 4.5 percent
(O+S). In 2009, the rate of active labor participation, for a long time the
Achilles' heel of the Dutch corporatist welfare state, stood at 66.1 percent, nearly at the same level as the national rate of 67.2 percent (O+S).
Due to frequent changes in the definition of the unemployed it is hard
to construct a consistent time series, but the overall data clearly point in
the same direction: a return to a job-growth trajectory in the 1990s that
continued in the first decade of the twenty-first century notwithstanding cyclical several swings.

A closer look at the labor market trends of non-Western migrants
in Amsterdam shows they are much more ambiguous than those for
the native Dutch. Clearly, the steady improvement of the Amsterdam
economy has been a sea that has lifted all boats, including those of non-
Western migrants. Although still behind the native Dutch, the rise in
active labor participation of non-Western migrants between 1996 and
2009 was larger than that of non-Western migrants (Economische
Zaken Amsterdam/Kamer van Koophandel Amsterdam 2011: 101–2). A
breakdown of the unemployed by group and gender between 2001 and
2009, however, makes clear that this rosy general picture hides some
less attractive features (see table 4.1). Among native Dutch, unemployment was consistently low, with rates between 2 and 5 percent—close
to full employment. Unemployment among migrants, on the whole,
was much higher. The overall rate for the Turkish population varied

Table 4.1. Unemployment Rates by National-Origin Group and Gender,
2001–2009

Group	2001	2003	2005	2007	2009
Surinamese/Antilleans (total)	8	14	20	12	11
Women	8	13	21	15	11
Men	8	14	18	10	10
Turks (total)	11	15	15	15	13
Women	12	22	18	20	25
Men	10	14	14	12	6
Moroccans (total)	18	19	28	20	21
Women	22	18	37	23	24
Men	16	20	24	19	19
Other non-Western migrants (total)	–	–	19	18	9
Women	–	–	25	19	11
Men	–	–	15	17	8
Western migrants (total)	–	–	10	8	4
Women	–	–	10	11	4
Men	–	–	10	6	4
Native Dutch (total)	3	5	5	4	3
Women	2	4	5	4	4
Men	3	5	5	3	2
Total (men and women)	5	8	10	8	6
Women	5	8	11	9	7
Men	5	8	10	7	5

Note: "National origin" refers to place of birth and not to nationality.
Source: O+S (2010).

between 11 and 15 percent, while that for the Moroccan population was even higher with rates between 18 and 28 percent. The Surinamese and Antilleans are somewhere in between the native Dutch and the former guest worker groups, with overall rates varying from 8 to 20 percent. Women, across the board, had higher rates of unemployment than men. This gender difference is much more pronounced among specific groups—namely Turks and Moroccans—than among the Surinamese, Antillean, and native Dutch populations. Behind the overall averages, one can find, then, a more complex layering of the Amsterdam labor market along ethnic and gender lines.

If one looks at the differences between first-generation non-Western migrants and the Dutch-born second generation (here those who have at least one parent born in a non-Western country), it becomes clear that the latter especially have benefited from the revival of the Amsterdam economy. The number of employed second-generation children of non-Western migrants rose from 26,000 in 2000 to 48,000 in 2008, an increase of 4.5 percentage points. The second generation has a significantly higher rate of active labor participation than the first generation (59.2 vs. 50.0 percent in 2007) and a much lower percentage living on some form of public support (11.6 percent for members of the second generation vs. 32.8 percent for the first generation in 2006) (O+S). A growing proportion of non-Western migrants generates its own employment (and, often, for others as well): the share of self-employed between 1999 and 2007 rose from 3.4 to 5.7 percent in 2007 for first-generation non-Western migrants and from 2.6 to 3.7 percent for the second generation. The majority of the second generation who are not part of the active labor force are still pursuing an education, thereby improving their chances of finding a good job. The increase in active labor participation of non-Western migrants has resulted in a considerable overall rise in average household income among them between 2000 and 2008, and this rise is much higher for the second generation than the first generation (Economische Zaken Amsterdam/Kamer van Koophandel Amsterdam 2011: 104).

Evidently, improvements in the general labor market situation have benefited not only native Dutch, but also non-Western migrants and their children, especially younger cohorts, who have been able to improve their labor market position. Though unemployment rates are still much higher for non-Western migrants than for native Dutch, the overall picture for the first decade of the twenty-first century is a far cry from that of the 1980s.

How was the Netherlands able to get out of the corporatist morass and why could the Amsterdam economy shift gears? The striking turn-around in the labor situation in Amsterdam in the 1990s took place against a background of gradual changes in the Dutch national institutional framework. In contrast to Esping-Andersen's implicit assumptions, institutional frameworks, despite displaying strong path-dependent characteristics, can be transformed through the accumulation of a whole series of small changes. After more than a decade of tinkering and, inevitably, nearly endless political bickering, a quite different institutional framework surfaced in the Netherlands in the early 1990s that led away from the corporatist dead-end postindustrial employment trajectory (Kloosterman 1994b; Visser and Hemerijck 1997; Van Zanden, 1997).

The institutional overhaul had already begun in 1982 with the so-called central accord of Wassenaar in which, in true corporatist fashion, the government, employers, and unions agreed to wage restraint in return for job creation through a shortening of working time—in effect eroding the protection of insiders and aiming at opening up jobs to outsiders on the labor market. This turned out to be the beginning of a long overhaul of the corporatist framework in the Netherlands; the overhaul involved a combination of more free-market oriented labor market policies (i.e., lowering of the minimum wage and, even more so, unemployment benefits in real terms while making access to these benefits more difficult) with more "social-democratic"- or "Swedish"-inspired active labor market policies to boost active labor participation. Steadily, the government also largely dismantled the legal and fiscal backing of the typical corporatist gender division of labor with a male breadwinner and the woman at home as the housewife.

The consequences of the changes were far-reaching. Downward pressure on wages—generated by high unemployment and after 1982 backed by the triad of government, employers, and employees—helped to restore the profitability of firms and thus put an end to layoffs and, later on, made it even possible to take on new workers. The drop in the minimum wage in real terms had a dampening effect on Baumol's cost disease (the rise of wages in service activities in line with those in manufacturing without, however, a concomitant rise in labor productivity resulting in increasing wage costs in services and, hence, an erosion of profitability). By lowering the threshold for paid employment, the reduced minimum wage also allowed for more growth at the lower end of the services sector. Furthermore, the active labor market policies undermined step by step the entrenched subcultures of unemployment and more generally put more pressure on the unemployed to look for (and eventually accept) work.

The changes in the Dutch labor market situation were not just top-down. Many people were consciously looking for ways to get around stifling corporatist regulations and, more specifically, legally binding collective agreements that stipulated wages. The success of the fast-growing number of temping agencies mediating temporary labor, the very rapid expansion of those seeking part-time employment (Kloosterman 1994b; Visser and Hemerijck 1997), and the rise of self-employment can be seen, partly, as bottom-up strategies to make the supply of labor both cheaper and more flexible and, thus, a better match for the demand generated by service activities (cf. Atkins and Steinglass 2011).

Although the results of the accumulated incremental changes were already evident at the end of the 1980s, the job-intensive growth path became clearer in the 1990s (Visser and Hemerijck 1997: 26). Job growth was mainly generated in services, notably in producer services, for example, financial services and consultancy and, to a lesser extent, personal services, for example, restaurants and fitness. This growth was driven by increasing demand for services—both domestic and foreign—and made possible by the combination of wage moderation, flexibilization, and upgrading of labor as younger cohorts entering the labor market had, on average, considerably higher educational qualifications than those who had entered the labor market before 1960 (Kloosterman and Elfring 1990). The newcomers on the labor market—children of the 1960s and 1970s—were not only better educated but also displayed a more individualistic attitude that was often better suited to service sector activities than the attitudes of the earlier collectivist generations which grew up in a society dominated by manufacturing and standardization. The rapid rise of female labor participation, the majority of it part-time, was not just the consequence of the expansion of the service sector but also the outcome of a strong emancipatory shift in the attitude of women toward paid work—and thus a clear move away from the corporatist (Christian Democratic) ideal of the nuclear family with its sharp division of labor between men (paid employment outside the home) and women (unpaid work at home).

The combination of more economic opportunities and a cultural shift is also reflected in the rise of self-employment among native Dutch and among the migrant population. Postindustrial economies offer more chances for small firms, but these opportunities have to be perceived and seized—requiring a different mind-set than that of an industrial worker. At first, the rise of entrepreneurship was stifled through regulation aimed at protecting established businesses; the clamp down on Turkish sweatshops in Amsterdam in the 1980s was a prime example of a heavy-handed and business-unfriendly approach toward new (migrant) businesses (Rath 2002). But in the 1990s a policy aimed at deregulation and opening up of economic opportunities to newcomers prevailed.

In the 1990s, then, the different pieces of the economic, sociocultural, and institutional aspects of the postindustrial puzzle gradually came together, and instead of a laggard the Netherlands became an example to be emulated, with a combination of strong economic growth, a rapid rise in employment, and a high level of welfare protecting citizens against the vagaries of market forces (decommodification). The contours of the emerging postindustrial society were in particular on display in Amsterdam, the Dutch capital and the largest and most "global" city of the Netherlands.

Given that total employment in services in Amsterdam rose from 87.3 percent in 1995 to 92.6 percent in 2010, deindustrialization has clearly run its course (see figure 4.3). What has emerged in postindustrial Amsterdam resembles closely what geographer Allen Scott (2008: 64–66) has labeled a cultural-cognitive urban economy with a broad palette of services (private and public), fashion-oriented neoartisanal production, and a range of cultural-products industries in which production is highly dependent on "intellectual and affective human assets" and "deeply penetrated by digital technologies" that enable "deroutinization/destandardization" and "radical flexibilization" (i.e., the ability to rapidly change the quantity of production and/or shift to another line of products). These activities—typically highly transaction intensive, characterized by a volatile demand for labor, and dependent on a thick institutional fabric—thrive when located in close proximity in urban environments. The reemergence of agglomeration economies (in which economic benefits accrue from being located in close proximity) thus strengthens the position of large cities, which already have a strong and viable base of knowledge-intensive activities (see figure 4.3).

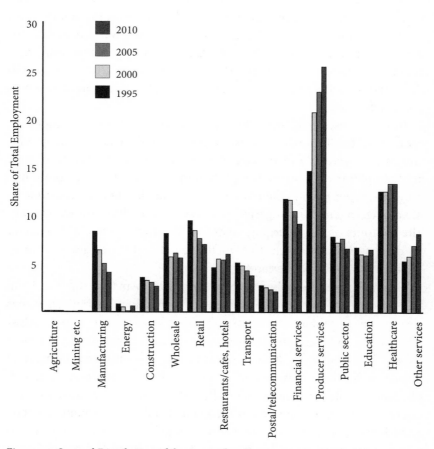

Figure 4.3. Sectoral Distribution of the Amsterdam Economy, 1995–2010
Source: O+S (2010).

Amsterdam, like other capital cities, turned out to be well positioned to reap the fruits of the fundamental transition to a cognitive-cultural economy. Although relatively small from an international viewpoint, its rich historic legacy of financial services, producer services, and cultural amenities and its longstanding role as an international transport and communication node in conjunction with a marked cosmopolitan orientation provided a very good base for a strong urban renaissance (Kloosterman and Lambregts 2007; Bosscher 2007a, 2007c; Engelen 2007; Fernandez 2011). Amsterdam together with other "capitals demonstrated a striking ability to recover, aided by their dominance of national and international business and transport networks. The upturn in world banking and finance since the 1980s consolidated their primacy" (Clark 2009: 243). Within the Dutch Randstad—the polycentric urban configuration in the western part of the Netherlands also comprising Rotterdam, The Hague, Utrecht, and a host of smaller cities—Amsterdam strengthened its position as a location for internationally oriented producer services and head offices (Lambregts and Kloosterman, forthcoming). Thus, Amsterdam clearly followed a "global city" trajectory and its economic profile became distinctly less similar to other Dutch cities between 1995 and 2008 (Van der Waal 2010: 42). In the Mastercard Worldwide Ranking 2008 of 75 international centers of commerce, Amsterdam ranked tenth, the only Dutch city on the list; only slightly smaller Rotterdam was conspicuously absent (Scott 2011: 293–94). In recent years, Amsterdam has also showed a strong growth in employment in cultural industries (e.g., advertising, audiovisual production, music, performance art, and publishing) and increased its dominance as the cultural capital of the Netherlands (Kloosterman 2004; Röling 2010; Van der Groep 2010; Deinema and Kloosterman, forthcoming). Amsterdam has consequently been one of the most successful urban economies within the country, often outstripping the already strong national growth rates (O+S) and with the highest average hourly wage level in the Netherlands (Groot et al. 2010). These relatively high wages and the high general rate of labor participation in combination with the presence of a large number of single- and two-earner households further boost job growth as they generate demand for a variety of personal services.

The success of the Amsterdam economy after 1990, however, cannot be solely attributed to the changes in the demand side of the labor market. The changes on the supply side are also important. We already saw that at the end of the 1980s, so-called new urbanites were opting for living in Amsterdam, and the inflow of highly educated young-sters in search of job opportunities, cultural amenities, and friends and (potential) partners has swelled. As the economist Edward Glaeser has observed, "[C]ities also attract young people because they are fun places to be young and single" (2011: 128). In 2010 alone, 13,000 young people with university degrees came to Amsterdam for the fleshpots, galler-ies, concert venues, and cafés (Tomesen 2011). Amsterdam is by far the most attractive city in the Netherlands in terms of cultural amenities (Marlet 2009). No less that 54 percent of the Amsterdam labor force in the years 2007–2009 was highly educated (higher vocational training or university degree), which is higher than the surrounding municipalities in the larger Amsterdam metropolitan area and much higher than the national average of 32 percent (Economische Zaken Amsterdam/Kamer van Koophandel Amsterdam 2011: 109). At the same time, the educa-tional characteristics of the local labor force were changing, including those of the children of non-Western migrants, who improved their levels of educational attainment.

The presence of highly educated workers has fueled cognitive-cul-tural productive activities of employees as well as of the self-employed. Much of the flexibility of the labor force that is needed to deal with the volatile environment of a cognitive-cultural economy comes from small businesses, especially one-person businesses with either full-time or part-time owners. Again, Amsterdam stands out with more than half of all firms in the city in 2009 one-person businesses (Economische Zaken Amsterdam/Kamer van Koophandel Amsterdam 2011: 107).

Amsterdam has thus become a preferred place to live and work in the Netherlands for highly educated workers. The upswing of the Amsterdam economy in the 1980s at first seemed to be set on a course of a mismatch whereby the local demand for highly educated labor did not fit the skill level of the local labor force; in the late 1980s, the mis-match created the paradoxical situation in Amsterdam of a growth of jobs along with a rise in the number of unemployed. With the increas-ing number of highly educated workers after 1990, the scope of this mismatch was gradually reduced and local demand and supply of labor became more in tune, hence pushing the number of unemployed down.

At first, the strong job growth was highly selective. Young, higher-educated, native Dutch workers (initially partly from outside Amsterdam) were generally preferred, but persistent strong demand effectively shortened the labor queue and, eventually, non-Western migrants and their children, especially the young and highly educated, benefited as well. Indeed, labor market indicators for the second generation show a significant improvement when compared to their first-generation parents. The second generation is increasingly found in cognitive-cultural economic activities (Brandellero 2011). Overall unemployment rates for non-Western migrants and their children are, however, still high and, in the case of Moroccans and Turks, very high. Many of these unemployed lost their jobs in the earlier phases of the urban transition of the Amsterdam economy and, given their limited educational attainments, never were able to get jobs in the formal sector again. The high unemployment rates will no doubt decline as first-generation guest workers enter retirement age and disappear from the unemployment statistics. How high unemployment rates will be among the second generation in the future remains to be seen. The especially high unemployment rates for Moroccans and Turks suggest that even with prolonged strong job growth, many individuals in these groups are still largely passed by. Among them, some will be seen as virtually unemployable due to age, health, criminal records, or other problems. In the case of orthodox Muslim women of Moroccan and Turkish descent, low labor participation rates are also caused by the fact that some are not allowed to work in environments where men (nonrelatives) and women are together. Another dynamic is at work as well. The large swings from year to year, which might partly be statistical artifacts but are too large to ignore, seem to indicate that the Amsterdam labor market has a secondary segment whose members are employed only when no others are available and who have very low job security.

Conclusions

Amsterdam has been through a strong period of growth in the last two decades. Its economy has recovered from the deep crisis of the 1970s and the 1980s, and the city has regained its position as a popular place to work, live, and recreate. The change of fate was driven by changes in the international and national economy favoring service sector activities as well as cultural industries, which were already prominent in Amsterdam. This pocket-sized global city, node of international financial and producer services, important global media hub, and cultural capital of the Netherlands thus represents a clear case of urban renaissance. A long piecemeal process of institutional change has enabled firms, workers, and a plethora of formal and informal institutions (from educational institutions to websites for expatriates in Amsterdam) in the Netherlands and Amsterdam in particular to come to grips with the structural transformation to a knowledge-intensive, flexible, and internationally oriented economy. Amsterdam has become an attractive place for highly educated, cosmopolitan workers from the Netherlands and abroad who benefit from the diverse production system and, to a lesser extent, from "soft factors" such as a vibrant urban atmosphere and many local amenities (Musterd and Murie 2010; Pethe et al. 2010). The influx of highly educated workers has even led to strong upward pressure on the housing market and, consequently, rents have gone up and are now the highest per square meter in the Netherlands (Groot et al. 2010).

The pronounced economic recovery did reach the established non-Western migrant population after a time lag, and avenues of upward social mobility have opened up for them. The urban renaissance has evidently benefited the highly educated parts of the population (both from native and migrant backgrounds) the most. At the same time, poverty remains rather limited in Amsterdam as the Dutch welfare state, despite years of cuts and tinkering, is palpably present in poorer neighborhoods and continues to prevent a slide into the abyss of destitution.

Notwithstanding the undeniable economic successes in Amsterdam, in terms of the improved labor market position of non-Western migrants, the danger still exists of concentration of long-term employment among specific ethnic/religious groups, which can contribute to processes of radicalization, criminalization, and alienation. Even before the current credit crisis started to have palpable effects, certain groups were less able to benefit from the long upturn. Both among Turks and Moroccans unemployment has decreased but stayed at high levels. Surveys, moreover, have shown that a large share of the Amsterdam population has negative views of Moroccans and Antilleans (not so much of Turks)—two groups that also have high crime rates (O+S 2010). These views might translate into a further worsening, even hardening, of the already weak labor market position of these groups, which could lead to the rise of local pockets of cultures of poverty outside of the mainstream society. In addition, there is a substantial population of mobile workers in the informal sector from eastern European Union member states and elsewhere who provide cheap, easily disposable labor outside the regulatory regime of the Netherlands.

In Allen Scott's penetrating analysis of the emerging urban form of cognitive-cultural capitalism in *Social Economy of the Metropolis*, his point of departure is that every historical phase of capitalism has its own distinctive urban form with its own corresponding, equally distinctive, type of social stratification. Although Scott's analysis is first and foremost based on the contemporary American urban experience (notably that of his hometown, Los Angeles), his sweep of generalization reaches much further as we find cognitive-cultural capitalism in other advanced economies as well. From a distance, Amsterdam appears to fit the picture of the "Resurgent City" as painted by Scott. Amsterdam indeed has a cognitive-cultural economy with a highly "flexible and malleable system of production" (Scott 2008: 12) that depends strongly on "intellectual and affective human assets" (ibid.: 64). We also see the contours of an emerging type of social stratification in Amsterdam with a "thick stratum of high-wage professional and quasi-professional workers" who are concerned with a broad range of knowledge-intensive and, typically, also transaction-intensive activities (ibid.: 12). Their activities are "complemented by and organically interrelated with a second stratum composed of poorly-paid and generally subordinate workers engaged in either manual labor . . . or low-grade service activities" (ibid.). Part of the Amsterdam migrant population indeed fits this bill. We also clearly see processes of extensive gentrification in Amsterdam in which former working-class neighborhoods such as De Pijp have been transformed into places of choice for highly educated workers; centrally located former port and industrial areas have also changed into a museum district, workplaces for cultural industries, and residential neighborhoods for new urbanites. The question, then, becomes whether the emerging social stratification system in Amsterdam is also driving a process of social polarization that "threatens human conviviality," something that, according to Scott (2008: 73), is happening in many American cities.

Although the underlying drivers of cognitive-cultural capitalism are more or less general, the concrete shape of corresponding social stratification in a particular city is still highly dependent on local circumstances. First, there has never been just one type of industrial capitalism and neither will there be just one type of cognitive-cultural capitalism. Different institutional frameworks are compatible with economies based on cognitive-cultural production and this will generate quite distinct trajectories of socioeconomic development with divergent outcomes in terms of social polarization (Kloosterman 2010). The extensive welfare state arrangements in Amsterdam—encompassing not only social benefits but also including access to housing, education, and healthcare—make a significant difference when it comes to social polarization. Second, size matters as does the morphological organization of urban space (Kloosterman 2010; Scott 2011). The relatively compact city of Amsterdam with its intensive 24/7 use of public space by pedestrians and bikers creates a very different urban atmosphere as compared to a more sprawled city dominated by cars. In Amsterdam, diversity is not just a statistical fact at the level of the city as a whole, but can be observed in its streets and public transport. Human conviviality is "out there" and makes the city livable and attractive for native Dutch and migrants alike.

There is, of course, no guarantee that this situation will continue. The riots in London in 2011, occurring even before the current economic crisis in Europe started really biting, have already showed that pressures and discontents may be brewing behind the façade of a seemingly peaceful and multicultural global city. Whatever happens in the near future, in recent decades Amsterdam has shown that government intervention (on a national and a local level) following a broad social-democratic program can accommodate winners and losers in the context of the rise of the cognitive-cultural economy, although admittedly with trial and error and sometimes irritatingly long time lags. Still, a strong safety net exists, helping to provide access to avenues of social mobility and sustaining human conviviality. Up to a certain extent, Amsterdam proves the point made by the late Tony Judt (2010), a British émigré in New York, on the need for government intervention to safeguard a decent society. I Amsterdam can thrive only if there is also a sense of We Amsterdam.

NOTES

1. This pessimistic atmosphere was beautifully captured in the novel *Advocaat van de hanen* (Lawyer of the Mohicans) by A.F.Th. van der Heijden, published in 1990 and, alas, so far translated only into German (*Der Anwalt der Hähne*). The movie (same name) based on the book came out in 1996.
2. I would like to express my thanks to Rogier van der Groep of O+S who helped me in gathering the data.

REFERENCES

Atkins, Ralph, and Matt Steinglass. 2011. "A Fix that Functions," *Financial Times*, August 4: 7.

Bosscher, Doeko. 2007a. "Een stad van en voor wie?'" in Piet de Rooy (ed.), *Geschiedenis van Amsterdam: Tweestrijd om de stad, 1900–2000*. Amsterdam: SUN.

———. 2007b. "Geen woning, toch een kroning: Herwonnen zelfbewustzijn," in Piet de Rooy (ed.), *Geschiedenis van Amsterdam: Tweestrijd om de stad, 1900–2000*. Amsterdam: SUN.

———. 2007c. "Amsterdam hoofdstad," in Piet de Rooy (ed.), *Geschiedenis van Amsterdam: Tweestrijd om de stad, 1900–2000*. Amsterdam: SUN.

Brandellero, Amanda M. C. 2011. *The Art of Being Different: Exploring Diversity in the Cultural Industries*. Ph.D. dissertation, University of Amsterdam.

Clark, Peter. 2009. *European Cities and Towns 400–2000*. Oxford: Oxford University Press.

Deinema, Michaël N., and Robert C. Kloosterman. n.d. "'Historical Trajectories and Urban Cultural Economies in the Randstad Megacity Region: Cultural Industries in Dutch Cities since 1900," in Johan Klaesson, Börje Johansson, Charlie Karlsson, and Roger R. Stough (eds.), *Metropolitan Regions: Preconditions and Strategies for Growth and Development in the Global Economy*. Berlin: Springer Verlag (forthcoming).

Economische Zaken Amsterdam/Kamer van Koophandel Amsterdam. 2011. *Economische Verkenningen. Metropoolregio Amsterdam 2011*. Amsterdam: Economische Zaken Amsterdam/Kamer van Koophandel Amsterdam.

Engbersen, Godfried, Kees Schuyt, Jaap Timmer, and Frans van Waarden. 1993. *Cultures of Unemployment: A Comparative Look at Long-Term Unemployment and Poverty*. Boulder, CO: Westview.

Engelen, Ewald. 2007. "'Amsterdamned'? The Uncertain Future of a Financial Centre." *Environment and Planning A* 39 (6): 1306–24.

Esping-Andersen, Gøsta. 1990. *Three Worlds of Welfare Capitalism*. Cambridge: Polity Press.

———. 1999. *Social Foundations of Postindustrial Economies*. Oxford: Oxford University Press.

Etnische Groepen in Amsterdam; Jaarbericht 1994. 1994. Amsterdam: Bureau voor Strategisch Minderhedenbeleid Gemeente Amsterdam.

Fernandez, Rodrigo. 2011. *Explaining the Decline of the Amsterdam Financial Centre: Globalizing Finance and the Rise of a Hierarchical Inter-City Network*. Ph.D. dissertation, University of Amsterdam.

Glaeser, Edward L. 2011. *The Triumph of the City*. London: Macmillan.

Groot, Henri de, Gerard Marlet, Coen Teulings, and Wouter Vermeulen. 2010. *Stad en land*. The Hague: Centraal Planbureau.

Hohenberg, Paul, and Lynn Hollen Lees. 1995. *The Making of Urban Europe 1000–1994*. Cambridge, MA: Harvard University Press.

Jobse, Rein B., and Sako Musterd. 1992. "Changes in the Residential Function of the Big Cities," in Frans M. Dieleman and Sako Musterd (eds.), *The Randstad: A Research and Policy Laboratory*. Dordrecht, Boston, and London: Kluwer Academic Publishers.

Judt, Tony. 2010. *Ill Fares the Land: A Treatise On Our Present Discontents*. London: Allen Lane.

Kloosterman, Robert C. 1994a. "Amsterdamned: The Rise of Unemployment in Amsterdam in the 1980s." *Urban Studies* 31 (8): 1325–44.

———. 1994b. "Three Worlds of Welfare Capitalism? The Welfare State and the Postindustrial Trajectory in the Netherlands after 1980." *West European Politics* 17 (4): 166–89.

———. 1996. "Post Industrial Experiences on the Amsterdam Labour Market." *New Community* 22 (4): 637–53.

———. 1998. "Migration in the Netherlands and the Emerging Post-Industrial Divide in Urban Areas," in *Organisation for Economic Co-operation and Development, Immigrants, Integration and Cities: Exploring the Links*. Paris: OECD.

———. 2004. "Recent Employment Trends in the Cultural Industries in Amsterdam, Rotterdam, The Hague and Utrecht: A First Exploration." *Tijdschrift voor Economische en Sociale Geografie* 95 (2): 243–52.

———. 2010. "This Is Not America: Embedding the Cognitive-Cultural Urban Economy." *Geografiska Annaler: Series B, Human Geography* 92 (2): 131–43.

Kloosterman, Robert C., and Tom Elfring. 1991. *Werken in Nederland*. Schoonhoven: Academic Services.

Kloosterman, Robert C., and Bart Lambregts. 2007. "Between Accumulation and Concentration of Capital: Comparing the Long-Term Trajectories of the Dutch Randstad and London Urban Systems." *Urban Geography* 28 (1): 54–73.

Lambregts, Bart, and Robert C. Kloosterman. n.d. "Randstad Holland: Probing Hierarchies and Interdependencies in a Polycentric World City Region," in Michael Hoyler (ed.), *Handbook of Globalization* (forthcoming).

Mak, Geert. 1992. *De engel van Amsterdam*. Amsterdam/Antwerpen: Atlas.

———. 1995. *Een kleine geschiedenis van Amsterdam*. Amsterdam/Antwerpen: Atlas.

Musterd, Sako and Alan Murie. 2010. "What Works for Managers and Highly Educated Workers in Creative Knowledge Societies," in Sako Musterd and Alan Murie (eds.), *Making Competitive Cities*. Chichester: Wiley-Blackwell.

O'Brien, Patrick. 2001. "Reflections and Mediations on Antwerp, Amsterdam and London in Their Golden Ages," in Patrick O'Brien, Derek Keene, Marjolein 't Hart, and Herman van der Wee (eds.), *Urban Achievement in Early Modern Europe:*

Golden Ages in Antwerp, Amsterdam and London. Cambridge: Cambridge University Press.

O+S (Onderzoek en Statistiek Amsterdam). 2010. "Hoofdstuk 4: werk en inkommen." *2010 Jaarboek.* http://www.os.amsterdam.nl/pdf/2010_jaarboek_hoofdstuk_04.pdf, accessed August 16, 2011.

Pethe, Heike, Sabine Haffner, and Philip Lawton. 2010. "Transnational Migrants in the Creative Knowledge Industries: Amsterdam, Barcelona, Dublin and Munich," in Sako Musterd and Alan Murie (eds.), *Making Competitive Cities.* Chichester: Wiley-Blackwell.

Rath, Jan. 2002. "Needle Games: A Discussion of Mixed Embeddedness," in Jan Rath (ed.), *Unravelling the Rag Trade: Immigrant Entrepreneurship in Seven World Cities.* Oxford: Berg.

Röling, Robert W. 2010. "Small Town, Big Campaigns: The Rise and Growth of an International Advertising Industry in Amsterdam." *Regional Studies* 44 (7): 829–43.

Roosblad, Judith. 2002. *Vakbonden en immigranten in Nederland (1960–1997).* Ph.D. dissertation, University of Amsterdam.

Sassen, Saskia. 2001 [1991]. *The Global City.* Princeton, NJ: Princeton University Press.

Scott, Allen J. 2008. *Social Economy of the Metropolis: Cognitive-Cultural Capitalism and the Global Resurgence of Cities.* Oxford: Oxford University Press.

———. 2011. "Emerging Cities of the Third Wave." *City* 15 (3–4): 289–321.

Taylor, Peter J. 2005. "Leading World Cities: Empirical Evaluations of Urban Nodes in Multiple Networks." *Urban Studies* 42 (9): 1593–1608.

Terhorst, Pieter, and Jacques van de Ven. 2003. "The Economic Restructuring of the Historic City Center," in Sako Musterd and Willem Salet (eds.), *Amsterdam Human Capital.* Amsterdam: University of Amsterdam Press.

Therborn, Göran. 1986. *Why Some People Are More Unemployed than Others: The Strange Paradox of Growth and Unemployment.* London: Verso.

Tomesen, Remco. 2011. "Het platteland wordt echt platteland, de stad echt stad. Nederland is er bij gebaat dat Amsterdam groter is. Aantrekkelijk Amsterdam." *De Pers*, March 14.

Van der Groep, Rogier. 2010. "'Breaking Out' and 'Breaking In': Changing Firm Strategies in the Dutch Audiovisual Industry." *Regional Studies* 44 (7): 845–58.

Van der Waal, Jeroen. 2010. *Unravelling the Global City Debate; Economic Inequality and Ethnocentrism in Contemporary Dutch Cities.* Rotterdam: Erasmus Universiteit.

Van Zanden, Jan L. 1997. *Een klein land in de 20e eeuw.* Utrecht: Het Spectrum.

Visser, Jelle, and Anton C. Hemerijck. 1997 *A Dutch Miracle: Job Growth, Welfare Reform and Corporatism in the Netherlands.* Amsterdam: Amsterdam University Press.

PART III

Is Islam in Amsterdam Like Race in New York City?

In Amsterdam, Islam is a major barrier facing immigrants; in New York City, race operates in a similar fashion. Yet if Islam in Amsterdam is like race in New York City in many ways, there are also profound differences between the two urban contexts.

That immigrants in New York are often seen through the prism of race is not surprising given the history of racial inequality in the United States and the demographics of the city. Race, following Foner and Fredrickson, refers to socially significant differences between human groups or communities differing in visible physical characteristics or putative ancestry that are believed to be innate and unchangeable (2004: 2–3). In contemporary New York, "race" is basically a color word, which is a legacy of slavery, legal segregation, and ghettoization in the United States as well as the long-time presence of a large African American population in the city.

Anti-Islam sentiment, to be sure, is hardly absent in New York. The number of Muslim immigrants from South Asia and the Middle East has grown in recent years; in the backlash after the September 11 attacks on the World Trade Center, they have sometimes been victims of discrimination and harassment and occasionally even hate crimes owing to their religion or nationality (Bakalian and Bozorgmehr 2009). The public controversy in 2010 over a plan to build a Muslim community center a few blocks from the World Trade Center site—a plan that was vocally supported by the Lower Manhattan Community Board and

Mayor Michael Bloomberg, but attacked by many Republican politicians such as former mayor Rudolph Giuliani—also no doubt reflected and reinforced anti-Muslim prejudices among many New Yorkers. Yet divisions based on race are a more central fault line—and more pervasive and persistent—in a city, as Mary Waters notes, that is deeply unequal in terms of race and highly racially segregated.

For much of the twentieth century, a black/white dichotomy dominated New York race relations, dating from the large inflow of African Americans from the South between World War I and the 1960s. The black/white binary has not disappeared, but has proved inadequate in light of the huge influx of not-black and not-white Asian and Latino immigrants in the last five decades. A new racial/ethnic hierarchy has evolved in New York City—in broad strokes, white/Asian//Hispanic/black. These categories are used in official statistics as well as in everyday discourse. Even if immigrants often prefer to be known by their group of national origin, they are often labeled "black," "Hispanic," or "Asian" by others. Ethnic distinctions based on European ancestry—Italian, Irish, and Jewish—have not vanished, yet they have "become so faint as to pale beside other racial/ethnic boundaries" and a common identity has emerged among "Euro-Americans" as whites in opposition to other racial groups in the city (Alba 1999). New York has become what is often called a majority-minority city, in which non-Hispanic whites are now 33 percent of the population; Hispanics, 29 percent; non-Hispanic blacks, 23 percent; and Asians, 13 percent.

Racial minorities may be numerically dominant in New York, but nonwhites, especially blacks and Latinos, continue to encounter barriers whatever their immigrant status or national origin. As the quintessentially racialized Americans, people of African ancestry confront especially acute difficulties, or, as Waters puts it, face more systematic and "brighter" boundaries than Asians and light-skinned Latinos. Black immigrants and their children—about one million New Yorkers—are more residentially segregated from, and less likely to marry, whites than are Latinos and Asians. More than half of the city's public schools are at least 90 percent black and Latino (Kleinfeld 2012). The children of black (and Latino) immigrants generally attend predominantly minority schools in poor neighborhoods with less experienced teachers, more limited curricula, higher turnover, and more dangerous environments than those that most white and Asian children go to. The New York second-generation study found that most native blacks and West Indians worked in predominantly black work sites, whereas Hispanics and Chinese were more likely to work in racially mixed workplaces (Kasinitz et al. 2008: 198). Drawing on that study in her chapter, Waters shows that native-born blacks and the young adult children of West Indian immigrants reported the most prejudice and discrimination, followed by Hispanic groups, then the Chinese, and then native whites and Russian Jews. Many blacks and Hispanics complained of being stopped and searched by the police and experiencing discrimination in stores and from teachers and school administrators; middle-class blacks and Hispanics were especially bitter about racist slurs and treatment in public spaces, in which they were evaluated on the basis of race alone and their class status was unknown or ignored.

If racial inequalities remain deeply entrenched in New York, it is also the case that nonwhite immigrants have profited from the African American presence in ways that are largely absent in Amsterdam. Many immigrant New Yorkers have benefited from federal government policies and legislation, including affirmative action and diversity outreach programs to improve minorities' access to higher education and professional positions. Implemented in the United States in the wake of the civil rights movement of the 1960s, these programs were originally justified as a response to the caste-like status of African Americans and then extended to other groups, especially Latinos. It has become widely accepted in New York that blacks and Latinos should be represented (and improve their representation) in important political bodies, universities, and corporate and government offices. Waters and her colleagues argue that affirmative action and other policies designed to redress longstanding American racial inequalities actually have ended up working better for immigrants and their children than for the native minorities for whom they were initially intended (Kasinitz et al. 2008).

There are additional contrasts with Amsterdam. Whereas immigrants and their second-generation children in Amsterdam are confronted with long established white working- and middle-class communities and structures, for the New York black and Latino second generation, the long-settled populations of African Americans and Puerto Ricans may be a more welcoming presence. Second-generation blacks and Latinos may feel excluded from white America, but they generally come to feel a part of the large black and Latino minority communities. Indeed, they can take advantage of organizations and programs (such as various ethnic studies programs at colleges and universities) established in post–civil rights America to meet the needs of African Americans as well as Latinos and Asians. There is now a sizable African American middle class in the New York area; incorporation into what has been called the African American middle-class "minority culture of mobility" provides role models and resources for upward mobility for black second-generation immigrants, including black professional and fraternal associations and organizations of black students in racially integrated high schools and universities (Neckerman, Carter, and Lee 1999). The other side of the coin is that immigrants often attempt to distance themselves from native blacks. Given that African Americans are generally seen by New Yorkers to be at the bottom of the racial hierarchy, it is not surprising that immigrants—especially those of African ancestry or close in phenotype to native blacks—often try to set themselves apart to avoid the stigma associated with African Americans and to claim superior status (Foner 2005; Itzigsohn 2009; Vickerman 1999; Waters 1999).

Although immigrants in Amsterdam often claim superior status to those in other immigrant-origin groups on the basis, for example, of having come to the country earlier, the absence of an equivalent native minority group rules out the kind of distancing that takes place in New York with regard to African Americans. It also rules out the possibility of assimilating into a native minority group, something that seems to be happening in New York among second-generation West Indians of African ancestry. Many struggle to have their West Indian identity recognized but find that without an accent or other cues to immediately signal their ethnicity to others, they are seen as African American in encounters with whites. Indeed, a gradual blurring of boundaries between African American and West Indian youth appears to be taking place (Vickerman 2013). At least at the current moment, assimilation into black America (including the growing black middle class) is an inevitability for most second-generation West Indians. Becoming American, to put it another way, means becoming black American (Foner 2011).

For West Indians and other black immigrants, foreignness is an advantage in the context of New York's racial hierarchy. This is in line with a more general feature of New York City brought out in Waters's chapter—that nativism, or intense opposition to an internal minority on the basis of foreign connections, is not strong. In fact, the city prides itself on its immigrant heritage and likes to celebrate present-day immigrants owing to a variety of factors, among them the ethnoracial and socioeconomic diversity of the immigrant flows there and the long and continuous history of immigration (see Foner, this volume). Members of the second generation, Waters states, experience exclusion based on the color of their skin, not foreignness. In Amsterdam, foreignness is a disadvantage for those of non–Western European origin, and indeed the commonly (and officially) used term "allochthones" (people born abroad or with one or both parents born abroad) often has negative connotations (Lucassen, this volume).

In Amsterdam, Islam (and cultural values and practices associated with it), not color-coded race, is the "bright boundary" and basis for exclusion of many immigrants and their children. Not that color is irrelevant as a symbolic marker of difference, particularly for the large number of Antilleans and Surinamese of African ancestry, who represent a significant share of the immigrant-origin population. Having origins in former Dutch colonies, these groups have recently come to be seen as quite Dutch in contrast to newly immigrated Muslims, whose cultural and religious differences stand out. To further complicate things, the term "black" is not always reserved for those of sub-Saharan African descent. In a practice that would seem strange to most Americans, "black" schools in Amsterdam refer to those where most students have a foreign background, especially Moroccans and Turks, although pupils of Surinamese and Antillean origin may be present, as well. Still, those of immigrant origin in Amsterdam are more likely to be stigmatized on the basis of culture—as Muslims—than color.

Partly this situation has to do with historical developments. Although colonialism and slavery in distant possessions gave rise to racist attitudes and structures in the Netherlands, they had much less impact on race relations there than internal slavery in the United States—and of course there is no large native minority population that has had a powerful role in shaping the social construction of race, and race relations, as in New York. The very term "race"—widely accepted and used in New York across the political and racial spectrum—is a suspect concept in the Netherlands given its association with Nazi racial laws about the superior "Aryan race" and inferior Jewish "race," and concern that using the term gives legitimacy to discriminatory tendencies by reifying races as distinguishable groups. In any case, Islam is associated in Amsterdam with Moroccans and Turks who not only comprise 28 percent of the immigrant-origin (and 41 percent of the non-Western-immigrant-origin) population in the city but also are seen as problematic immigrant-origin groups in terms of poverty, unemployment, education, and crime rates (see Lucassen, this volume; Vermeulen et al., this volume).

A key question is whether the use of allegedly deep-seated cultural differences associated with Islam as justification for hostility and discrimination against immigrants and their descendants is a kind of cultural racism. Scholars who use the term "cultural racism" to describe the reaction to certain new immigrant groups in Europe have argued that race is, in effect, coded as culture, the central feature of this process being that the qualities of groups are seen as fixed, made natural, and confined within a "pseudo-biologically defined culturalism" (Solomos and Back, quoted in Fredrickson 2002: 8). In George Fredrickson's conceptualization, culture and religion can become essentialized to the point that they serve as functional equivalents of biological racism—culture, in other words, can do the work of race when peoples or ways of life are seen as unchangeable as pigmentation (Fredrickson 2002: 8, 141, 145). Others have argued that the hostility toward Muslims is better understood as an expression of nativism, highlighting the supposed foreignness of Islam (Duyvendak 2011). This would imply that the religious barrier is, in the end, permeable.

However Islam is conceptualized—in terms of race, religion, or culture—Muslims are the most stigmatized and disadvantaged group in Amsterdam. Their culture is commonly seen as a barrier to socioeconomic advancement. Muslims are often labeled uncivilized and backward in terms of their values and practices by many in the general public as well as politicians both on the populist right and the more cosmopolitan left. Moroccans, in particular, have been marginalized as criminals, problem youth, and religious extremists (Vermeulen et al., this volume).

What Justus Uitermark, Jan Willem Duyvendak, and Jan Rath refer to as a culturalist discourse has been prominent in Amsterdam's public life in recent years, especially in the wake of the World Trade Center attacks of September 11, 2001, and murder of Theo van Gogh by a Dutch youth of Moroccan background in 2004. Islam is widely portrayed as irreconcilable with and constituting a threat to Western values such as free speech and equal rights for women and homosexuals—which are at the core of what Duyvendak and his colleagues elsewhere have called a progressive monoculture of the Dutch majority that developed in the past few decades. For the Dutch, Muslims' "strict sexual morals remind [them] too much of what they have recently left behind" (Peter van der Veer, quoted in Duyvendak et al. 2009: 138) and, particularly among people on the left, the painful wresting free from the strictures of their own religions (Buruma 2006: 69).

The chapter on Islam in Amsterdam complicates the picture, showing how views and policies toward Islam have shifted among the city's political leadership—and how Islam in the Netherlands has itself begun to change. During his mayoralty from 2001 to 2010, Job Cohen and others in the city government tried to bring Islam more into the mainstream by, among other things, attributing to ethnic cultures an array of beliefs and behaviors disparaged by the Dutch as "uncivil" and arguing that they were antithetical to true Islamic teachings. Many Muslim leaders, moreover, presented Islam as an integrating force counteracting misogyny, delinquency, and crime, and rejected elements of their ethnic cultures concerning, for example, gender relations in the family.

The chapter concludes by noting that the mayor who succeeded Cohen ended attempts to create a cultural center for debating Islam and spoke out against Muslim civil servants who refused to shake hands with members of the opposite sex. There are other clouds on the horizon, including the possibility of stalled mobility—and high rates of unemployment—for Moroccan and Turkish young people and the attraction of some to extremist Islamic groups. Yet there are also some encouraging signs. Islam, as the chapter makes clear, continues to change in the Dutch context in part as a result of actions by many Muslim leaders. Some scholars predict that as members of the second generation assume leadership in religious associations and institutions, they will generally strive for a more liberal version of Islam than their parents practiced, one that is focused on integration into Western European society and viewed more positively by the wider population (Lucassen 2005: 157–58, 207). A study of the second generation in the Netherlands suggests that most will become less religious altogether. Although the vast majority of second-generation Turks and Moroccans surveyed in 50 Dutch cities identified as Muslim, they reported weaker religious identities and less engagement in religious practices than the first generation (Maliepaard, Lubbers, and Gijsberts 2010). Over time, the native Dutch are likely to grow used to, or at least more used to, Islamic religious observance, especially as Islam becomes more Europeanized. Increased day-to-day interactions with Muslims in schools, neighborhoods, and other social settings are also likely to heighten comfort with people of Muslim background; as the proportion of European-born and well-educated Muslims grows, their participation in mainstream political and economic life will seem more and more "natural."

Predicting the future, of course, is a risky business, and we have to wait to see whether, and to what extent, Islam in Amsterdam—and race in New York—remain barriers for inclusion not only for immigrants but also their second- and third-generation descendants. In Amsterdam, the chapter by Uitermark and his colleagues argues, Islam itself has been undergoing transformation, and it remains to be seen if, and how, racial boundaries in New York City will blur in the context of future developments, including rising rates of intermarriage and opportunities for economic advancement (e.g., Alba 2009; Foner 2005; Lee and Bean 2010).

NANCY FONER AND ROGIER VAN REEKUM

REFERENCES

Alba, Richard. 1999. "Immigration and the American Realities of Assimilation and Multiculturalism," *Sociological Forum* 14: 2–23.

———. 2009. *Blurring the Color Line*. Cambridge, MA: Harvard University Press.

Bakalian, Anny, and Mehdi Bozorgmehr. 2009. *Backlash 9/11: Middle Eastern and Muslim Americans Respond*. Berkeley: University of California Press.

Buruma, Ian. 2006. *Murder in Amsterdam*. New York: Penguin.

Duyvendak, Jan Willem. 2011. *The Politics of Home: Belonging and Nostalgia in the United States and Europe*. New York: Palgrave Macmillan.

Duyvendak, Jan Willem, Trees Pels, and Rally Rijkschroeff. 2009. "A Multicultural Paradise? The Cultural Factor in Dutch Integration Policy," in Jennifer Hochschild and John Mollenkopf (eds.), *Bringing Outsiders In: Transatlantic Perspectives on Immigrant Political Incorporation*. Ithaca, NY: Cornell University Press.

Foner, Nancy. 2005. *In a New Land: A Comparative View of Immigration*. New York: NYU Press.

———. 2011. "Black Identities and the Second Generation: Afro-Caribbeans in Britain and the United States," in Richard Alba and Mary Waters (eds.), *The Next Generation: Immigrant Youth in a Comparative Perspective*. New York: NYU Press.

Foner, Nancy, and George Fredrickson. 2004. "Immigration, Race, and Ethnicity in the United States: Social Constructions and Social Relations," in Nancy Foner and George Fredrickson (eds.), *Not Just Black and White: Historical and Contemporary Perspectives on Immigration, Race, and Ethnicity in the United States*. New York: Russell Sage Foundation

Fredrickson, George. 2002. *Racism*. Princeton, NJ: Princeton University Press.

Itzigsohn, José. 2009. *Encountering American Faultlines: Class, Race, and the Dominican Experience*. New York: Russell Sage Foundation.

Kasinitz, Philip, John Mollenkopf, Mary C. Waters, and Jennifer Holdaway. 2008. *Inheriting the City: The Children of Immigrants Come of Age*. Cambridge, MA: Harvard University Press.

Kleinfield, N. R. 2012. "Why Don't We Have Any White Kids?" *New York Times*, May 13.

Lee, Jennifer, and Frank Bean. 2010. *The Diversity Paradox: Immigration and the Color Line in Twenty-First Century America*. New York: Russell Sage Foundation.

Lucassen, Leo. 2005. *The Immigrant Threat: The Integration of Old and New Migrants In Western Europe Since 1850*. Urbana: University of Illinois Press.

Maliepaard, Mieke, Marcel Lubbers, and Merove Gijsberts. 2010. "Generational Differences in Ethnic and Religious Attachment and their Interrelation: A Study Among Muslim Minorities in the Netherlands." *Ethnic and Racial Studies* 33: 451–71.

Neckerman, Kathryn, Prudence Carter, and Jennifer Lee. 1999. "Segmented Assimilation and Minority Cultures of Mobility." *Ethnic and Racial Studies* 22: 945–65.

Vickerman, Milton. 1999. *Crosscurrents: West Indian Immigrants and Race*. New York: Oxford University Press.

———. 2013. "Jamaicans: Balancing Race and Ethnicity," in Nancy Foner (ed.), *One Out of Three: Immigrant New York in the Twenty-First Century*. New York: Columbia University Press.

Waters, Mary C. 1999. *Black Identities: West Indian Dreams and American Realities*. Cambridge, MA: Harvard University Press.

5

Nativism, Racism, and Immigration in New York City

MARY C. WATERS

When immigrants enter a new society the history and institutions of that society shape the opportunities and obstacles they will encounter. Most comparisons of the integration of immigrants in Europe and the U.S. begin with an acknowledgement of that fact. The United States' long history of immigration is often held up as a resource that provides a model or pathway for current immigrants to follow, one that is lacking in European countries. On the other hand, America's dark history of slavery and racism is seen as a roadblock or barrier to incorporation for today's nonwhite immigrants and their children.

In this chapter I explore the interplay between these two historical patterns and how they manifest themselves in the local history and context of New York City. My argument is that it is important to make a distinction between *racism* and *nativism*. *Racism* can be defined as the belief that "socially significant differences between human groups or communities that differ in visible physical characteristics or putative ancestry are innate and unchangeable" and when "such a sense of deep, unalterable difference [. . . is] accompanied by the notion that 'we' are superior to 'them' and need to be protected from the real or imagined threats to our privileged group position that might arise if 'they' were to gain in resources and rights" (Foner and Fredrickson 2004: 2–3). *Nativism* is defined as an "intense opposition to an internal minority on the ground of its foreign (i.e. 'un-American') connections" (Higham 1963: 4). In American history blacks have been subject to virulent racism, and European immigrants were subject to virulent nativism. Asians and Hispanics were subject to both, although the degree to which their exclusion and suffering was due to one or the other is a subject of scholarly debate.[1]

New York City is a context in which nativism is present, but not very strong, especially in comparison to other parts of the country. This is primarily because of New York's distinct demography and history. First, New York City's demographic makeup is advantageous. Its immigrant stream is very diverse with no one immigrant group dominating the flow. The diversity of origins of New York's immigrant population means that it is harder to stereotype immigrants in New York as undocumented, unskilled, Latino immigrants. This is the stereotype most often invoked in the American South and Southwest where nativist movements are currently strongest. The city also has fewer undocumented immigrants than many other areas of the country, and it also has both a recent history of white immigration and a current flow of white immigrants. In addition, the city gets both low-skilled and very-high-skilled immigrants (Kasinitz et al. 2008). All of these factors are likely to reduce native fears of immigrants.

Secondly, the successful history of New York as an immigrant receiving city leads to an ideology of inclusion and a tolerance for diversity that is much stronger in the city than elsewhere in the U.S. (Foner 2000, 2007). The vitality of the city as a global crossroads and the diversity of its inhabitants is self-consciously understood as a positive factor, not a negative one, and this ideology affects the politics, policies, and discourse about immigration in the city. Thus nonwhite immigrants enter a city that is very welcoming and hospitable to immigrants *qua* immigrants.

On the other hand, New York's demography and history do not provide immunity to American racism. In fact its demography and its history have entrenched a great deal of racial inequality in the city that is not easily eradicated and that shapes the experiences of both natives and new immigrants. The large African American and native Puerto Rican communities in the city are highly segregated from whites, with substandard schools, high crime rates, high rates of imprisonment, unemployment, and health inequality. This reinforces racial stereotypes associating race with crime, drugs, lack of education, violence, and hopelessness. Thus nonwhite immigrants enter a city that remains deeply unequal in terms of race, highly segregated, and occasionally hostile.

As if this paradox was not enough, both of these phenomena—nativism and racism—are changing in the wider society. Events since the Civil Rights Movement in the 1960s have led to declines in the grip of racial inequality on the life chances of nonwhites and better race relations than the U.S. has ever experienced (although with quite a long way to go). And the rapid growth of Mexican immigration and most especially undocumented immigration since the early 1990s has led to a growth of nativist rhetoric and punitive laws targeting both legal and illegal immigrants and even their children (Massey and Sánchez R. 2010). These American conditions have improved vis-à-vis race in the last few decades and deteriorated vis-à-vis immigration.

The current wave of immigration to the U.S. began at about the same time as the passage of the Civil Rights Act that finally ended de jure segregation and discrimination on the basis of race. The Civil Rights Act of 1964 and the Immigration Act of 1965 were both a result of the Civil Rights Movement, and the rationale for the 1965 act was to finally remove the racial quotas that had been the core of American immigration decisions since the 1920s. Even though the law set out specifically to allow equal access to immigration among all the countries in the world, most of the lawmakers who passed it did not understand that the result of the new system would be to change the racial distribution of immigrants coming to the United States. The immigration to the U.S. since the early 1970s has been predominantly nonwhite and has changed the racial distribution of the entire U.S. population. At the same time the changes in the status of native minorities—mostly African Americans, but also native-born Hispanics, American Indians, and Asians—in the post–Civil Rights era have meant that the nature of race relations is increasingly complicated and contested.

Progress has most definitely occurred for native minorities, at the same time as racism has persisted. The election of Barack Obama was heralded by many as a symbol of this new postracial society. At the same time national statistics on race show persisting gaps between whites and blacks on every important measure of wealth and well-being (Massey and Denton 1993; Oliver and Shapiro 1995; Conley 1999;

Grodsky and Pager 2001; Wakefield and Uggen 2010). Nonwhite immigrants have entered a society that is still very much stratified by race and yet they are also assimilating into a changing landscape of race relations. This is further complicated by the fact that the very presence of the immigrants and their descendants is a major part of that change.

So, scholars have been debating the implications of immigration for American race relations, and the implications of American race relations for the experiences of immigrants and their children. This national debate centers on a number of key questions. What characterizes post–Civil Rights race relations? Does racism still limit the life chances of people of color? Do we need affirmative action and diversity policies to avoid segregation in work, schools, and universities or is it enough that these institutions can no longer legally discriminate against nonwhites? How much does our system of racial classification and identification, designed to monitor and combat discrimination, serve to perpetuate racial divisions and boundaries that would naturally disappear without the elaborate classification system we have created? Are the experiences of African Americans similar to those of Latinos and Asians? Do immigrants experience discrimination? If they do, is it because of their racial status as nonwhite or their status as immigrants or foreigners? Are immigrants and their children "racialized" and do they face a future as stigmatized minorities or are they assimilating into a diverse mainstream where they will follow a path similar to the successful incorporation of immigrants and their children from Europe who came in the past (Alba and Nee 2003; Telles and Ortiz 2008)?

This debate is far from decided as the evidence about the first and second generation of the post-1965 immigration is in the process of being analyzed and reported. In addition, the theoretical models we use to understand both race and immigration are only recently being integrated. Sociological models to understand race and to understand immigration were developed separately and until recently did not intersect (Waters 1999a, 1999b). Race scholarship and immigration scholarship had moved on parallel tracks, each addressing different questions and sometimes seeing different phenomena in the same places. Scholarship on American cities in the 1980s is a prime example. Scholars specializing in the study of African Americans wrote about deindustrialization, declining jobs in cities, rising unemployment, and the desolation of public housing projects and the lack of stores and other institutions in ghettos. At the same time, scholars of immigration were describing many of the same cities as magnets for new immigrants, sites of investment in neighborhoods, rising home owner-ship, and the home to small businesses and even manufacturing.

New York City is a site where all of these paradoxes are present. Home to a large and long-standing population of native African Americans and Puerto Ricans, and a gateway city with a very large and diverse immigrant population, New York is a place where race and immigration intersect. Identified as a quintessential immigrant-absorbing city (Glazer and Moynihan 1963; Foner 2007; Kasinitz et al. 2008), it is also one of the most racially segregated cities in the country. New York City has main-tained a level of discrimination high enough that it can be considered "hypersegregated" (Massey and Denton 1993; Iceland 2009). Its index of dissimilarity between blacks and whites was 83 in 1980 and just under 84 in 2000, meaning that 84 percent of either whites or blacks would have to move to achieve an even spatial distribution in the city (Rosenbaum and Argeros 2005). (Nationally the index of dissimilarity of blacks from whites was 65.1 in 2000 [Lewis Mumford Center 2001].) New York has recently had a black mayor, and it has a diverse city council and congres-sional representatives, yet it is also famous throughout the country for some of the most violent and stark racial incidents and riots in the last few decades. While it is home to some of the most diverse residential neighborhoods in the country—Elmhurst in Queens, for example—it is also home to neighborhoods that have become synonyms for white racial violence against blacks—Howard Beach and Bensonhurst.

Racial Distribution of the Population

From 1971 to 2000, 19.9 million legal immigrants arrived in the United States, along with millions more undocumented, eclipsing the 18.2 mil-lion immigrants who came in the 30-year period from 1891 to 1920 (once remembered as the high-water mark in American immigration). Between 2000 and 2010 the foreign-born population grew by about nine million, despite the Great Recession in 2008, which slowed immi-gration, especially of the undocumented. As a result, the foreign-born population has steadily increased since 1960, rising from 9.7 million in that year to 40 million in 2010. The foreign born of the early twenty-first century are more numerous than ever before, but at 12.9 percent of the population in 2010, they constitute a smaller proportion of the total population than they did a century ago, when they were 14.7 percent.

Another 10 percent of the U.S. population are the children of immigrants—referred to by scholars as the second generation. So currently at least one in five Americans are first or second generation. Only 12 percent of the foreign born in the United States are from Europe. The largest group (53 percent) are from Latin America (including Central America, South America, and the Caribbean), while 28 percent are from Asia, and 7 percent are from other regions of the world, such as Africa and Oceania. Mexicans are the largest single group of the foreign born and now comprise 30 percent of all foreign born (Grieco et al. 2012). After Mexico, the top ten countries of origin of the foreign born are China, India, the Philippines, El Salvador, Vietnam, Cuba, Korea, the Dominican Republic, and Guatemala.

This immigration has transformed the major ethnic-racial groups in America. In 1970, 88 percent of the U.S. population was white, 11 percent was black, and less than 1 percent consisted of American Indians, Asians, and Hawaiians. Hispanics, who can be of any race, were only 5 percent of the total 1970 U.S. population. By 2010, the effects of immigration were readily apparent in the demographics of the country—64.7 percent of the population was non-Hispanic white, 12.2 percent was non-Hispanic black, 4.5 percent was Asian, and 16 percent was Hispanic. American Indians increased in number over the 30 years (through new people claiming or discovering their Indian heritage) but still were only 1.5 percent of the population (the remainder identified with two or more races) (Kaiser Family Foundation 2010).

In addition to changing the relative numbers of different races and ethnic groups in the United States, immigration has also changed the generational distribution within American race and ethnic categories. Tables 5.1 and 5.2 provide the national statistics. Asians are the most impacted by immigration. In 2010, only 7 percent of Asians were third generation or higher, 66 percent were foreign born, and 27 percent were second generation. The six largest Asian groups include the long-established Chinese at 25 percent of the total Asian population, followed by Filipinos at 19 percent, Asian Indians at 16 percent, and Koreans,

Vietnamese and Japanese, each at 10 percent. As Roberto Suro and Jeffrey Passel (2003: 6) point out, in the mid-twentieth century the Latino population in the U.S. was dominated by the three-plus generation—it was primarily a group distant from immigrants who could be considered a native minority and primarily composed of Mexican Americans and Puerto Ricans. By 2010 the majority (72 percent) of Latinos were first or second generation—but more than a fourth were third generation or higher. In addition to long-time Mexican Americans and Puerto Ricans, the Latino group includes immigrants and their children with origins in the Caribbean and Central and South America. Indeed only whites, blacks, and American Indians in 2010 had a

Table 5.1. Race and Ethnic Distribution in the United States, 2010

Race/Ethnicity	Percent
White (non-Hispanic)	64.7
Black (non-Hispanic)	12.2
Hispanic	16.0
Asian (non-Hispanic)	4.5
American Indian	0.8
Two or more races	1.5
N=310.2 million	

Source: Kaiser Family Foundation (2010).

Table 5.2. Race and Ethnicity by Generation in the United States, 2010

Generation	Black	Asian	Hispanic	Non-Hispanic White	Proportion of total population that is of this generation
1st	8.4	65.7	40.1	4.5	13.6
2d	5.2	27.2	32.0	5.9	11.2
3d	89.5	6.8	27.2	89.5	75.1
Total N (in millions)	37.8	13.9	49.6	200.6	310

Source: Calculated from the 2010 Current Population Survey IPUMS (King et al. 2010).

majority of nonmigrant stock. Even blacks—the group whose experience most racial policies in the United States are designed to address—
were 13.6 percent first or second generation, as African Americans have
been joined by groups such as Nigerians, Haitians, West Indians, and
Cape Verdeans. In their generational distribution they are more similar to non-Hispanic whites, who are about 10 percent first or second
generation.

New York City is considerably more diverse than the nation as a
whole. Table 5.3 provides the racial distribution of the city according
to the pooled 2006–10 American Community Survey. White non-Hispanics were 33.7 percent of the city population, followed by Hispanics
at 29.2 percent, black non-Hispanics at 23.2 percent, and Asians at 12.5
percent. Another 1.2 percent of the population provided two or more
races in the survey, and American Indians were a negligible 0.2 percent
of the city's population. Thirty-six percent of the city's population is foreign born, and the share of each racial group that is first generation also
varies a lot. Non-Hispanic whites are the least impacted by immigration, but even so a little over a quarter (27 percent) of them are foreign
born. Almost a third (32 percent) of non-Hispanic blacks are foreign
born, and a large majority of Asians (72 percent) and about half of Hispanics are foreign born (52 percent).

While whites are a minority in the city, "traditional" native minorities are also a minority. Nancy Foner (2007) points out that in the late
1990s African Americans and Puerto Ricans who were themselves
native born with native-born parents were just about 25 percent of the

Table 5.3. Race and Ethnicity in New York City, 2010

Race/Ethnicity	N	Percent
White (non-Hispanic)	2,723,853	33.7
Hispanic	2,281,115	29.2
Black (non-Hispanic)	1,874,089	23.2
Asian (non-Hispanic)	1,012,014	12.5
Two or more races	95,260	1.2

Source: American Community Survey 2006–10 pooled estimate. United States Census
Bureau. http://www.census.gov/acs/www.

city's total population. Although official statistics and everyday discourse describe race relations in New York City in terms of the familiar government-sanctioned ethnoracial categories—white, black, Hispanic, Asian, and American Indian—relations among racial and ethnic groups in New York are simultaneously a story of immigrants and their children and their relations with natives and with each other.

The Changing Contours of Racism and Nativism

Howard Winant (2006: 989) summarizes the contradictory nature of current race relations: "In the post–World War II era, the postcolonial era, it has been possible to claim that race is less salient than before in determining life chances; this is the nonracialist or color blind argument. At the same time social organization continues to function along racial lines; race consciousness operates in the allocation of resources, the dynamics of social control, and the organization of movements for equality and social justice."

While the right wing of American politics increasingly argues that we have now achieved a race-neutral society and should no longer measure or classify by race, the left is in the ironic position of defending the nation's vast racial statistical system in order to monitor and expose continuing racial inequalities. Many scholars have found similar patterns in the changes in white racial attitudes since the Civil Rights Movement. Overt racism and conscious support for de jure racial discrimination are confined to a small (but dangerous) fringe of the white population. Most whites hold what Douglas Massey (2007: 74) summarizes as "a conscious rejection of principled racism, on the one hand and the persistence of negative sentiments and beliefs about African Americans on the other." This constellation of racial attitudes has been labeled symbolic racism (Kinder and Sears 1981), modern racism (McConahay 1983), laissez-faire racism (Bobo, Kluegel, and Smith 1997), color-blind racism (Bonilla-Silva 2003), and aversive racism (Dovidio and Gaertner 2004).

Yet most studies of racism and prejudice have been done under the old race relations paradigm—testing white attitudes toward blacks and much more rarely, blacks' attitudes toward whites. Only very recently has this research begun to include attitudes toward Hispanics and Asians.

Empirically, there is a great deal of evidence that the brightness of the boundary between blacks and whites is much stronger than the boundary separating whites from Asians and Hispanics (Alba 2005). For one thing, because of the ways in which racial statistics are structured in the U.S. a lot of Hispanics consider themselves to be whites, and are considered by whites to be white. Half of Hispanic immigrants report their race to be white in the U.S. census (Foner and Alba 2010: 803). Intermarriage with whites is much higher among Asians and Hispanics than blacks (Perlmann and Waters 2004). While residential segregation also exists between Asians and whites and Hispanics and whites, it operates differently between blacks and whites. Levels of segregation for blacks are at the same high level regardless of the socioeconomic status of African Americans. It is not just poor African Americans who are segregated from whites in neighborhoods. For Asians and Hispanics segregation decreases as their socioeconomic status increases, which suggests less resistance on the part of whites. These different experiences have led some scholars to suggest that the color line in the U.S. has shifted from one in which the greatest divide is between whites and nonwhites, to one where the important divide is between blacks and nonblacks, with Asians and Hispanics facing a future in which they will be able to step over the color line to join whites while leaving African Americans behind (Gans 1999; Loewen 1988; Lee and Bean 2010).

The question of how race will affect the integration of nonwhite immigrants and especially the second and later generations in the U.S. has generated disagreement. The theory of segmented assimilation argues that race will have very negative consequences for the children of immigrants, channeling them into segregated neighborhoods, substandard schools, and oppositional identities (Portes and Zhou 1993; Portes and Rumbaut 2001). Latinos are especially seen as subject to racial exclusion that results in a lack of intergenerational mobility and stalled progress (Telles and Ortiz 2008; Massey and Sánchez R. 2010). Other scholars see a much more optimistic outcome for Latinos and Asians, with a trajectory more like that of European immigrants in the twentieth century rather than a racialized group like African Americans (Alba and Nee 1999; Alba 2009; Smith 2001; Kasinitz et al. 2008).

Massey and Sánchez R. (2010) argue that the hostile context of reception that Latino immigrants are currently experiencing is creating a reactive ethnicity that is hardening boundaries between Latinos and native whites. Based on interviews with both documented and undocumented first- and second-generation immigrants in the area between New York and Philadelphia, including some interviews in New York City, these authors argue that Latinos are rejecting an American identity: "Most arrive with dreams of social or material advancement and initially perceive the United States as a land of opportunity. Over time they encounter a harsh world of work and experience the indignities of prejudice, discrimination, and blocked opportunities, and most eventually come to see the United States as a place of inequality and racism" (Massey and Sánchez R. 2010: 21).

Massey and Sánchez R. are correct to point out the growing anti-immigrant opinions in the U.S. since the recession of 2008, and the targeting of undocumented immigrants that has been occurring all over the country since the 1990s. Yet I believe they are incorrect in interpreting this as a racial phenomenon. The targeting of undocumented immigrants may have the potential to become a racial phenomenon but as of yet it is best characterized as nativism. The difference is that while both racism and nativism targeted toward Latino immigrants leads to discrimination and prejudice, racism is based on differences believed to be permanent and innate, while nativism is based on difference owing to nationality. Traditionally in the United States, immigrants and their children have become Americans. Blacks have always been Americans, but have not been accepted as equal Americans with whites.

In his perceptive study of third- and later-generation Mexican Americans in California and Kansas, Tomás Jiménez (2010) argues that most later-generation Mexican Americans experience discrimination not because they are Mexican American per se, but because they are associated with new Mexican immigrants in the eyes of native-born Americans. In other words, Mexicans are not discriminated against in American society because of their culture or beliefs about their racial inferiority, but rather because Americans question their right to be in the country. Jiménez argues that Mexican Americans are experiencing a racialized form of nativism, not due to a legacy of colonialism but rather because of contemporary immigration. He writes that "instances in which race matters in the lives of Mexican Americans are virtually always linked to notions of Mexicans as foreigners, as seen in situations in which respondents were mistaken for immigrants." Mia Tuan (1998) makes a similar argument about Asian Americans.

This distinction matters a lot for the future integration of nonwhite immigrants and their descendants in the United States. Exclusion based on race is about a permanent or at least very long lasting boundary which will give rise to reactive ethnicity and societal cleavages. Nativism could have the same result, but it does not have to. Anti-immigrant attitudes in the United States are always ambivalent, as the country has an ideology of acceptance of immigrants. Anti- immigrant attitudes tend to follow the unemployment rate, rising in bad times and declining in good times. Because of birthright citizenship and rapid language and cultural assimilation the children of immigrants do not have the same recognizable difference from natives that immigrants themselves do.

Evidence from the New York Second-Generation Study

The study of second-generation immigrants in the New York City metropolitan area that I conducted with Philip Kasinitz and John Mollenkopf sheds some light on this issue.[2] The study drew representative samples of young adults (age 18–32) from five ethnic groups: Dominicans, South Americans, West Indians, Chinese, and Jews from the former Soviet Union.[3] We also interviewed samples of African Americans, Puerto Ricans, and whites with native-born parents. Altogether, we completed telephone interviews with 3,415 respondents and did further in-person, in-depth interviews with a subsample of approximately 10 percent (for a more complete overview of the study, see Kasinitz et al. 2008).

We reached three conclusions about the kinds of inclusion and exclusion these young people were experiencing. First we found that their patterns of socioeconomic mobility and educational and occupational achievement in young adulthood were strongly racially patterned. They were entering and experiencing a racially stratified city. The white Russian immigrants and the Chinese were doing the best, followed by the lighter-skinned South Americans, the West Indians, the darker-skinned Dominicans, and then the native Puerto Ricans and African Americans.

Second, we found that race was not experienced the same way by all of the "nonwhite" respondents. African Americans, and those who "look like" or could be confused with African Americans (such as

West Indians and dark-skinned Latinos), have more negative experiences than other nonwhite groups. They face more systematic and "brighter" racial boundaries than do Asians and light-skinned Latinos (Alba 2005). This, we argue, creates more formidable obstacles for those defined as black, as opposed to those who are just "nonwhite," to full incorporation into American society (see also Hattam 2007).

Yet, even for those who are defined as black, race is far from the monolithic barrier it was in the nineteenth and early twentieth centuries. While racial prejudice is alive and well in twenty-first-century New York, there are many spheres of life in which it has lost its potent punch. Most previous works on the second generation have seen being a racial minority as a distinct disadvantage in the U.S., and those in the second generation often do face serious racial barriers. At the same time, at least some of them, precisely because they have been defined as "nonwhite," have also benefitted from the institutions, political strategies, and notions of rights developed in the aftermath of the Civil Rights Movement. Ironically, affirmative action and other policies designed to redress long-standing American racial inequities turn out to work better for immigrants and their children than they do for the native minorities for whom they were designed (Skrentny 2001; Graham 2001).

Finally, we found that the children of immigrants in New York were not experiencing exclusion based on the fact that they were the children of immigrants. They did not feel like they needed to choose between their parents' cultures and American culture. Unlike stories of earlier European second-generation young people who had to change their names to less ethnic ones to get jobs or go to college, or who were ashamed of their parents' language, our respondents saw no conflict between their ethnic and American identities. Indeed many of them thought their bilingualism and combination of cultures were advantages rather than disadvantages. On balance, the majority of second-generation respondents did not perceive either America or being American as something racial. Even those who had experienced a great deal of discrimination tended to see themselves as American and to see America as a place that accepted their culture and their identity.

We speculated that this is very much tied to their coming of age in New York. Multiculturalism is relatively easy for New Yorkers. The history of the city's incorporation of immigrants, the sheer diversity of its population, and the relative openness of its institutions to a wide variety of groups create a kind of on-the-ground diversity that is perceived as particularly welcoming and inclusive.

Indeed, when we asked young people about cultural inclusion we got generally positive stories. They did not find it hard to keep the music or food or religion of their parents. The exclusion that they experienced was based on the color of their skin, not their cultural difference. We asked a series of questions about discrimination that made that clear.

We asked respondents about their own experiences with discrimination: "Within the past year, did you feel like someone was showing prejudice toward you or discriminating against you?" (For native whites, we added the phrase "because of your ethnicity.") This question is inclusive of experiencing both negative actions (discrimination) and negative attitudes (prejudice). We then asked whether the respondent had experienced this prejudice or discrimination at work, when buying something in a store or waiting for a table at a restaurant, by the police, at school or when looking for work. The pattern of responses is presented in table 5.4.

The general pattern is that native-born blacks and West Indians report the most prejudice and discrimination, followed by the Hispanic groups, then the Chinese, and then the whites and Russian Jews. Clearly

Table 5.4. Experience of Prejudice by Group

	Percentage experiencing prejudice				
	At Work	Shops/ Restaurants	From Police	At School	Looking for Work
South Americans	20	41	22	17	17
Dominican	19	37	25	14	20
Puerto Rican	26	40	22	15	22
West Indian	30	57	35	17	26
Black	35	55	34	15	33
Chinese	14	41	13	25	12
Russian Jew	8	12	8	11	9
White	14	15	6	9	6

Note: South Americans includes people whose parents are from Colombia, Ecuador, and Peru.
Source: New York Second-Generation Study (Kasinitz et al. 2008).

this suggests a predictable hierarchy based on skin color. Groups clearly of African descent (and most likely to be seen as "like" African Americans) experience the most discrimination, followed by Latinos, then Asians, with whites reporting the least discrimination.

Dominican males are much more likely than South American and Puerto Rican males to report problems with the police (in all groups, problems with the police were far more common for men than for women). Indeed, the Dominican males are closer to the African American and the West Indian males in their perceived levels of prejudice from the police. It is worth noting that among native white males the number that report having experienced "prejudice or discrimination by the police" is actually far *lower* than the number that have actually been *arrested*. We also asked a question about whether respondents thought that the police favor whites in New York City. Most respondents in every group agreed with that statement although West Indians and native blacks were most likely to agree. There were no significant gender differences in any group except for the Dominicans, where more males than females thought the police favored whites (79 percent vs. 61 percent).

The locations where respondents are most likely to have encountered discrimination also vary by group, as indicated in table 5.4. Shopping and dining out are the places where every group most commonly experiences discrimination, ranging from 12 percent of Russian Jews who report such problems to 57 percent of West Indians. But among the Chinese, discrimination while shopping was followed by discrimination in school (25 percent), which is striking given that the group was generally the most successful in educational attainment. The Chinese report much lower levels of discrimination while looking for work or from the police—around 13 percent. For West Indians, being "hassled" by the police was the next most likely arena (35 percent), followed by work (30 percent), looking for work (26 percent), and in school (17 percent).

Respondents clarified these survey patterns in our in-depth interviews. Often different ethnic groups are referring to different phenomena when they answer the questions on discrimination and prejudice. When the Chinese discuss discrimination at school, it turned out they were discussing discrimination from peers, primarily black and

Hispanic students in their schools who teased or bullied them. They also experienced what might be seen as "positive discrimination": fellow students who tried to copy from their papers in school because they were assumed to be very smart, or teachers who put them in the hardest math class just because they were Chinese.

The "discrimination" that the Hispanic and black respondents were thinking of was much more likely to come from white teachers or administrators who assumed that they were not smart. They described being put in bilingual education classes when they did not need them and being criticized for not speaking English correctly. They described sometimes blatant racism from white teachers as well as guidance counselors who steered kids into non-college-track courses. Those who went on to college described discrimination from white peers at college—one Dominican woman told us that when she was moving into her freshman dorm room her roommate insisted on being present so that she would not steal anything. They also complained about white professors who had low expectations of their nonwhite students.

Negative experiences with the police were very common among black and Hispanic young men. They described being stopped if they were "driving while black," or stopped on the street or on the subway because they "fit the description." Most young men were very angry about their experiences with the police and most had been advised by parents or teachers or friends to just "take it" and not to talk back because that could lead to far greater trouble. So most of the young men ended up "swallowing" a lot of anger.

Encounters with the police seem to have a particularly deep and long-lasting effect on young people, particularly young men. Part of this may be because, no matter how unfairly one is treated, it is generally imprudent, or actually dangerous, to argue back. This inability to respond leaves one with a bitter sense of frustration. Further, it is hard to dismiss a police officer who treats one badly as simply "ignorant" or a lout, as one could with a peer. The police are armed representatives of the state. Negative treatment by them, in some way, represents negative treatment by the larger society. And if a group, such as African Americans, already has ample reason to feel excluded and stigmatized, repeated negative encounters with the police can reinforce this perception in ways they may not for whites.

Finally, anonymous encounters with shopkeepers, security guards, and particularly with the police in public spaces are powerful because they are so purely "racial." In such confrontations class differences do not count—as the frequent, bitter complaints of middle-class African Americans make clear (Feagin 1991). Nor do ethnic differences. Many of the victims of some of New York's most notorious police brutality cases have been black immigrants. A police officer rarely has a basis for knowing if a young man on a public street is African American or West Indian, middle class or poor. If the police officer discriminates, it is on the basis of race alone.

By contrast, many respondents from many groups reported hearing racial slurs on the street or on subways. Unlike encounters with the police, these incidents were described as hurtful but not overly dramatic, perhaps because the victim had more power to respond. Indeed, some young men responded to slurs by threatening or actually engaging in physical violence. These incidents contributed to a sense that other people were identifying them racially and ethnically and that they had to stand up for themselves. But most people remembered them as a regrettable aspect of dealing with other "ignorant kids," and in contrast to encounters with the police, these incidents generally did not leave lasting scars or deep anger.

The model presented in figure 5.1 captures the differences in the experiences and consequences of different types of discrimination across the groups in our study. Not all "nonwhites" are alike. The "closer" you are perceived to be to African Americans the more serious the discrimination. Groups differ in the degree and kind of discrimination they experience. So after African Americans, West Indians face the most discrimination, followed by Dominicans and Puerto Ricans. South Americans experience much less. Chinese experience discrimination even less and Russians—as whites—the least.

A first set of racial incidents in public spaces (experienced by Dominicans, West Indians, Puerto Ricans, and African Americans especially on the streets, in stores, and from the police) do not leave much control to the nonwhite victim and thus lead to discouragement and confrontation with whites. The respondents try to avoid racial discrimination by avoiding white neighborhoods so they will not be targeted or try to dress nicely so that cabs will stop for them or restaurants will give them

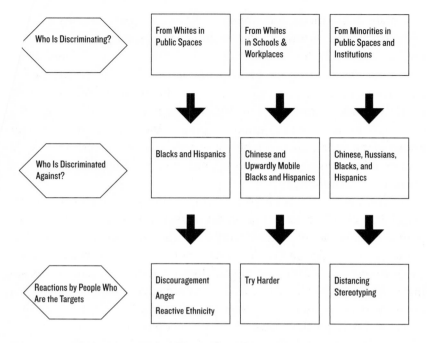

Figure 5.1. Different Types of Racial Discrimination Experienced by the Second Generation

good service. They may try to signal their middle-class status to differentiate themselves from the "ghetto poor," or, in the case of Dominicans, West Indians, and Puerto Ricans, also try to signal their ethnic difference from African Americans. But in impersonal encounters on the street or in job applications, often the only thing whites know about them is their race and such techniques cannot always prevent racist treatment.

A second set of racially discriminatory incidents in schools and workplaces (more common among Chinese, Russians, South Americans, upwardly mobile blacks, Dominicans, and Puerto Ricans) lead less to discouragement and more to increased efforts to overcome racial stereotypes. When discrimination by whites occurs in an institutional setting where the nonwhite victim perceives some degree of control over it, such discrimination is experienced as a challenge—there is a felt need to try harder to succeed. So workplace discrimination is often interpreted not as a reason to give up, but as a reason to show how good one can be, to show that one is better than all the other workers so that individual characteristics can end up trumping racial stereotypes.

Respondents defined as black experience these kinds of incidents but they require integrated settings—schools, workplaces, churches—to even be exposed to whites' discriminatory practices up close. As a result poor African Americans, West Indians, and Dominicans don't usually experience as much of this sort of discrimination because they spend so much time in segregated neighborhoods, schools, and workplaces. Ironically, it is better-off blacks and Hispanics, who are more likely to be in integrated settings, who thus have the "opportunity" to be the victim of this sort of discrimination (see also Hochschild 1996; Vickerman 1999).

Finally the third set of racially discriminatory encounters—intergroup tensions—is quite common in multiethnic New York. The different ethnic and racial groups compete for resources at work, in schools, and in neighborhoods. The immense diversity in New York City means that there is a great deal of complexity in who is discriminating against whom. Often in-group favoritism—such as black supervisors wanting to hire black workers—is perceived as racism by other nonwhite employees who are vying for the same jobs. This sort of ethnic rivalry accounts for a great deal of the reported discrimination among all groups and it certainly makes young people highly conscious of ethnic differences. Yet the vast number of crosscutting rivalries also means that while there may be clear ethnic hierarchies among nonwhites, they are less associated with any permanent or systemic sense of inferiority or superiority than are rivalries between whites and nonwhites.

The use of similar racial talk to describe many different types of phenomena can also mask social progress. The more integrated a person's life, the more likely he or she is to experience discrimination in a number of spheres. Chinese, the most successful second-generation group in our study, are also the group most likely to be in integrated schools, workplaces, and neighborhoods where they are in the minority among other groups. In contrast, black and Latino respondents are more likely to be in segregated schools and neighborhoods, especially during their earliest years of education where they tend to comprise part of the majority group. For those of them who are upwardly mobile, it is often not until college and the workplace that they finally have enough contact with other groups and particularly with whites to have much opportunity to be discriminated against.

Understanding Discrimination

Our study shows that the term "discrimination" is being used to describe all kinds of perceived unfairness. African Americans' experiences, however, are the benchmark against which we can compare the experiences of all the groups. African Americans are most likely to report discrimination when looking for work and being at work. They, along with West Indians, report the highest levels of discrimination while shopping and from the police. And the discrimination they experience while shopping is very different than what is reported by other groups—it is not due to social class. Better-educated African Americans are *more* likely than the less well educated to report discrimination—the opposite of what occurs among native whites. Indeed, upward mobility in terms of class status may actually expose African Americans to more rather than less discrimination in their everyday lives. Such situations are often understood as an indication that "race," an ascribed and immutable characteristic, is trumping class, which most Americans see as an achieved characteristic. Needless to say, this is the sort of discrimination that is the most frustrating for its victims, since there is so little that an individual can do about it.

Indeed, our data show that different types of discrimination produce different reactions. When it is possible to demonstrate one's individuality in school or at work, respondents in our study tended to react by trying to "outshine" those who doubt them. It is in impersonal instances, such as when a police officer or store keeper who knows nothing about someone except his or her race treats that person poorly, that discrimination wreaks its most debilitating and anger-inducing effects. This, we argue, is the specific kind of racism that could lead to what Alejandro Portes and Rubén Rumbaut (2001) call "reactive ethnicity." While Chinese, South Americans, and Russian Jews are also sometimes treated unfairly because of their race or ethnicity, their experiences are qualitatively and quantitatively different from the experiences of people with dark skin.

Thus the fact that children of immigrants have come to be categorized as members of native "minority groups" does not mean their experience has been the same as that of the native minorities. They clearly do suffer much of the same prejudice and discrimination, but they do not inherit the scars and handicaps of a long history of racial exclusion. Nor, for them, are everyday incidents of discrimination likely to be seen as connected to deep and pervasive power asymmetries. These incidents are not trivial, but they can be challenged and they do not engender hopelessness.

Finally, even if the children of immigrants are coming to be seen (and to see themselves) as members of a "minority," we must ask if, at this historical juncture, that is always a bad thing. Too often social scientists have assumed that being "racialized" as "black" or "Latino" can only have negative consequences for the children of immigrants, a view they often share with immigrant parents. They are partially right. Pervasive racism can indeed be soul crushing, and the nihilism of the American ghetto can lead young people down many a self-destructive path. However, African American communities have always been more complex than this view implies, maintaining their own institutions and paths of upward mobility (Neckerman, Carter, and Lee 1999). In post–Civil Rights America, the heritage of the African American struggle for racial justice has given young people new strategies, vocabularies, and resources for upward mobility (see Massey et al. 2007).

This may partially explain the pervasiveness of the notion of "discrimination" among the current generation of second-generation and native white young adults. If the African American experience of discrimination has been more harsh than that of other groups, the African American civil rights struggle has also provided a heroic model for opposing discrimination. Today's children of immigrants are quick to take up this model even when, ironically, they are better positioned to make use of it than are African Americans. While their immigrant parents are often willing to quietly accept unfair treatment, the second-generation children are far more willing to challenge discrimination whenever they see it. In the post–Civil Rights era, this is one of the ways in which they are becoming American.

They have the advantage of becoming American in New York where they feel very much included as Americans even if they experience discrimination as nonwhite Americans. Their experiences might be very different in other parts of the country where they might be more likely to experience both the sting of nativism and racism.

Areas of the country that are coping with large numbers of immigrants without a history of absorbing immigrants in the past are more likely to have sharper divisions between immigrants and natives (Waters and Jiménez 2005). These new destinations are also places where the majority of immigrants are Latino and in many cases undocumented, stoking nativist concerns (Massey 2008). In the southern and midwestern United States, the combination of rapid in-migration to areas that have had no recent experience with immigration, and sometimes no history of immigration at all, along with a preponderance of unskilled undocumented immigrants, have created a potent stew of anti-immigrant feeling and behavior. Daniel Hopkins (2010) finds that a combination of national anti-immigrant rhetoric (mostly from the Republican Party and right-leaning media) with a sudden growth in immigration leads to local anti-immigrant policies. With the failure of comprehensive immigration reform at the federal level, many states and local towns and counties have passed laws directed toward immigrants. Restrictive local laws against immigrants sanction landlords who rent to undocumented people, target day laborers gathering in public places, authorize police to inquire about legal status and share that information with federal authorities, and restrict undocumented immigrants from any local aid or services. In 2010 state legislatures considered 1,400 legislative bills targeting immigration, and passed 208 laws (Johnston and Morse 2011).[4]

Immigrants and their children in New York City are not directly affected by these anti-immigrant developments. It is almost impossible to imagine such negative legislation being enacted in New York or other gateway cities where the majority of immigrants continue to live. This is especially true now that many decades of immigration have created a large population of citizen first- and second-generation Latinos who wield strong voting power in states like New York, California, Texas, and Florida.

Yet this does not mean that the rising tide of nativism might not affect intergroup attitudes in these gateway cities. Scholars such as Douglas Massey (2011) have argued that anti-immigrant attitudes are racializing Latinos, and that what began as nativist fears may crystallize into racialized discrimination that will consign Mexican immigrants and their children into a permanent underclass. Whether the tolerance and acceptance immigrants and their children experience in New York City will spread to the rest of the country, or the intolerance and exclusion that characterizes other parts of the country will spread to New York, is an open question. Meanwhile, the race to fix ongoing racial inequality is even more pressing, as immigration increases the numbers of people facing ongoing racial inequality.

NOTES

1. There is also a large literature about European immigrants during the period after 1880 being defined as "nonwhite" and as races separate from whites (Jacobson 1998). While some historians and sociologists would argue that these immigrants were racialized in a way similar to blacks, none would argue that what they experienced was as virulent as what blacks experienced. The best empirical investigation of this difference remains Stanley Lieberson's 1980 book, *A Piece of the Pie.*

2. The sample included the four boroughs of Manhattan, Brooklyn, Queens, and the Bronx but excluded Staten Island, because it had a much lower concentration of immigrants and their children. It also included the close suburbs of Long Island, Westchester, New Jersey, and Connecticut. See Kasinitz et al. (2008) for more details.

3. We interviewed about 400 from each background and oversampled Chinese to learn both about those whose parents came from the mainland and those from Taiwan or Hong Kong. Our Russian sample was restricted to about 300.

4. It is important to note that even in new destinations some local governments are passing pro-immigrant legislation, "welcoming" immigrants to their areas, or declaring themselves "sanctuaries" where police are prohibited from enforcing immigration laws (Ramakrishnan and Wong 2010).

REFERENCES

Alba, Richard. 2005. "Bright vs. Blurred Boundaries: Second-Generation Assimilation and Exclusion in France, Germany, and the United States." *Ethnic and Racial Studies* 28: 20–49.

———. 2009. *Blurring the Color Line: The New Chance for a More Integrated America.* Cambridge, MA: Harvard University Press.

Alba, Richard, and Victor Nee. 1999. "Rethinking Assimilation Theory for a New Era of Immigration," in Charles Hirschman, Philip Kasinitz, and Josh DeWind (eds.), *The Handbook of International Migration: The American Experience.* New York: Russell Sage Foundation.

Blackmun, Harry. 1978. Opinion, *University of California Regents vs. Bakke* (438 U.S. 265).

Bobo, Lawrence, James R. Kluegel, and Ryan A. Smith. 1997. "Laissez-Faire Racism: The Crystallization of a 'Kinder, Gentler' Anti-Black Ideology," in Steven A. Tuch and Jack Martin Greenwood (eds.), *Racial Attitudes in the 1990s: Continuity and Change*. Greenwood, CT: Praeger.

Bonilla-Silva, Eduardo. 2003. *Racism Without Racists: Color-Blind Racism and the Persistence of Racial Inequality in the United States*. Lanham, MD: Rowman and Littlefield.

Conley, Dalton. 1999. *Being Black, Living in the Red: Race, Wealth, and Social Policy in America*. Berkeley: University of California Press.

Deaux, Kay. 2006. *To Be an Immigrant*. New York: Russell Sage Foundation.

Dovidio, John F., and Samuel L. Gaertner. 2004. "Aversive Racism," in Mark P. Zanna (ed.), *Advances in Experimental Social Psychology, Volume 36*. San Diego: Academic Press.

Feagin, Joe R. 1991. "The Continuing Significance of Race: Antiblack Discrimination in Public Places." *American Sociological Review* 56: 101–16.

Foner, Nancy. 2000. "Beyond the Melting Pot Three Decades Later: Recent Immigrants and New York's New Ethnic Mixture." *International Migration Review* 34: 255–62.

———. 2007. "How Exceptional is New York? Migration and Multiculturalism in the Empire City." *Ethnic and Racial Studies* 30: 999–1023.

Foner, Nancy, and Richard Alba. 2008. "Immigrant Religion in the U.S. and Western Europe: Bridge or Barrier to Inclusion?" *International Migration Review* 42: 360–92.

———. 2010. "Immigration and the Legacies of the Past: The Impact of Slavery and the Holocaust on Contemporary Immigrants in the United States and Western Europe." *Comparative Studies in Society and History* 52: 798–819.

Foner, Nancy, and George M. Fredrickson. 2004. "Immigration, Race, and Ethnicity in the United States: Social Constructions and Social Relations," in Nancy Foner and George M. Fredrickson (eds.), *Not Just Black and White: Historical and Contemporary Perspectives on Immigration, Race, and Ethnicity in the United States*. New York: Russell Sage Foundation.

——— (eds.). 2004. *Not Just Black and White: Historical and Contemporary Perspectives on Immigration, Race and Ethnicity in the United States*. New York: Russell Sage Foundation.

Gans, Herbert. 1999. "The Possibility of a New Racial Hierarchy in the Twenty-First Century United States," in Michele Lamont (ed.), *The Cultural Territories of Race: Black and White Boundaries*. Chicago: University of Chicago Press.

Glazer, Nathan, and Daniel P. Moynihan. 1963. *Beyond the Melting Pot: The Negroes, Puerto Ricans, Jews, Italians, and Irish of New York City*. Cambridge, MA: MIT Press and Harvard University Press.

Graham, Hugh Davis. 2001. "Affirmative Action for Immigrants? The Unintended Consequences of Reform," in John D. Skretney (ed.), *Color Lines: Affirmative Action, Immigration and Civil Rights Options for America*. Chicago: University of Chicago Press.

Grieco, Elizabeth, Edward Trevelyan, Luke Larsen, Yesenia D. Acosta, Christine Gambino, Patricia de la Cruz, Tom Gryn, and Nathan Walters. 2012. "The Size, Place of Birth, and

Geographic Distribution of the Foreign-Born Population in the United States: 1960 to 2010." U.S. Census Bureau. http://www.census.gov/population/www/techpap.html.

Grodsky, Eric, and Devah Pager. 2001. "The Structure of Disadvantage: Individual and Occupational Determinants of the Black-White Wage Gap." *American Sociological Review* 66: 542–67.

Harris, Marvin. 1964. *Patterns of Race in the Americas*. Westport, CT: Greenwood Press.

Hattam, Victoria. 2007. *In the Shadow of Race: Jews, Latinos and Immigrant Politics in the United States*. Chicago: University of Chicago Press.

Higham, John. 1973. *Strangers in the Land: Patterns in American Nativism, 1860–1925*. New York: Atheneum.

Hochschild, Jennifer L. 1996. *Facing Up to the American Dream: Race, Class, and the Soul of the Nation*. Princeton, NJ: Princeton University Press.

Hopkins, Daniel J. 2010. "Politicized Places: Explaining Where and When Immigrants Provoke Local Opposition." *American Political Science Review* 104 (1): 40–60.

Iceland, John. 2009. *Where We Live Now: Immigration and Race in the United States*. Berkeley: University of California Press.

Itzigsohn, José. 2009. *Encountering American Fault Lines: Race, Class and the Dominican Experience in Providence*. New York: Russell Sage Foundation.

Jacobson, Matthew Frye. 1998. *Whiteness of a Different Color: European Immigrants and the Alchemy of Race*. Cambridge, MA: Harvard University Press.

Jiménez, Tomás R. 2010. *Replenished Ethnicity: Mexican Americans, Immigration and Identity*. Berkeley: University of California Press.

Johnston, Gillian, and Ann Morse. 2011. "2010 Immigration-Related Laws and Resolutions in the States." National Conference of State Legislatures. www.ncsl.org/default.aspx?tabid=21857.

Kaiser Family Foundation. 2010. "Distribution of U.S. Population by Race/Ethnicity, 2010 and 2050." http://facts.kff.org/chart.aspx?ch=364.

Kasinitz, Philip. 1992. *Caribbean New York: Black Immigrants and the Politics of Race*. Ithaca, NY: Cornell University Press.

———. 2004. "Race, Assimilation and Second Generations, Past and Present," in Nancy Foner and George Fredrickson (eds.), *Not Just Black and White: Historical and Contemporary Perspectives on Immigration, Race, and Ethnicity in the United States*. New York: Russell Sage Foundation.

Kasinitz, Philip, John Mollenkopf, Mary C. Waters, and Jennifer Holdaway. 2008. *Inheriting the City: The Children of Immigrants Come of Age*. Cambridge and New York: Harvard University Press and Russell Sage Foundation.

Kessler, Ronald C., Kristin D. Mickelson, and David R. Williams. 1999. "The Prevalence, Distribution and Mental Health Correlates of Perceived Discrimination in the United States." *Journal of Health and Social Behavior* 40: 208–30.

Kinder, Donald R., and David O. Sears. 1981. "Prejudice and Politics: Symbolic Racism Versus Threats to the Good Life." *Journal of Personality and Social Psychology* 40: 414–31.

King, Miriam, Steven Ruggles, J. Trent Alexander, Sarah Flood, Katie Genadek, Matthew B. Schroeder, Brandon Trampe, and Rebecca Vick. 2010. Integrated Public

Use Microdata Series (IPUMS), Current Population Survey: Version 3.0. [Machine-readable database]. Minneapolis, MN: Minnesota Population Center [producer and distributor].

Lee, Jennifer, and Frank Bean. 2010. *The Diversity Paradox:Immigration and the Color Line in 21st Century America*. New York: Russell Sage Foundation.

Lieberson, Stanley. 1980. *A Piece of the Pie: Blacks and White Immigrants Since 1880*. Berkeley: University of California Press.

Loewen, James W. 1988. *The Mississippi Chinese: Between Black and White*. New York: Waveland Press.

Massey, Douglas S. 2007. *Categorically Unequal: The American Stratification System*. New York: Russell Sage Foundation.

———. 2011. "Isolated, Vulnerable and Broke." *New York Times* (opinion page), August 4. http://www.nytimes.com/2011/08/05/opinion/hispanic-families-isolated-and-broke.html.

——— (ed.). 2008. *New Faces in New Places: The Changing Geography of American Immigration*. New York: Russell Sage Foundation.

Massey, Douglas S., and Nancy A. Denton. 1993. *American Apartheid: Segregation and the Making of the Underclass*. Cambridge, MA: Harvard University Press.

Massey, Douglas S., Margarita Mooney, Kimberly C. Torres, and Camille Z. Charles. 2007. "Black Immigrants and Black Natives Attending Selective Colleges and Universities in the United States." *American Journal of Education* 113: 243–71.

Massey, Douglas S., and Magaly Sánchez R. 2010. *Brokered Boundaries: Creating Immigrant Identity in Anti-Immigrant Times*. New York: Russell Sage Foundation.

McConahay, John. 1983. "Modern Racism and Modern Discrimination: The Effects of Race, Racial Attitudes, and Context on Simulated Hiring Decisions." *Personality and Social Psychology Bulletin* 9: 551–58.

Mollenkopf, John M. 2000. "Assimilating Immigrants in Amsterdam: A Perspective from New York." *Netherlands Journal of Social Sciences* 36 (2): 15–34.

Neckerman, Kathryn M., Prudence Carter, and Jennifer Lee. 1999. "Segmented Assimilation and Minority Cultures of Mobility." *Ethnic and Racial Studies* 22: 945–65.

Oliver, Melvin L., and Thomas M. Shapiro. 1995. *Black Wealth, White Wealth: A New Perspective on Racial Inequality*. New York: Routledge.

Pager, Devah. 2007. *Marked: Race, Crime and Finding Work in an Era of Mass Incarceration*. Chicago: University of Chicago Press.

Perez, Anthony Daniel, and Charles Hirschman. 2009. "The Changing Racial and Ethnic Composition of the US Population: Emerging American Identities." *Population and Development Review* 35: 1–51.

Perlmann, Joel, and Mary C. Waters. 2004. "Intermarriage Then and Now: Race, Generation and the Changing Meaning of Marriage," in Nancy Foner and George Fredrickson (eds.), *Not Just Black and White: Historical and Contemporary Perspectives on Immigration, Race, and Ethnicity in the United States*. New York: Russell Sage Foundation.

Portes, Alejandro, and Rubén Rumbaut. 2001. *Legacies: The Story of the Immigrant Second Generation*. Berkeley and Los Angeles: University of California Press; New York: Russell Sage Foundation.

Portes, Alejandro, and Min Zhou. 1993. "The New Second Generation: Segmented Assimilation and Its Variants among Post-1965 Immigrant Youth." *Annals of the American Academy of Political and Social Science* 530: 74–96.

Ramakrishnan, S. Karthick, and Tom Wong. 2010. "Partisanship, Not Spanish: Explaining Municipal Ordinances Affecting Undocumented Immigrants," in Monica W. Varsanyi (ed.), *Taking Local Control: Immigration Policy Activism in U.S. Cities and States*. Stanford, CA: Stanford University Press.

Rosenbaum, Emily, and Grigoris Argeros. 2005. "Holding the Line: Housing Turnover and the Persistence of Racial/Ethnic Segregation in New York City." *Journal of Urban Affairs* 27: 261–81.

Skrentny, John. 2001. *Color Lines: Affirmative Action, Immigration and Civil Rights Options for America*. Chicago: University of Chicago Press.

Smith, Robert C. 2005. *Mexican New York: Transnational Lives of New Immigrants*. Berkeley: University of California Press.

Steele, Claude. 1997. "A Threat in the Air: How Stereotypes Shape the Intellectual Identities and Performance of Women and African Americans." *American Psychologist* 52: 613–29.

Suro, Roberto, and Jeffrey Passel. 2003. "The Rise of the Second Generation: Changing Patterns of Hispanic Population Growth." Washington, DC: Pew Hispanic Center.

Telles, Edward, and Vilma Ortiz. 2008. *Generations of Exclusion: Mexican Americans, Assimilation and Race*. New York: Russell Sage Foundation.

Tuan, Mia. 1998. *Forever Foreigners or Honorary Whites?* New Brunswick, NJ: Rutgers University Press.

Vickerman, Milton. 1999. *Crosscurrents: West Indian Immigrants and Race*. New York: Oxford University Press.

Wakefield, Sara, and Christopher Uggen. 2010. "Incarceration and Stratification." *Annual Review of Sociology* 36: 387–406.

Waters, Mary C. 1999a. *Black Identities: West Indian Immigrant Dreams and American Realities*. Cambridge, MA: Harvard University Press.

———. 1999b. "Sociology and the Study of Immigration." *American Behavioral Scientist* 42: 1264–67.

Waters, Mary C., and Tomás R. Jiménez 2005. "Assessing Immigrant Assimilation: New Empricial and Theoretical Challenges." *Annual Review of Sociology* 31: 105–25.

Western, Bruce, and Becky Pettit. 2005. "Black-White Wage Inequality, Employment Rates and Incarceration." *American Journal of Sociology* 111: 553–78.

Winant, Howard. 2006. "Race and Racism: Towards a Global Future." *Ethnic and Racial Studies* 29: 986–1003.

Zolberg, Aristide R., and Long Litt Woon. 1999. "Why Islam Is Like Spanish: Cultural Incorporation in Europe and the United States." *Politics & Society* 27: 5.

6

Governing through Religion in Amsterdam

The Stigmatization of Ethnic Cultures and the Uses of Islam

JUSTUS UITERMARK, JAN WILLEM DUYVENDAK, AND JAN RATH

Introduction

Islam is being transformed in each and every corner of the world, and Europe is definitely no exception.[1] Muslims in Europe—the *dramatis personae* of this religion—have demonstrated a wide and continuously changing variety of affiliations to Islam. As the overwhelming majority of the 13–15 million Muslims living in Western Europe are predominantly first- and second-generation immigrants,[2] the transformation of this religion cannot be understood without also addressing the process of integration in the receiving society. As first- or second-generation immigrants, European Muslims find themselves in an environment in which the expression of their faith is not a matter of course. It has involved and continues to involve discussions and occasionally conflicts with representatives of the receiving society, while the introspections of Muslims themselves about the meaning of their religion and its practices are changing and evolving as well under these conditions. Some try to be faithful to what they see as the true Islam and deepen their connections with major regions of the Muslim world. Others refuse to proclaim their faith any longer, and cherish silent agnosticism or indifference. Still others seek to wrest Islam from ethnic or cultural traditions and rethink religion in relation to liberal democracy. The highly secularized wider society, to be sure, is scrutinizing these processes with a keen eye, and many people loudly voice their aversion to Muslims.

Amsterdam is an interesting place to reflect on the ongoing reinvention of Islam. If we take the number of Turkish and Moroccan immigrants and their Dutch-born children—the largest immigrant groups in Amsterdam—as a crude proxy for the number of Muslims, then there are about 110,000 Muslims in the city (14 percent of the population).[3] The city represents a highly secularized landscape and many regard it as a capital of vice. But what is more, the local government has assumed an active role in mediating the relationship between Muslim immigrants and others within the city. Especially since 9/11 and the (more or less coinciding) appointment of the social democrat Job Cohen as mayor (2001–10), the city has engaged with Islam and Muslim associations.

This engagement should be understood against the background of fierce disputes over minority integration. Many intellectuals and politicians feel that ethnic minorities are not well integrated. Problems like educational underachievement, unemployment, (youth) delinquency, radicalization, misogyny, homophobia, disrespect for women in the form of harassment, and so forth are all considered to be problems stemming from a lack of civic integration. The lack of integration, in turn, is diagnosed as resulting from a lack of cultural citizenship; immigrants are regarded by many as lacking loyalty to Dutch society, economic independence, and democratic engagement. While a few prominent figures have explicitly called for a "civilizing offensive" to diffuse Dutch norms of citizenship among immigrants (Van den Brink, 2004; Van den Brink and De Ruijter 2003), it has become "common sense" among the Dutch public, policymakers, and politicians that ethnic minorities are not sufficiently integrated and that the government should induce, educate, or enforce them to be better citizens (Schinkel 2007; Van der Berg 2007). We realize the term "civilizing" carries a lot of baggage associated with colonialism and colonial rule. Frantz Fanon (1986), for instance, documented how colonial subjects were targeted by civilizing offensives—they had to show they conformed perfectly to an idealized image of French *citoyennes* to be recognized as rights-bearing subjects. Such baggage is part of the reason why we think the term "civilizing" is applicable here: the central idea informing attempts at civilizing is that the targeted groups are not seen to be fully part of the nation's civil community and have to be incorporated culturally to protect the nation's integrity (Weber 1976), and that is exactly what Dutch policymakers think and do.

The Dutch government has introduced mandatory civic enculturation courses and tests for non-Western immigrants to teach the Dutch language and also to convey the image of the Netherlands as a place where people work hard, are considerate of their social environment, and have respect for women and homosexuals (Suvarierol 2012). The government has also introduced "education courses" to teach immigrant parents how to raise their children, when to take out the trash, and so on (Van der Berg 2007). In areas where many immigrants live, the government has been undertaking so-called house visits where officials (the police, the housing corporation, social workers) enter homes in order to detect illegalities and to offer or force residents to participate in social programs. All these sorts of measures are part of a "civilizing offensive" that uses both persuasion and force to promote the civic integration of target groups. Islam figures into this because many have argued that a commitment to Islam implies a lack of commitment to Dutch society. This is most virulently expressed by Geert Wilders of the Freedom Party, who believes that Islam is a totalitarian ideology akin to National Socialism, but there are many others who have suggested in less ferocious ways that Muslims fail to live up to the norms of citizenship.

Whereas many have blamed Islam for *causing* integration problems, the Amsterdam government has felt that Islam and Muslim institutions might contribute to *solving* these problems. In the government's attempts to promote integration and influence the transformation of Islam, we observe a process we describe as *civilizing through Islam*; Islam has been used to argue for and promote civic integration. The government and its partners used Islam to "civilize" minorities by arguing that certain behaviors and beliefs were not just uncivil but also antithetical to true Islamic teachings (see Ramadan 2004). Beliefs and behaviors deemed problematic were ascribed to "ethnic culture" instead of religion. And while ethnic culture was degraded and blamed, Muslim associations and liberal Muslims claimed that Islam should be valued and embraced.

In this chapter, we analyze how the Amsterdam government has engaged with Islam and Muslim leaders and institutions. As background to the analysis of local politics, we first elaborate the notion of integration that is central to Dutch discourses of ethnic diversity. Then we explain how religion, and especially Islam, came to be seen as a tool for integration by the Amsterdam government. We show how the Amsterdam government selectively supported some Muslim associations and groups while disciplining others. The concluding section explains why the Amsterdam government's intimate engagement with Islam has come to an end.

Integration as a Distinct Governmental Logic

To understand the specificity of the Dutch ways of dealing with immigrants and ethnic diversity compared to American ways, it is necessary to consider the concept of *integration*. In the Netherlands, as elsewhere in Europe, the concept of integration is *de rigueur*, and this is evidently related to a widespread discomfort with the international migration that occurred after World War II. Unlike the United States and other classic countries of immigration, the Netherlands has *not* regarded itself as a country of immigration and even resisted the possibility that it could become one. While waves of immigrants have found their way to the Netherlands in the past (see Lucassen's chapter in this book), the arrival of immigrants in the post–World War II era has typically been seen as a disturbance of the nation rather than a condition for continued vitality (Rath 1999, 2009).

Over the last five or six decades, when mass immigration did take place and new and hitherto unfamiliar ethnic and religious diversity proliferated, the long-established Dutch were concerned that the presence of maladjusted groups would undermine the unity, integrity, and good traditions of the nation-state. Minority groups were expected to undergo *rites de passage* and demonstrate their credentials before they could be accepted as full-fledged members of the nation-state (Duyvendak 2011; Rath 1993; Rath et al. 2001, 2004). This implied shedding their ethnic, cultural, and religious particularities. In this light, integration policies were regarded as a condition *sine qua non* for the well-being of the immigrants, but even more so of Dutch society at large.

It would be an oversimplification, however, to assume that the explanation for this reaction can be found within the realm of immigration and diversity only. In fact, the social engineering project of "controlled integration" of marginal social categories has a long history and is rooted in the late nineteenth century when the Dutch modern nation-state developed, industrialization and urbanization took off, a new proletariat of factory workers emerged, a working-class movement came to the fore, and the contours of the welfare state began to take shape.

The late nineteenth century was (politically) dominated by what was called "the social question" (*de sociale quaestie*). This social question referred to the inhumane living and working conditions of the emerging working class, female and child labor, and extreme poverty as a consequence of underpayment and unemployment. In response, well-off liberals and socialist activists mobilized forces to improve these appalling conditions. Some of the enlightened "advocates" were motivated by moral repugnance, others feared revolts by the "dangerous classes," and still others were driven by the ideal to create a better world. Around the turn of the twentieth century both at the national and municipal levels—especially in municipalities dominated by social democrats—a plethora of measures was taken to improve poverty relief, unemployment relief, education, social housing, and health care (De Regt 1984). The educated, better-paid, and better-organized workers appeared to be more susceptible to the ideals of higher culture and what they saw as civilized conduct, and increasingly felt uncomfortable with the rough, illiterate, unorganized underclass. Their quest for distinction was satisfied by adopting a more cultivated and respectable lifestyle. In order to morally improve the working poor, the elites offered a series of educational activities and established a wide array of institutions for them: evening classes, libraries, outdoor pursuits, theatrical and singing groups, youth organizations, alcohol-free canteens (Dercksen and Verplanke 1987). According to Ali de Regt (1984), these moral improvements took on the character of a "civilizing offensive" based around typical middle-class norms and values such as order, neatness, industriousness, thrift, and devotion to duty.

The "moral improvement" soon acquired a less voluntary character. In Amsterdam, for instance, in the beginning of the twentieth century the local government identified "socially weak families" as a problem group and called them "inadmissible" (*ontoelaatbaar*): they were denied council housing. Instead, they were offered a place in "housing schools" (*woonscholen*), special residential areas under the supervision of wardens, who educated them into becoming respectable citizens. A set of real or alleged features warranted the label of "inadmissible": causing nuisance, being troublesome, lacking cleanliness, failing to pay the rent, alcohol abuse, child neglect, delinquency, and mental deficiency (De Regt 1984). The combination of these features was seen as a syndrome dominating the lives of the "socially weak" and damaging an integrated society. The targeting of "antisocial families," as they came to be known, to redress their lack of integration continued until the late 1950s. During this decade, the government's approach to antisocial families was further institutionalized and professionalized. Academic researchers studied the problem of antisocial families, new educational institutions were set up to train young people to become professional social workers, and a new ministry—the Ministry of Social Work—was established.

During the 1960s, under the pressure of progressive social movements, the Dutch government shifted gears and reconsidered this approach. It then took the position that the lack of integration of these families was not so much related to their moral or material condition per se, but to their stigmatization as "antisocials." The professionals and ministerial departments responsible for targeting "antisocial families" subsequently identified new "problem groups" that were in need of well-intended care: immigrants and travelers (Rath 1999). This *path dependency* was fostered by the dramatic expansion of the welfare state in the second half of the twentieth century and—later—the development and implementation of all sorts of urban renewal programs. Until the early 1990s most welfare state provisions were general and unconditional, but in more recent years the state has become more demanding and intrusive. Fewer provisions were available, and as far as individuals in need called upon the state or semiprivate institutions for support, more strings were attached. A dense web of state institutions was developed and concerned with deprived neighborhoods, and the general service providers of the past were refigured as disciplinary institutions aiming to govern the minutiae of clients' personal lives (Uitermark and Van Beek 2010). Such a project is a contemporary variant of the "civilizing offensive" that was pressed upon the underclass earlier. Then as now, a sense of moral outrage and fear informed the actions of civil servants and other officials who tried to educate and discipline the "dangerous classes" with language courses, house visits, and education in morals and democracy (Rath 1999; Van den Berg and Duyvendak 2012). The images of contemporary immigrants are in some respects similar to the image that paternalistic elites previously held of urban paupers: they lack the culture to be responsible citizens but they can, in principle, be inculcated with this culture and integrated into bourgeois society, provided they have good and especially stern guidance. The new concerns over immigrant integration thus fit with a long tradition of extensive and occasionally intrusive state intervention.

Especially after 9/11, there were fierce debates on how integration should be understood and promoted. The role of Islam in particular became a wedge issue in Dutch politics. Politicians like Frits Bolkestein (Liberal Party VVD in the 1990s), Pim Fortuyn (leader of his own Lijst Pim Fortuyn [LPF] party, in 2002), Ayaan Hirsi Ali (initially Labor Party PvdA, later Liberal Party VVD), and Geert Wilders (initially Liberal Party VVD, later the Freedom Party PVV) argued that a commitment to Islam inhibits or even prevents integration into Dutch society. These politicians are the most prominent representatives of what could be called a culturalist discourse—emphasizing that Western and Islamic cultures are irreconcilable and successful integration into Dutch society requires Muslims to shed their norms and values, including those regarding gender, family, and sexuality on which the Dutch majority now has a progressive consensus (Duyvendak, Pels, and Rijkschroeff 2009). Shrill anti-Muslim statements are nothing unusual in modern-day Dutch politics. The maverick filmmaker Theo van Gogh, for example, referred to Muslims as "goat fuckers." In a speech before the Dutch Parliament on September 6, 2007, to give another example, Wilders stated, "Islam is the Trojan Horse in Europe. If we do not stop Islamification now, Eurabia . . . will just be a matter of time. . . . We are heading for the end of European . . . civilization as we know it."

While culturalist criticisms of Islam and Muslims were strongly articulated, other political figures framed integration issues differently. Some politicians, for instance, refused to comment on Islam as they viewed religious affairs as a personal matter, while others argued that the real problem was rooted not in the cultural or religious identity of minorities, but in their weak class position. Several mayors of Amsterdam, including Ed van Thijn (1983–94), Schelto Patijn (1994–2001), and Job Cohen (2001–10), all Labor Party PvdA, argued that the strong focus on the cultural and religious identity of minorities created an extra obstacle for their integration and undermined social cohesion. It should be noted that these politicians, too, felt that Muslim immigrants were not sufficiently integrated into mainstream Dutch society and that the state should develop policies to achieve integration. But they took a different position from the culturalists in the sense that they did not consider religion, and specifically Islam, as antithetical to integration. Job Cohen in particular gained fame and notoriety as he resisted the tendency to blame immigrants for their lack of integration (cf. Cohen 2002). In direct opposition to Ayaan Hirsi Ali, Pim Fortuyn, and Geert Wilders, he argued that religion, and specifically Islam, could play a role in facilitating integration.

Religion as a Tool for Integration

After the turn of the twenty-first century, the government, and especially Amsterdam's mayor, Job Cohen, developed a discourse that revolved around the idea that all groups within society had an obligation to defend civil unity. It was the task of administrators to stand above and connect the different groups—an approach that developed under the slogan "Keeping things together" (*De boel bij elkaar houden*).

What defined Cohen's position—and made the apparently mundane ambition to "keep things together" into a highly controversial slogan— was his insistence that Muslims are an integral part of the civil community. On several high-profile occasions, he argued for mutual understanding and expressed his concern over the backlash against Muslims after 9/11 and the murder of Theo van Gogh (2004) by a young Dutch-born Moroccan, who targeted Van Gogh for making a film with Ayaan Hirsi Ali that depicted abused women with passages from the *Quran* written on their skin. Whereas the "culturalist" discourse often portrays

Muslims or radical Muslims as intruders or violators, Cohen argued that Islam and its institutions can in fact help to integrate newcomers and indeed provide cement that can keep together a society threatened by disintegration:

> We now deal with an inflow of people for whom religion often is the most important guide in their lives. That raises the question of acceptance by the secularized society that surrounds them and their integration in this society. As far as this last issue is concerned: religion is for them an easy and obvious entry when they try to connect to the Netherlands. Where would they find that connection if not initially with their compatriots? This is why the integration of these migrants in Dutch society may best be achieved via their religion. That is almost the only anchor they have when they enter the Dutch society of the 21st century. (2002: 14)

Cohen's emphasis on religious institutions, like mosques, as vehicles for integration was something new. Previously, Amsterdam political leaders had almost completely ignored mosques and Muslim associations on the grounds that they might serve a large constituency but do not qualify as government partners because they are religious institutions. Cohen's discourse created a sense among administrators and civil servants that minority associations, and especially Muslim associations, should be incorporated into governance networks.

After the violent events of the early 2000s, a discourse developed based on the idea that the commitment of moderate Muslims was necessary to curb the threat posed by extremism. This view informed subsequent institutional reforms and projects carried out under the banner of Us Amsterdammers (Wij Amsterdammers)—a policy program created by top-level civil servants under the direct supervision of the mayor and deputy mayors, based on the premise that diversity can lead to explosive conflicts that need to be suppressed before they materialize. Whereas before ethnic groups were the policy objects, now the population was divided into different groups according to their putative civil virtues. While the precise articulation of this principle of differentiation has varied among individual administrators and policy documents, the continuum usually runs from ethnic minorities who passionately defend liberal democracy to those who passionately attack many of its principles.

For example, immediately after the assassination of Van Gogh, Us Amsterdammers distinguished among five groups of Muslims:

1. Muslims who are completely integrated into Dutch society and experience no tension whatsoever between Islam and modernism. They actively resist radical Islam;
2. Muslims who accept the rules of the game of liberal democracy but feel some tension between Islam and modernism. They resist radical Islam;
3. Muslims who experience strong tension between Islam and modernism but who accept the Dutch constitutional order. They are willing to provide information to the government on Islamic extremism;
4. Muslims for whom political Islam provides a sense of identity and meaning. They approve of the assassination, passively reject the Dutch constitutional order and passively support jihadis;
5. The jihadis who recruit and train extremists, maintain breeding places for them, spread hatred of the West, and want to commit extremist acts. This group consists of about 150 people [an estimate by the Dutch intelligence agency] and strong networks around them. (Gemeente Amsterdam 2004: 4–5)

The non-Muslim population, according to Us Amsterdammers, also consists of five groups:

1. Those who accept Islam within the context of the Dutch liberal state and actively strive for the recognition of Islam within the Netherlands;
2. Those who accept Islam within the context of the Dutch liberal state;
3. Those who have difficulty with Islam and exclude and stigmatize Muslims;
4. Those who want Islam to disappear from the Netherlands and who exclude and stigmatize Muslims;
5. Those who (want to) undertake violent action against Muslims. (Gemeente Amsterdam 2004: 5)

These categorizations give an impression of the ways in which administrators perceived the population of Amsterdam: there is a rough division between Muslims and non-Muslims and both groups are internally differentiated according to their putative civil virtue. Policies thus are based on a certain civil hierarchy: some people are regarded as better citizens than others and it is the government's task to ensure that people move up in the hierarchy.

How Islam Is Used in Amsterdam's "Civilizing Offensive"

These categorizations also suggest a line of action: the municipality and its administrators should form coalitions with those who embrace liberal democracy, wish to reduce polarization and fight against extremism, and isolate and prosecute those who seek to undermine liberal democracy. The government therefore designed its institutions by embracing a liberal elite, accommodating Muslims critical of Dutch society, and disciplining deviant or defiant Muslims.

Embracing the Liberal Elite

The government's "civilizing offensive" involved and was promoted with and by a small but prominent group of Muslims who were also members of the Labor Party. They advocated what came to be seen as a "liberal" interpretation of Islam that is compatible with or even prescribes integration into Dutch society. Ahmed Aboutaleb, Haci Karacaer, Ahmed Marcouch, and Ahmed Larouz—all members of the Labor Party with a Muslim background—were among the most visible representatives of this particular understanding of Islam after the assassination of Theo van Gogh. Larouz, Marcouch, and Karacaer staged a press conference in De Balie, one of Amsterdam's most prestigious cultural centers. Larouz read a statement on behalf of the government-funded association Islam and Citizenship, asking people to stay calm after this "attack on our society." Karacaer, director of the Muslim Federation Milli Görüş, was "visibly shocked" by the event according to a newspaper report and uttered, "I wish I could undo all this." Ahmed Marcouch declared on behalf of the Union of Moroccan Mosques in Amsterdam and Surroundings (UMMAO) that "this was not a religious act, even if the assassin committed it in the name of Allah."[4] A day after the assassination, Ahmed Aboutaleb, the deputy mayor for diversity from 2004 till 2006, reprimanded the visitors of the Al Kabir Mosque, where he publicly expressed anger that people close to the assassin had not intervened. He called upon the Moroccan and Muslim community to produce "counter poison" and not allow extremists to "hijack their religion." He also said that if Muslims didn't like the Netherlands, they were free to leave—they should "pack their bags" because "there are planes flying to Morocco every day" (Hajer and Uitermark 2008: 7).

These key figures thus argued that incivilities like the assassination are antithetical to Islam. But they also reprimanded rather than represented Turkish and Moroccan Muslims. They became key figures in the "civilizing offensive" that simultaneously sought to bring Islam into the mainstream and marginalize interpretations of Islam antithetical to liberal democracy. Some parts of that "civilizing project" were hardly controversial, such as the Ramadan festival. Consultants for Larouz's firm Mex-It, which advises on diversity, integration, and emancipation, conceived the festival after the assassination of Theo van Gogh in 2004 to improve the image of Islam and involve the Amsterdam population in the celebration of this Muslim feast. The municipal government contributed funds, but the Mex-It organization was also very effective—much more so than any other immigrant or Muslim association had been—in attracting funds from commercial sources, including banks, consultancy agencies, and privatized welfare agencies eager to improve their positions in a market where more and more customers have Muslim backgrounds. Newspapers and television stations widely covered the festival's activities. Although controversial issues were debated, the focus was on mundane topics such as food, fashion, and business.

Other government-sponsored projects in which the liberal elite were involved aroused strong opposition and controversy. One was the plan to establish the so-called Wester Mosque in the Amsterdam neighborhood of De Baarsjes. The media drama began in the early 1990s when conflict arose between the Turkish federation Milli Görüş and the neighborhood council of De Baarsjes over the construction of the mosque (Lindo 1999). The neighborhood council and a group of local residents protested its size and the height of the minaret, but Milli Görüş insisted it had the right to build anyway. The very fact that

Milli Görüş represented an orthodox—some would say fundamental-ist—tendency of Islam evidently added to the controversy. After some years of stalemate, Milli Görüş pushed forward a leadership that prom-ised that the center would become a vehicle for emancipation rather than an orthodox bastion. The new and very visible leadership—with Haci Karacaer as charismatic figurehead—spoke out against funda-mentalist tendencies and in favor of integration. Karacaer, representing Milli Görüş, participated in the commemorations of World War II and unequivocally denounced the attacks of 9/11. The apotheosis was per-haps Karacaer's performance at Amsterdam's gay monument where he declared he would struggle for the rights of other minorities even if that brought him into conflict with his own constituency. Milli Görüş had become transformed—in media representations—from a hypercon-servative association into a liberal vanguard of Dutch Muslimhood. A housing association now agreed to a joint-venture to construct homes on a plot adjacent to the mosque; the neighborhood council agreed to fully support the project. But all this changed in 2007. According to media sources, "conservative hardliners" sponsored by the German headquarters of Milli Görüş had engineered a "coup" against the "liber-als" sponsored by the Amsterdam municipality (e.g., Beusekamp 2006). The downfall of the liberal leaders robbed the proponents of "liberal Islam" of what had been their most widely covered success story (Uiter-mark and Gielen 2010). Cohen's government suffered a direct blow when it became known that it had covertly given an indirect subsidy of two million euro for the construction of the complex.

These two examples show that the government intervened directly to strengthen the power of liberal Islam. The government sought to strengthen the position of Muslims who were critical of their own (eth-nic and religious) communities and who argued powerfully and pas-sionately for integration. So strong was this desire that the government attempted to rewrite the rules of the game by giving itself the discretion to subsidize religious projects.[5]

Accommodating Critical Muslims

The "liberal Muslims" we have described distinguished themselves through sharp criticisms of their own communities and a passionate commitment to integration. A sizable segment of the Muslim population, however, was much more critical of Dutch society than were the liberal Muslim elite. For the sake of convenience, we refer to this segment as "critical Muslims," though this category lumps together actors as diverse as illiterate first-generation mosque representatives who vaguely sense that politicians are against Islam and second-generation intellectuals who eloquently counter Islamophobia in newspapers and on television. These critical Muslims did not receive nearly as much recognition and resources as the liberal Muslim elite. Nevertheless, there were attempts to incorporate them into governance networks. Through supporting projects that would lead Muslims to enter into public debates, government officials and political leaders hoped to reduce the power of radical discourses.

What kinds of projects received support? One example is Muslim Youth Amsterdam (Moslimjongeren Amsterdam), which has brought together youths from different ethnic backgrounds and mosques. In 2004, the deputy mayor for diversity, Ahmed Aboutaleb, decided that this type of coalition was needed after research reported that mosques, and especially Moroccan mosques, developed few initiatives that were engaged with the wider civil society. The Amsterdam government also supported cultural centers such as Mozaïek and Argan in the staging of public debates. Unlike the prestigious cultural centers in the central Amsterdam canal area (such as De Balie, Rode Hoed, and Felix Meritis), Mozaïek and Argan attracted large numbers of people from groups that have been notoriously difficult for the media and administrators to reach, such as orthodox Muslims and Moroccan youths.

These associations, venues, and events offered entry points for journalists in search of "Muslim youth," political parties in search of new talent, and companies looking for new hires. The fact that these settings were constantly in the media spotlight affected how they functioned. In one sense, the media coverage was a crucial part of the attraction for Muslim youth. The presence of important politicians and television cameras also added to the prominence of debates that took place in various associations and events. The preference for high-profile debates, however, limited their role as settings for the inculcation of mainstream civic values and encouragement of participation in mainstream institutions. Although volunteers and professionals often intended to engage in long-term efforts to build institutional networks among Muslim youth, such ambitions were easily forgotten when the next spectacular event took place. Associations in this volatile environment functioned more as portals for political talent than as organizing platforms for the "unintegrated" Muslims and Moroccans who dominated news reports.

Disciplining Defiant Muslims

Precisely because participation in government-supported associations and debates requires a measure of civic engagement, they did not attract the problematic groups that have typically filled media and policy documents: isolated women, dropouts, delinquent youths, and (potential) extremists. To deal with these groups, the Amsterdam government, like other governments, intensified its investments in repressive and disciplinary institutions in the first decade of the new century: more discretion and personnel for the police, more camera surveillance, more state funds and discretion for security personnel, stricter enforcement of the legal requirement to attend school, and so on. But in addition to these repressive measures, the government sought to win over the hearts and minds of potentially dangerous groups and to stimulate "integration" or "participation."[6]

To discipline the most defiant groups, the government increasingly called upon Islam, Muslim authorities, and Muslim associations. This development, which took place throughout Amsterdam, reached its zenith in Slotervaart, a postwar neighborhood on the city's western outskirts that became a laboratory for new governance institutions. After it became clear that Van Gogh's assassin lived in Slotervaart, journalists, academics, policy makers, and politicians flooded the neighborhood. Media scrutiny and political interest further intensified when Labor Party member Ahmed Marcouch ran for and became chair of the neighborhood council in 2006—the first Moroccan to achieve this position in the Netherlands. Marcouch's discourse was tough on those who exhibited what was seen as uncivil behavior and full of praise for those who exhibited civil qualities. Referring to Marcouch's background as a police officer, the German weekly *Der Spiegel* called him the "sheriff of Slotervaart" (cited in Jongejan 2007). Indeed, Marcouch had no sympathy whatsoever for youths hanging out on the streets after midnight or adults forsaking their parental responsibilities. But his policies were disciplinary rather than simply repressive: the goal was to weave a network of surveillance and control around the life worlds of perpetrators and potential perpetrators. The neighborhood government of Slotervaart set up a rapid response unit of "street coaches" (usually martial arts practitioners) to keep watch on the neighborhood and intervene whenever youths were loitering, skipping school, or causing a nuisance. The neighborhood council also financed programs to teach parents about the intricacies of the school system and tried to stimulate them to be actively involved in their children's educational performance. Such disciplinary interventions have surged in many locations in the Netherlands (Van den Berg 2007) and elsewhere in Europe (Crawford 1997, 2006) in recent years.

In Slotervaart, religion has been used to try to convince target groups that they need to cooperate. The policy document in which the council laid out its strategy against radicalization states,

> The emphasis will be on the opportunities offered by religion and culture in upbringing, strengthening one's own identity and developing a positive self-image. Next to that, there will be a search for points of contact (*aanknopingspunten*) in religion and culture for creating a bridge to Dutch society. Dichotomous world views will be countered with religious prescriptions. This offers the opportunity to convince parents that their wish to give their children an Islamic identity does not entail a clash with Dutch norms and values. (Stadsdeel Slotervaart 2007: 8–9)

The council's position was that delinquents and radicals should be confronted by religious authorities to demonstrate that their behavior is not in accordance with proper Islamic conduct. This policy was one manifestation of the reconfiguration of the government's relationship to both parents and civil society associations. At a time when many secular and neighborhood associations in Amsterdam had lost government subsidies and accommodations, associations catering to groups close to potential radicals or delinquents retained or consolidated their roles as intermediaries. For instance, the Amsterdam government provided assistance for recruiting participants in child-rearing courses through Islamic associations. The government organized debates within mosques and provided guidance to mosques wishing to represent and explain themselves in the media. The government also supported mosques in organizing dialogues among their constituents and with other religions in an effort to better communicate and explain Islam to members of the wider Dutch society.

One of the goals of government-subsidized programs for Turkish and Moroccan Muslim parents was to bring their religious conceptions in sync with the requirements of educational and other social environments. In her evaluation of a course for Moroccan parents offered as part of the anti-radicalization policy, Amy-Jane Gielen shows that parents and especially mothers were not primarily interested in religion or culture, but in their children's achievements at school and in the labor market; most of all, they did not want their children to drop out of school or fall into the hands of local criminals (Gielen 2008). However, in the course, religious precepts were used to delegitimize cultural beliefs or practices that supposedly inhibited success in Dutch society. For instance, in discussing whether it was permissible to spank a child, some mothers complained that child protection laws were too strict and Dutch society does not allow them to discipline their children the way they think best. Others suggested that Islam requires parents to adopt a gentle approach and expressly forbids hitting children. These mothers felt that their ethnic culture holds women back and that greater knowledge of Islam would lead to a reevaluation of the mother's role. As one mother put it, "I do not find traditions and being Moroccan very important, because I think we mostly have bad traditions. The fact is that a girl is kept down, while a boy is allowed to do anything he likes. Islam is against this" (quoted in Gielen 2008: 15).

Attempts to "civilize" cultural practices through the mobilization of religious discourse were not unique to Slotervaart; throughout the city similar initiatives were taken, with and without government support. For instance, the women's association of Milli Görüş received subsidies from the city for a project on female emancipation. In this particular project, an imam explained to men that much of the behavior they consider as "religious" is, in fact, "cultural," and quite possibly in contradiction to the Quran. The women's association website is full of texts (by men) that argue that the well-being of women is central to Muslim belief. It is worth looking in detail at the minutes of one meeting published on the Internet since they focus on honor killings, a topic that arouses great concern in the Netherlands. The two panelists—an imam and a chairman—asked what the assembled men thought of when they heard the word "honor." Most of the men thought of women, some more specifically of wives, daughters, or mothers. One also thought of tradition and an old saying: the most important things in a man's life are a horse, a wife, and a weapon. Women, the men agreed, carried honor while the consensus was that men had to defend it. And what if honor was violated? One man had the impression that "she must die," others suggested marriage or prevention, and one stressed that sufficient proof must exist (because the Prophet emphasized this). Then came the question: what would the men do if someone from their family lost their honor? Here we translate some of the discussion provided in the report:

PARTICIPANT 1: The person should question himself first. What is my share in this?

PARTICIPANT 2: We raise the children. If my daughter does that, then I am responsible. But I did not raise my wife. What is my share [of the responsibility] when my wife walks down the wrong path? You should also question yourself to see if you give enough attention to your wife.

PARTICIPANT 3: To give a frightening example, that person could be killed.

PARTICIPANT 4: I would take a weapon and kill.

CHAIRMAN: You say "I will kill my wife or sister"? If it is your little brother, do you kill him too?

PARTICIPANT 4: Why do we discuss? Because the Dutch want it that way? Our religion is pure and that is why it forbids these kinds of things.

IMAM: I do not know what you are saying; what has this to do with the topic? These are our problems.

CHAIRMAN: We prepare these programs and questions. It has nothing to do with the wish of the Dutch. The Dutch do not have honor and honor killings, but our society does. And such bad things are done on behalf of Islam. We work to prevent these problems. (Report published online by the women's section of Milli Görüş in 2006)

The Turkish men in this meeting tended to regard honor violence as a good or at least a normal part of their ethnic culture. However, the imam, Osman Paköz, reframed honor violence as a bad thing, finding it especially reprehensible that it is carried out on behalf of Islam. In what followed in the discussion, the chair and the imam used Islam as a way to argue against honor killings.

These are just some examples of a much more general process taking place in the Muslim community in Amsterdam. In interviews, meetings, brochures, and websites, Muslims have routinely mobilized religion to criticize ethnic culture. Religion is seen as God given and making people pure—and differentiated from ethnic culture, which has come to stand for that which is all too human. Islam has been used to argue against arranged marriages, gender inequality, and insolence. This kind of discourse has been in circulation not only among governmental elites and among higher-class Muslims but has also found strong support among, for instance, isolated lower-class Muslim women (Van Tilborgh 2006)—an indication that the "civilizing"-by-Islam was not exclusively a government-instigated process and perhaps not even primarily a process that trickled down from ("highly civilized") elites to ("less civilized") lower classes (cf. Elias 1994).

In sum, in the decade of Job Cohen's mayoral administration, the government, with the help of minority associations, governed through (specific interpretations of) Islam. While Moroccan and Turkish cultures were negatively viewed as being overly traditional and negative for women, Islam was seen by the government as a "civilizing force." In complete contradiction to the culturalists who had dominated the national debate on integration, local policy makers and their associates mobilized Muslim discourses to argue against misogyny, delinquency, intolerance, and crime. As a side effect of this transformation, secular and critical minority associations and voices were marginalized because they were not as willing to participate in Islam-inspired "civilizing" missions and were more oriented toward struggling against discrimination within Dutch society.

Conclusions

Between 2001 and 2010, the Amsterdam government developed alternative discourses and institutions to promote minority integration. While many national politicians and opinion makers vocally argued that Islam itself was a problem or that Islam contributed to integration problems,

Job Cohen's government adopted the opposite view and attempted to use Islam to promote integration. Cohen and his government feared that the intense and often negative focus on Islam would further marginalize Muslims and lead to social disintegration. But this fear triggered counterforces: as integration politics heated up at the national level, more time, energy, and resources were devoted to the discursive and institutional incorporation of Turkish and Moroccan migrants, who were increasingly represented as Muslims. The controversies over Islam were divisive in some ways, but also brought together groups and individuals that were previously apart. The commitment to use Islam to encourage integration bound together a coalition stretching from progressive politicians like Cohen to orthodox Muslims opposing radicalism. Islam thus fused into governance and was mobilized to extend the influence of the government. The government even created new civil society associations: it invested heavily in those promoting liberal Islam, sponsored individuals and organizations providing critical or orthodox alternatives to radical Islam, and created disciplinary institutions to "civilize" groups that supposedly were not integrated enough. In short, we can observe the emergence of a governance configuration that differentiated among groups according to their civil virtue and in which Islam was used, both by the government and by Muslims, to integrate minority groups who were seen as being too stuck in their ethnic cultures.

These attempts at "civilizing" minorities represent a reinvention of the civilizing projects developed in the late nineteenth and first half of the twentieth centuries. Now, as in the past, elites, and especially elites from social-democratic circles, embarked on civilizing projects for a variety of reasons: out of fear that the groups seen as uncivilized would rebel, to promote cultural emancipation, and ensure that lower-class groups would engage in work instead of crime. And in both the present and earlier periods, elites used extensive and intrusive state institutions to penetrate the grassroots, create a web of surveillance, and diffuse certain discourses. While the motivations and means were roughly the same in both eras, the discursive content was quite different in that, in the contemporary period, religion was used to incorporate lower-class and ethnic groups that were otherwise believed to be out of the government's reach.

While the intention to use Islam to "civilize" minority groups bound together a large variety of groups, there were also contradictions. Political opponents severely criticized the Amsterdam government for favoritism and breaching the division between church and state. Job Cohen especially was routinely portrayed as a weakling who was more interested in appeasing Muslims—notably in "drinking tea" with them—than in enforcing the law and supporting native Dutch. His successor, Eberhard van der Laan (Labor Party, as of 2010), appears determined not to walk down the same path—he discontinued attempts to create a cultural center for debating Islam, spoke out against Muslim civil servants who refused to shake hands with members of the opposite sex, and generally refrained from articulating a broad vision of integration. The role of Amsterdam as a prime milieu where the relations between Islam and governance were refigured appears to have ended for the time being.

However, as we noted, the strategy to use Islam to argue against stigmatized cultural practices and beliefs is not simply imposed from above. Many Muslims in the trenches of civil society appear to have adopted the idea that their pure religion should take precedence over, and negate, their ethnic cultures. While obviously they do not *en masse* renounce their ethnic cultures, it has been common to use Islam to criticize and reconsider those elements of their ethnic culture that they have come to reject and question, including patriarchal familial relations and overly strict practices of child rearing. It has also become common to appeal to Islam to advocate commitment to school, open debate, and work. The transformations of Islam appear not to depend on direct government intervention and will thus proceed long after the government's attempts to govern through using Islam have discontinued.

NOTES

1. This chapter is based in part on Uitermark (2012); Uitermark and Duyvendak (2008); Rath (1999); and Rath, Penninx, Groenendijk, and Meyer (2004).
2. This is a very rough estimate; see EUMC (2006) and OSI (2010).
3. See http://www.os.amsterdam.nl/tabel/7221/, accessed May 15, 2012. Such a "guess-timate," however, is quite problematic (Demant, Maussen, and Rath 2007).
4. Cited in the daily newspaper *NRC Handelsblad*, "Zondaar doden is een zonde," November 3, 2004.

5. The philosophical legitimation for this is the principle of "compensating neutrality," which stipulates that some forms of religion can be stimulated to increase choice. If one accepts the idea that fundamentalist or radical Islam is much more powerful than liberal Islam, it is justified, according to the principle of compensating neutrality, to support the latter. It is an interesting paradox that the very same administrators who have argued that most Muslims are not fundamentalist or radical also argue that fundamentalist or radical Islam is so strong that the government needs to compensate for the weakness of liberal Islam.

6. On one of the municipality's poster campaigns, the slogan was "Civil enculturation, that means participation" (*Inburgeren, datbetekentmeedoen*). Participation is defined as participation in those institutions where native Dutch or native Dutch ways of doing things dominate. So participation in an ethnic association, in a household, or in a network of friends is not, according to the conception of government policy, participation.

REFERENCES

Alba, Richard, and Victor Nee. 1997. "Rethinking Assimilation Theory for a New Era of Immigration." *International Migration Review* 31 (Winter): 826–74.

———. 2003. *Remaking the American Mainstream: Assimilation and Contemporary Immigration.* Cambridge, MA: Harvard University Press.

Bagley, Christopher. 1973. *The Dutch Plural Society: A Comparative Study in Race Relations.* Oxford: Oxford University Press.

Beusekamp, Willem. 2006. "Milli Görüs is om de tuin geleid." *De Volkskrant*, November 15.

Bovenkerk, Frank (ed.). 1978. *Omdat zij anders zijn. Patronen van rasdiscriminatie in Nederland.* Meppel: Boom.

Cohen, Job. 2002. *Vreemden.* Leiden: Cleveringa-lezing.

Crawford, Adam. 1997. *The Local Governance of Crime: Appeals to Community and Partnerships.* Oxford: Clarendon.

———. 2006. "Networked Governance and the Post-Regulatory State?" *Theoretical Criminology* 10 (4): 449–79.

Demant, Froukje, Marcel Maussen, and Jan Rath. 2007. *The Netherlands: Preliminary Research Report and Literature Survey.* London: Open Society Institute.

Dercksen, Adrianne, and Loes Verplanke. 1987. *Geschiedenis van de onmaatschappelijkheidsbestrijding in Nederland, 1914–1970.* Meppel: Boom.

De Regt, Ali. 1984. *Arbeidersgezinnen en beschavingsarbeid. Ontwikkelingen in Nederland 1870–1940. Een historisch-sociologische studie.* Meppel: Boom.

Duyvendak, Jan Willem. 2011. *The Politics of Home: Belonging and Nostalgia in Western Europe and the United States.* Basingstoke: Palgrave.

Duyvendak, Jan Willem, Rally Rijkschroeff, and Trees Pels. 2009. "A Multicultural Paradise? The Cultural Factor in Dutch Integration Policy," in Jennifer L.

Hochschild and John H. Mollenkopf (eds.), *Bringing Outsiders In: Transatlantic Perspectives on Immigrant Political Incorporation*. Ithaca, NY: Cornell University Press.

Elias, Norbert. 1994. *The Civilizing Process*. Oxford: Blackwell.

EUMC. 2006. *Muslims in the European Union: Discrimination and Islamophobia*. Vienna: European Monitoring Centre on Racism and Xenophobia.

Fanon, Frantz. 1986. *Black Skin, White Masks*. London: Pluto Press.

Gemeente Amsterdam. 1999. *De kracht van een diverse stad. Uitgangspunten van het diversiteitsbeleid van de gemeente Amsterdam*. Amsterdam: Gemeente Amsterdam.

Gemeente Amsterdam. 2004. *Analyse conflictpotentieel*. Amsterdam: Gemeente Amsterdam.

Gielen, Amy-Jane. 2008. *Een kwestie van identiteit*. Amsterdam: A.G. Advies.

Hajer, Maarten, and Justus Uitermark. 2008. "Performing Authority: Discursive Politics after the Assassination of Theo van Gogh." *Public Administration* 86 (1): 5–19.

Jongejan, Bettie. 2007. "Marcouch: de 'sheriff van Klein Marokko.'" *Trouw*, July 31.

Lijphart, Arend. 1975 [1968]. *The Politics of Accommodation: Pluralism and Democracy in the Netherlands*. Berkeley: University of California Press.

Lindo, Flip. 1999. *Heiligewijsheid in Amsterdam. Ayasofia, stadsdeel de Baarsjes en de strijd om het Riva-terrein*. Amsterdam: Het Spinhuis.

OSI (Open Society Institute). 2010. *Muslims in Europe: A Report on 11 EU Cities*. London: Open Society Institute.

Ramadan, Tariq. 2004. *Western Muslims and the Future of Islam*. Oxford: Oxford University Press.

Rath, Jan. 1993. "La construction sociale des minorités ethniques aux Pays-Bas et ses effets pervers," in Marco Martiniello and Marc Poncelet (eds.), *Migrations et minorités ethniques dans l'espace Européen*. Bruxelles: De Boeck.

———. 1999. "The Netherlands: A Dutch Treat for Anti-Social Families and Immigrant Ethnic Minorities," in Mike Cole and Gareth Dale (eds.), *The European Union and Migrant Labour*. Oxford: Berg.

———. 2009. "The Netherlands: A Reluctant Country of Immigration." *Tijdschrift-voorEconomische en SocialeGeografie* 100 (5): 665–72.

Rath, Jan, Rinus Penninx, Kees Groenendijk, and Astrid Meyer. 2001. *Western Europe and its Islam*. Leiden/Boston/Köln: Brill.

———. 2004. "Making Space for Islam in the Netherlands," in Roberta Aluffi Beck-Peccoz and Giovanna Zincone (eds.), *The Legal Treatment of Islamic Minorities in Europe*. Leuven: Peeters.

Schinkel, Willem. 2007. *Denken in een tijd van sociale hypochondrie: aanzet tot een theorie voorbij de maatschappij*. Kampen: Klement.

Stadsdeel Slotervaart. 2007. *Actieplan Slotervaart. Het tegengaan van radicalisering*. Amsterdam: Stadsdeel Slotervaart.

Uitermark, Justus. 2012. *The Dynamics of Power in Dutch Integration Politics: From Accommodation to Confrontation*. Amsterdam: University of Amsterdam Press.

Uitermark, Justus, and Krijn van Beek. 2010. "Gesmoorde participatie: Over de schaduwkanten van 'meedoen' als staatsproject," in Imrat Verhoeven and Marcel Ham (eds.), *Brave burgers gezocht. De grenzen van de activerende overheid*. Amsterdam: Van Gennep.

Uitermark, Justus, and Jan Willem Duyvendak. 2008. "Civilizing the City: Populism and Revanchist Urbanism in Rotterdam." *Urban Studies* 45 (7): 1485–03.

Uitermark, Justus, and Amy Jane Gielen. 2010. "Islam in the Spotlight: Discursive Politics in an Amsterdam Neighborhood after 9/11 and the Assassination of Theo van Gogh." *Urban Studies* 47 (6): 1325–42.

Van den Berg, Marguerite. 2007. "*Dat is bij jullie toch ook zo?*" *Gender, etniciteit en klasse in het sociaal kapitaal van Marokkaanse vrouwen*. Amsterdam: Aksant.

Van den Berg, Marguerite, and Jan Willem Duyvendak. 2012. "Paternalizing Mothers: Feminist Repertoires in Contemporary Dutch Civilizing Offensives." *Critical Social Policy* 32: 556–76.

Van den Brink, Gabriël. 2004. *Schets van een beschavingsoffensief. Over normen, normaliteit en normalisatie in Nederland*. Amsterdam: Amsterdam University Press.

Van den Brink, Gabriël, and Dick de Ruijter. 2003. *Marginaal of modern? Bestuurlijk advies inzake burgerschap onder migranten in Rotterdam*. Utrecht: Nederlands Instituut voor Zorg en Welzijn.

Van Tilborgh, Yolanda. 2006. *Wij zijn Nederland. Moslima's over AyaanHirsi Ali*. Amsterdam: Van Gennep.

Weber, Eugen. 1976. *Peasants into Frenchmen: The Modernization of Rural France, 1870–1914*. Stanford, CA: Stanford University Press.

PART IV

How Are Immigrants Entering the Precincts of Power in New York City and Amsterdam?

Politics are a central element in the urban landscape. The huge influx of immigrants has inevitably changed political dynamics in Amsterdam and New York City, bringing hundreds of thousands of new voters onto the political scene. At the same time, the way immigrants have entered the precincts of power has been shaped by the structure of political arrangements and the nature of the political culture in each city as well as characteristics of the immigrant groups themselves.

The focus of the two chapters in this section is on the ability of people of immigrant origin to obtain official political positions—a critical measure of political incorporation. Richard Alba and Nancy Foner (2009) have argued that electoral success by immigrant-origin groups can be viewed as the gold standard for measuring political inclusion, giving individuals from immigrant backgrounds entry into the inner precincts of power and seats at the table when decisions are made, although here we would expand this to include appointment to executive positions. Following Alba and Foner, there are four reasons why success in gaining political positions, through election or appointment, is so important. It is a direct measure of integration into the mainstream in the same sense that entry into high-status occupations is; the occupation of political office by members of an immigrant-origin group often gives the group a voice in government decisions that can directly affect it; and politicians in office not only usually play a role in routine decisions but also may be able to exert influence on the appointment of individuals to public positions. In addition, success of a group's members in obtaining valued political positions can nurture and strengthen a sense of identification with and allegiance to the society and its institutions.

The chapters on Amsterdam and New York analyze this process of political inclusion through different lenses. Looking at Amsterdam, Floris Vermeulen, Laure Michon, and Jean Tillie seek to explain why the major immigrant groups—Moroccans, Turks, and Surinamese—have not had the same success in gaining elected as well as appointed political positions. Across the Atlantic, John Mollenkopf highlights the dynamics of ethnic succession in New York City politics, examining the way ethnic and racial groups have jostled for position and fared in winning elected office, from white ethnics (Jews and Italians) and native minorities (native-born blacks and Puerto Ricans) in the early and mid-twentieth century to post-1965 immigrant groups who are entering the precincts of power today.

To what extent have immigrant-origin groups been able to obtain elected office? The bad news is that in neither city have they achieved elected office in city government equivalent to their share of the population or electorate. The good news is that they are making definite progress. As of 2009, 18 percent of the members of New York City's 51-seat city council had recent immigrant roots, certainly a vast improvement from no representation before 1991; in 2010, 16 percent of the representatives on Amsterdam's 45-seat city council were immigrants or children of immigrants, an increase from 9 percent in 1990 (although a slight decline from 20 percent in 2006). Since 2002, Amsterdam has had a number of deputy mayors as well as district mayors and deputy district mayors of Moroccan and Surinamese origin; in 2009, New York City elected a Taiwanese immigrant (who came to New York as a young child) as comptroller, the second highest elected office in the city.

The figures may be rather similar, but behind them are remarkably different political contexts. At the most basic, the political systems in Amsterdam and New York are worlds apart. In Amsterdam, the multiparty system involves party lists and preferential voting, so that voters choose a party and candidates on the party's list. Although the parties decide the order of candidates on the list, voters can select a candidate with a low position who may earn a seat if he or she gets enough votes.

Amsterdam's mayor is appointed by the crown after a process of consultation between national party leaders and the municipal council.

New York City—like other American cities—has what is called a first-past-the-post system, with single member districts in which voters can cast one vote each and the candidate with the most votes wins. In contrast to Amsterdam, and some other U.S. cities like Los Angeles, New York has a strongly partisan system. If ever there was a "blue" city it is New York. Registered Democrats outnumber Republicans nearly six to one. In all but the mayoral race, the main route to winning elected office is through the Democratic Party. Immigrants today, as in the past, have penetrated and become absorbed into the regular Democratic Party establishment by taking over its lower rungs—and then using lower-level positions as stepping stones to higher office, a major prize being a seat in the U.S. Congress. The main power in the city government is the office of the elected mayor, who defines and manages a $68 billion budget. Surprisingly for a liberal Democratic city, since 1989 New York has had a series of Republican mayors who have been elected by forging effective racial coalitions; in the case of billionaire Michael Bloomberg, he also used his enormous personal wealth in his campaigns. New York City also sends a number of representatives to state and federal legislative bodies: in 2011, 65 elected representatives to the New York State Assembly, 25 to the State Senate, and 11 to the U.S. Congress. There is no equivalent in Amsterdam. Because Dutch national elections are not districted, members of parliament have no representative relationship to a city or region.

Each system has advantages and disadvantages for immigrant representation—although it is not clear which one, overall, is better in this regard. One way that Amsterdam is clearly ahead, however, is that noncitizens are allowed to vote in local elections after five years of legal residence in the country. In New York, noncitizens do not have the right to vote, a situation that disenfranchises a very significant proportion of the population, especially in light of the continuous large inflow of new arrivals from abroad (nearly a third of the immigrants living in New York City in 2010 came there between 2000 and 2010). If noncitizens could vote in New York City elections, the political impact of immigrant-origin groups would be much larger, enabling them to put more of their own into office and wield more political influence. As of this writing, the city council is considering a proposal to allow nonciti-zen legal residents to vote in local elections, but even if successful, legal challenges, among other things, would block or delay implementation.

In addition to structural features of the political system, another contrast between the two cities stands out: the presence of a huge native minority population in New York (and its absence in Amsterdam). That immigrants in New York enter a city with a large native minority popu-lation—more than 700,000 Puerto Ricans (all of whom, by the way, are eligible to vote as adults since Puerto Ricans born on the island are U.S. citizens by birth) and about a million African Americans—means that immigrants have been able to join in alliances with native minorities to elect politicians who speak for their interests. To be sure, West Indians (the largest immigrant-origin black group) and African Americans as well as Dominicans (the largest immigrant-origin Latino group) and Puerto Ricans have sometimes competed for votes in elections at the local (rather than citywide) level. Yet they also often unite politically. West Indians vote like African Americans in most instances—and share deep concerns over racial prejudice and discrimination—parting ways, as Mollenkopf puts it, only when one of their own is running against an African American. Immigrant and native blacks are the second larg-est ethnoracial group in New York City's electorate (after whites), with native and immigrant Hispanics the third-largest segment. Indeed, black, Asian, and Latino council members represent a majority (albeit a bare majority) of the New York City Council, and the city had an Afri-can American mayor (David Dinkins) for one term in the early 1990s.

Moreover, immigrants in New York City have benefited from the gains won as a result of the civil rights struggles of the 1950s and 1960s in the United States. One tangible result in New York City of the 1965 federal Voting Rights Act, a civil rights law originally designed to enfranchise African Americans who had been deprived of politi-cal power, was that, as amended, it led to city council redistricting and the deliberate creation of districts for West Indians and Dominicans in 1991. Successful attempts by African Americans to win office in the wake of the civil rights movement have also provided a model for immigrant-origin politicians to follow. As John Mollenkopf and Jen-nifer Hochschild observe, the civil rights movement of the 1960s has acquired canonical status as a model for combining vigorous protest with political mobilization and electoral success (2010: 28–29). Not only does Amsterdam lack a native minority population with whom immigrants and their adult children can join political forces, but, like the Netherlands as a whole, it has had "little experience with . . . voting rights laws, minority advocacy groups . . . and other politics and organizational strategies intended to help mitigate the consequences of centuries of racial hierarchy" (ibid.: 28).

And this leads to a third difference in the two cities that affects the ability to enter the precincts of power: the legitimacy of ethnic politics. In New York City, ethnic politics is an accepted—and expected—way for aspiring leaders to mobilize their base and attain political representation. This has been true for well over a century. As Nancy Foner notes in her chapter, the fact that Irish, Italian, and Russian Jewish immigrants in earlier eras used ethnic appeals to gain entry into the political system gives legitimacy to similar strategies among contemporary immigrant-origin politicians. The efforts of today's Latino, Asian, and West Indian politicians in New York to gain local office by wooing the ethnic vote are viewed as a natural ethnic succession—and taken for granted as part of the way things are done. Indeed, Mollenkopf states that *not* to use ethnic appeals would be political suicide. No mainstream elected official in the city, he writes, would ever say that political leaders "should not represent, speak for, and be sensitive to the needs of specific ethnic constituencies."

In Amsterdam, as in New York City, the gateways to political power are to a large extent managed by a single party, the social democratic PvdA, and the immigrant-origin population forms an important electoral constituency. But this has certainly not led to the kind of ethnic politics typical of New York. Already in the 1990s and particularly in the new millennium, the established political elite has come to view ethnic politics as problematic and undesirable—and is highly suspicious of attempts to use group-based resources for political purposes. The formation of minority alliances does not provide people of immigrant background with a feasible strategy for obtaining political positions. More and more, representing a particular ethnic group has come to be seen as the opposite of successful political incorporation, namely as ethnic withdrawal from mainstream society. The result, Vermeulen, Michon, and Tillie argue, is that individuals and groups using group-based resources for political aims have trouble gaining access to appointed political positions. The antipathy to ethnic politics by mainstream political parties, they emphasize, has been on the rise. In the 1980s, local government policy in Amsterdam still sought to bolster group-based resources, for example, establishing minority councils for different immigrant-origin groups to advise politicians on how to solve problems facing the groups. By the turn of the twentieth-first century, however, a resistance to ethnically segmented incorporation had set in, and, among other things, minority advisory councils were abolished, subsidies for immigrant organizations were phased out, and overt ethnic politics was seen as illegitimate by the political elite and policy makers. In this new context, the argument goes, the political parties' wariness of group-based political mobilization has been particularly harmful to Turkish politicians seeking appointment to what Vermeulen and his coauthors call executive political positions. With strong ties in a well-organized Turkish ethnic community, they are seen by political parties as representing group-based interests.

The Turkish example indicates that a group's cultural and social characteristics can influence the ability of its members to win elected office. In Amsterdam, the very features of the Turkish community that have created problems in obtaining appointed executive positions have contributed to relative success in being elected to the city council. Between 1994 and 2010, Turks were represented in the city council proportionate to their number in contrast to Moroccans and Surinamese, whose representation lagged behind their share of the population. Vermeulen, Michon, and Tillie argue that high organizational density and strong ethnic networks among Turks support political participation and underpin "civic virtues" that are spread throughout the community and create a politically interested group.

Other features of immigrant groups come into play in New York. The sheer size and residential concentration of Dominicans and West Indians are significant factors in their electoral achievements. They are among the largest immigrant-origin groups in the city, with more than half a million people each. While the high rates of residential segregation among West Indians and Dominicans bring severe disadvantages, they have been a benefit when it comes to politics. Being concentrated in large numbers in neighborhoods in central Brooklyn (West Indians) and upper Manhattan (Dominicans) has provided a base for many successful West Indian and Dominican politicians. Political attitudes and traditions brought over from the home country can also affect political incorporation in New York; Mollenkopf points out that West Indians come from "democratically active and even fractious" countries, Dominicans from a society with a "robust tradition" of political competition in the post-Trujillo era, and Jews from the former Soviet Union arrive with a strong anticommunist orientation, which at least initially drew many to the Republican Party. The activities of homeland-based political parties in New York can have an impact, as well. While involvement in homeland politics is often thought to draw migrants away from political engagement in the United States, the reverse often happens. Dominican political parties, for instance, which are very active in New York, may stimulate and provide experience, skills, and organizational resources for engagement in New York City politics. And the way particular groups concentrate in the city's economy can also enter into the picture. West Indians, to give a pertinent example, are heavily concentrated in ethnic niches, such as work in hospitals and nursing homes and in public transportation, that are unionized and in which the unions are active in mobilizing members to vote.

Juxtaposing the two accounts of political incorporation in Amsterdam and New York—and teasing out some of the contrasts and parallels—thus sheds light on a broad range of factors that help explain how immigrant-origin groups are achieving political influence and positions as well as the barriers they face in seeking greater representation. These factors have to do with social, political, and cultural features in the two urban contexts, although distinctive characteristics of immigrant groups also seem to play a role. One of the most striking contrasts is that the political scene in New York provides immigrant-origin groups with a rich and institutionalized set of opportunities to engage in ethnic politics, with groups emulating each other's strategies and routinely forming alliances across ethnic lines. In Amsterdam, immigrants are increasingly expected not to represent ethnically specific constituencies, narrowing the margins for ethnic politics.

This said, in both Amsterdam and New York immigrants and their children are making significant inroads in gaining elected positions, which is perhaps not surprising given that both are liberal, progressive cities—and that large inflows from abroad date back about half a century so that major groups have had time to gain at least some political clout. It is also clear that immigrant-origin groups still have a long way to go before they achieve influence and power on a par with their number. Just when, how, and indeed whether they will do so are among the topics that must await future study.

NANCY FONER AND ROGIER VAN REEKUM

REFERENCES

Alba, Richard, and Nancy Foner. 2009. "Entering the Precincts of Power: Do National Differences Matter for Immigrant Minority Political Representation?" in Jennifer Hochschild and John Mollenkopf (eds.), *Bringing Outsiders In: Transatlantic Perspectives on Immigrant Political Incorporation*. Ithaca, NY: Cornell University Press.

Mollenkopf, John, and Jennifer Hochschild. 2010. "Immigrant Political Incorporation: Comparing Success in the United States and Western Europe." *Ethnic and Racial Studies* 33: 19–38.

7

The Rise of Immigrant Influence in New York City Politics

JOHN MOLLENKOPF

Introduction

While we have known that immigrants and their children have made up a majority of New York City's residents since the Federal Government's Current Population Survey (CPS) began to collect data on parents' place of birth in 1994, it may come as a surprise that they are now approaching a majority of its voting-age citizens as well. The November 2008 CPS indicates that 58 percent of the population and 48 percent of voting-age citizens are either immigrants or have at least one immigrant parent. (Native-born minority groups with native parents, such as African Americans and Puerto Ricans, constitute another 23 percent of the residents and 26 percent of the voting-age citizens.) Conversely, native-born whites with native-born parents, the nation's dominant population and voting group, now account for only one in four of New York City's potential voters and fewer than one in five residents. As a result, New York City constitutes an important laboratory both for how immigrants and their children become mobilized and represented within city politics (or not) as well as how those of immigrant descent interact with native-born minorities (and native-stock whites) in the political arena.

Only a few other U.S. or Western European cities come close to this level of potential political participation by immigrant-origin voters.

While the CPS samples are only marginally reliable for other big U.S. cities, the CPS suggests that only Los Angeles, where first- and second-generation residents make up 49 percent of the voting age citizens, San Jose,
with 46 percent, and Miami, with 41 percent, are comparable to New
York. New York differs markedly from Los Angeles, San Jose, and Miami,
however, both in having a larger African American population and a far
more diverse immigrant population. Moreover New York's immigrant
population is not dominated by one national-origin group, such as Mexicans in Los Angeles and San Jose or Cubans in Miami. New York presents an unusually diverse array of potentially competing or cooperating
native-stock and immigrant-origin ethnic groups. These features mean
that we can think of New York City not as an outlier in having a unique
set of immigrants, but as having a mixed set of immigrants who are more
representative of the foreign-born population in the country as a whole.

As the major immigrant gateway to the U.S. between 1850 and
1950, foreign-born people and their children already made up a significant proportion of New York City's population and electorate by
the early twentieth century. Indeed, the city's political history is often
told through the incorporation of succeeding waves of immigrants
(McNickle 1993). This is especially true if we also include African
Americans who came north between World War I and the 1960s and
Puerto Ricans who arrived in large numbers in the late 1940s, 1950s, and
1960s. After the end of the last great wave of immigration in 1930, the
Census Public Use Microdata Sample reported that native-born whites
with native parents made up just 22 percent of the city's voting-age citizens. That number is similar today. (The main difference, of course, is
that most of the rest then were white immigrants and their children,
whereas most are black, Hispanic, and Asian now.)

New York City's long history of struggle over how immigrants
and their descendants are to be integrated into its political processes
resulted in mechanisms and dynamics that continue to exert influence
today. As William Faulkner wrote in Requiem for a Nun, "The past is
never dead. It is not even past." In reaction to the great wave of immigration at the turn of the twentieth century, political institutions, political
cultures, and political dynamics formed both to limit and provide openings to mobilize immigrant voters and represent their interests. (Among
the most incisive analyses of this process are Shefter [1994], Morawska

[2001], and Smith [2003].) The momentum of the political order leads its main actors, including rising new groups, declining old ones, the major and minor parties, and various other organized groups with political weight (unions, business groups, religious institutions, and so on) to pursue well-established strategies, although groups may change these strategies in the course of implementing them. This momentum is embedded both in how the city charter and state election law define various governmental capacities and political processes as well as in the everyday interactions among parties, candidates, and interest groups.

The strongly partisan nature of New York's political system distinguishes it from American "reformed" cities (in which party candidates do not contend in local elections) as well as European cities (which have multi-party systems). New York City voters directly elect a strong executive (the mayor) separately from the relatively large city council (51 members). The mayor in turn sets policy, names department heads, determines the budget, and issues contracts (the last in conjunction with the city comptroller.) The main route to winning elected office (with the exception of the mayoralty) lies through a Democratic Party primary.[1] Between the individual city councilors, who do not exercise much power, and the mayor, who does, are two other citywide offices, comptroller and public advocate, as well as five relatively symbolic borough presidents. The city council, public advocate, and comptroller have difficulty checking the power of the mayor, although the comptroller is also influential because he or she manages the city's huge pension funds, must approve contracts, and audits city departments. Most assuredly, the key "precinct of power" is located at the mayor's end of City Hall, not the city council's end, nor across the street in the comptroller's office. Being a member of the New York City Council means belonging to a partisan hierarchy within which it is difficult to be an independent operator. Finally, party-related resources remain important to winning elections, notwithstanding the decline of party influence in urban America.[2] While the candidate-centered resources that determine outcomes in nonpartisan elections, such as money, media visibility, and support from elite organizations, are also important, especially in mayoral races, they are arguably less so for lesser offices in New York, particularly because of the city's generous public campaign finance system.

To break into elected office, even at the bottom rung of the ladder, the city council, rising minority and immigrant groups have had to wrestle their way through Democratic primaries. While these primaries present a number of obstacles, the Democratic partisan tilt of the general electorate can favor minority groups (including immigrant ethnic groups) because whites are less likely to register as Democrats than are members of minority groups. The latter thus make up a larger share of Democratic primary voters than they do of general election voters. The Democratic partisan tilt gives racial minorities a small advantage that counterbalances the many other factors—low levels of education, income, and home ownership—that tend to depress minority voter turnout compared to that of native whites. The Democratic advantage in registration and general election voting often leads to uncompetitive general elections, lowering overall turnout rates, including those in Democratic primaries. On the one hand, a relatively small core base can reelect Democratic incumbents, but on the other this leaves them vulnerable to insurgencies. As a result, county and district leaders also seek to designate—and often succeed in electing—favored immigrant ethnic candidates when new groups threaten to oust incumbents from older, declining groups. Still, the system leaves openings for challenges "from below"—although once elected, these candidates are generally absorbed into the "party regular" establishment.

Stepping back in time, a common feature of the city's history has been challenges by rising new immigrant ethnic groups to political party establishments whose leadership is based in previous ethnic waves (Mollenkopf 2003; Shefter 1976). During the second half of the nineteenth century, German and Irish immigrants gradually seized the reins of power from the older British political establishment; in the first half of the twentieth, Jews and Italians battled the Irish. In the second half of the twentieth century, African Americans (many with West Indian ancestry) and then Puerto Ricans sought empowerment within a white Catholic and Jewish political establishment. Today's immigrants are only the latest in the sequence of ethnic succession in city politics.

The patterns of ethnic succession have been varied. In most cases, this succession has involved penetrating and being absorbed into the regular Democratic Party establishment by taking over its lowest rungs. This typically has begun with efforts to displace incumbents in districts where the new population groups have been growing rapidly. Aware of the shifting ethnic composition of these districts, county party organizations have sometimes designated a loyal but appealing young member from the rising group to run for office while easing out an aging legislator (often by rewarding him or her with a judgeship). Sometimes, however, the county organizations have been slow to take such a step, the incumbent was unwilling to go, or the county organization wanted to slap down an insurgent, and the organization faced a real battle. Once in a while, the incumbent loses and the insurgent candidate wins. But unless there are enough other "reform" or "insurgent" legislators for him or her to join—which rarely happens—the newly elected member has little choice but to join the party establishment, thereby renewing it.

Historically, city- or countywide insurgencies based on ideology or principle sometimes fostered ethnic succession within the Democratic Party. Examples include the transformative mayoralties of Republicans Fiorello LaGuardia in the 1930s and John Lindsay in the 1960s, and to a lesser extent Democrat David Dinkins in 1989 (Mollenkopf 1992; Shefter 1994; Lowi 1964). When these broader insurgencies succeeded in winning the mayoralty, they promoted changes in the patterns of political mobilization at the neighborhood level, hastening the advent to power of new ethnic groups within the Democratic Party. Yet after these mayoral challenges, which tended to last only one or two terms, mayors continued to face the hegemony of the "regulars" within the Democratic Party and the new local officials became part of a renewed establishment. The current rise of a "Progressive Caucus" in the city council may offer a potential departure from this pattern, however.

New York thus offers two kinds of paths for new immigrant groups to break into the precincts of power: achieving power on the margins by gaining elected office (usually in the city council and state legislature, with the U.S. Congress and citywide office coming later) and rising up within a weakly organized but persistent regular Democratic organization, or achieving power within a citywide framework by being part of a wider insurgent majority that wins the mayoralty. In either case, it has been rare for rising ethnic minority candidates to appeal only to their own group, or even count on its effective mobilization as a *sine qua non* for success. Certainly at the borough or citywide level, and often even for a council or state legislative seat, the winner must bring diverse ethnic groups into a coalition, so that appealing too overtly to just one group might alienate others. At the same time, no mainstream New York City elected official would ever say that political leaders should not represent, speak for, and be sensitive to the needs of specific ethnic constituencies. To do otherwise would constitute political suicide.

Racial-Ethnic Succession in New York City Politics from 1950 to 1990

These dynamics are apparent in the 40-year period between 1950 and 1990. In 1950, New York City's foreign-born population—23 percent of the city total—was at a low ebb (1950 Census Public Use Microdata File and table 7.1). Less than 10 percent of the city's population was black, less than 3 percent Hispanic, and few were Asian; whites provided 90 percent of the eligible voters. In other words, New York was a white— and largely blue-collar—city.[3]

The 1.8 million foreign-born residents of New York City in 1950 reflected the great 1880–1920 immigrant wave. The largest group was Central European in origin, with 322,000 born in Russia, 184,000 in Germany, 179,000 in Poland, 118,000 in Austria, and 52,000 in Hungary. (Another 320,000 were children of immigrants from these places.) Apart from the Germans, who included Protestants and Catholics, the great majority were Central and East European Jews, giving the city the largest and most diverse Jewish community in the world, more than a million residents. At the same time, 355,000 had been born in Italy and 137,000 in Ireland, with 190,000 more being children of Italian immigrants and 89,000 children of Irish immigrants. The city thus had more than a million white Catholic residents of immigrant origin. (It also had a few hundred thousand residents born in Great Britain or whose parents were born there.)

New York's political leadership in the 1950s reflected this Jewish and Catholic immigration-origin base. In 1933, Fiorello LaGuardia had been elected the first mayor of Italian ancestry (though his mother was Jewish). He was succeeded by William O'Dwyer (Irish) in 1945, Vincent Impellitteri (Italian) in 1950, and Robert Wagner (German Catholic) in 1953. The city council, which was elected through a form of proportional representation between 1938 and 1947, had Irish, Italian, and Jewish

Democratic leadership as well during this period. The main political cleavage was between the more liberal Jewish Democrats (often in alliance with African American and Puerto Rican voters) against the more conservative white Catholic Democrats.

At the same time, the city was on the cusp of a dramatic racial and ethnic transition. The restrictions on international migration from federal legislation in the 1920s as well as the Depression and World War II meant that the city's wartime demand for new labor was filled by migration from the American South and Puerto Rico. By 1950, the city was home to 719,000 non-Hispanic blacks, 45,000 of whom had been born in the West Indies, as well as 192,000 people born in Puerto Rico and 67,000 whose parents were born there. These numbers swelled in the succeeding decades. If the first half of the twentieth century had featured political competition between Jews and Catholics in New York City, the second featured efforts by blacks and Puerto Ricans to break into a political system dominated by white ethnics.

New York's black population in the 1950s and 1960s was concentrated in Harlem in upper Manhattan and Bedford-Stuyvesant in north-central Brooklyn. Although the first black was elected to the state sssembly in 1917 and the first Puerto Rican in 1937 (both as Republicans), the first significant African American breakthrough into Democratic politics occurred when Hulan Jack, a Tammany Hall legislator from Harlem born in the West Indies, won the Manhattan borough presidency in 1953, making him a member of the powerful Board of Estimate. (He had been elected to the assembly in 1940.) Similarly, Adam Clayton Powell, pastor of a major Harlem church, became the first black city councilman in 1941 and first black congressman from New York in 1944. A stalwart of the Brooklyn Democratic organization, Bertram Baker, also born in the West Indies, was elected its first black Assembly member in 1944, while his protégée Shirley Chisholm became Brooklyn's first black member of the U.S. House of Representatives—and the first black woman in the chamber—in 1968. Her parents had migrated from Barbados, where she spent part of her youth, and Guyana.

Another key figure in Harlem politics, Percy Sutton, was Malcolm X's lawyer and founder of Inner City Broadcasting. He became a state assemblyman in 1965, Manhattan borough president in 1966, and a mayoral candidate in 1977 (Green and Wilson 1989). His close friend and ally David Dinkins was elected to the state assembly in 1965, served many years as city clerk, and was elected Manhattan borough president in 1985. In 1989, Dinkins became New York City's first (and so far only) black mayor. It is worth noting that the major tacticians of the Manhattan and Brooklyn regular Democratic parties, J. Raymond Jones and Wesley McDonald Holder, were both born in the Caribbean (St. Thomas and Guyana, respectively) (Walter 1989), but black politicians from West Indian backgrounds did not highlight their immigrant ancestry in this era.

Puerto Ricans have been less segregated than African Americans, but have also been racially stereotyped. Their biggest population concentration was neither in Manhattan nor Brooklyn (though both have Puerto Rican neighborhoods), but in the Bronx, one of the smaller boroughs of the city and its poorest. Following in the path forged by the initial African American elected officials, Puerto Rican politicians began to win elected office in the 1960s and 1970s. Herman Badillo became the Bronx borough president in 1965 and the first Puerto Rican congressman in 1970, while Fernando Ferrer joined the city council in 1982, became Bronx borough president in 1987, ran for but failed to win the Democratic nomination for mayor in 2001, and was the Democratic nominee in 2005 but lost the general election (Jennings 1977; Sánchez 1996).

In the period between 1950 and 1990, therefore, the main story of ethnic minority empowerment in New York City was that of native-born blacks and Hispanics seeking to achieve political influence commensurate with their population numbers. This drive culminated in the narrow victory of David Dinkins in his mayoral race against Rudolph W. Giuliani in 1989, with most African Americans, Hispanics, and white liberals from educated and professional backgrounds favoring Dinkins and the great majority of white Catholics and Jews outside of Manhattan favoring Giuliani (Mollenkopf 1992).

This achievement was made possible by a profound and disconcerting set of demographic changes. As table 7.1 shows, the white share of New York City's population dropped by half between 1950 and 1990, leaving whites considerably less than half the resident population, though still a majority of the electorate, while the black and Hispanic populations more than doubled and the Asian population grew twenty-fold. The aging white immigrant population of 1950, almost two million

Table 7.1. Population and Voting-Age Citizens by Race and Nativity in New York City, 1950–2009 (Percentages)

Group	1950 Population	1950 Voting Age Citizens	1990 Population	1990 Voting Age Citizens	2009 Population	2009 Voting Age Citizens
Native whites	65.1	62.6	35.2	46.0	27.5	35.4
Foreign whites	22.3	25.5	8.3	8.1	7.8	7.9
Native blacks	8.5	8.5	19.6	20.8	16.3	17.6
Foreign blacks	0.7	0.6	6.0	3.2	7.3	6.7
Native Hispanics	2.6	2.3	15.3	14.4	16.3	15.1
Foreign Hispanics	0.4	0.3	8.5	3.5	11.3	6.8
Asians	0.3	0.2	6.8	3.6	12.5	9.6
Total	7,891,957	5,667,928	7,322,564	4,568,310	8,387,216	5,159,575

Note: Asians are not broken out by nativity because the vast majority of them are immigrants.
Sources: 1950 and 1990 Microdata files, Decennial Census, 2009 American Community Survey.

people, slumped to about 600,000 by 1990. As the minority share of the city's population grew, white flight accelerated, particularly during the traumatic decade of the 1970s, which featured racial conflict, a fiscal crisis, and sharp economic decline.

The immediate political impact of disinvestment, white flight, racial polarization, and fiscal crisis was to sharpen political competition between whites and members of minority groups. The adventurous and inclusive liberal experimentalism of the Lindsay administration in the late 1960s and early 1970s was discredited, many parts of the white electorate shifted in a more conservative direction, and outer-borough Jews and Catholics tended to vote more alike instead of competing as they had in the past. As the city recovered economically and fiscally, it was led by Mayor Edward Koch (from 1978 through 1989), a formerly liberal Congressman from Greenwich Village who campaigned on restoring fiscal discipline, restraining union demands, and ending social programs aimed at bolstering minority politicians. The city also recovered demographically, despite continued decline of the white population, partly because native-born minority populations continued to grow, but mainly because of the huge inflow of new immigrant groups.

By 1990, therefore, New York City was no longer a white, blue-collar city, but a multiracial mosaic in which no racial/national-origin group was the majority, although native-born whites remained the largest group and were still a bare majority of the voters. Class had colors, in the sense that whites worked predominantly in the professional and managerial occupations and the most skilled trades, whereas African Americans and Puerto Ricans were clustered in service work (and many were outside the labor force and dependent on social provision), although African Americans had made great strides in public employment (Waldinger 1996). Meanwhile, the steadily emerging new immigrant communities were taking on the blue-collar roles vacated by the departing white working class as well as lower-level service jobs, as many native minorities were able to move into better positions.

In this context, it was no wonder that the 1989 mayoral race was highly racially polarized. David Dinkins's victory symbolized the long-awaited breakthrough of a progressive governing coalition driven by an alliance of minority and white liberal voters. This breakthrough was short-lived, however (Mollenkopf 1992, 2003). In the wake of a difficult mayoralty marked by a severe economic downturn, rising crime, and continuous racial controversy, Dinkins narrowly lost the 1993 election to Republican Rudolph W. Giuliani, who in turn was succeeded narrowly by Republican Michael Bloomberg in 2001 (who then won reelection in 2005 and, more controversially, in 2009) on the basis of a white Jewish and Catholic outer-borough electoral core similar to the one critical to Edward Koch's mayoral victories in 1981 and 1985.

Racial-Ethnic Succession in New York City Politics from 1990 to 2013

While the ability of African American and Puerto Rican voting blocs to form a citywide electoral majority proved short-lived, candidates from these backgrounds continued to make steady headway in winning city council, state assembly, and state senate seats. It is an irony of history that they would join white Catholics and Jews in the following decades as politically established but demographically declining constituencies facing the emergence of new groups that in some cases sought to displace them. As table 7.1 shows, the white share of the city's total population and potential electorate continued to decline between 1990 and 2009. International migration, a significant background factor slowing the fall of the city's population between 1970 and 1980, emerged as a driving force, helping the city's overall population to rebound to record numbers. Unlike Newark, Detroit, or St. Louis, New York City did not become more black—or even more native minority—as it became less white. Instead, it received a growing number of immigrants from all racial backgrounds. By 2009, whites remained a third of the city's population, but mainly because immigrants from the former Soviet Union bolstered the total.

In 2009, according to the Current Population Survey (CPS), some three million of New York City's 8.3 million residents were foreign born and another two million were their children. People living in immigrant families made up almost three-fifths of the city's residents, almost half its voting-age citizens, and two-fifths of its actual voters. Table 7.2 shows the makeup of New York City shortly after the 2008 presidential election as captured by the November CPS.[4] The table breaks down the composition of the population, the potential electorate (voting-age citizens), and those who actually cast votes by race and immigrant generation, distinguishing those born abroad, born in the U.S. to immigrant parents, and born in the U.S. with native-born parents.

A number of politically important conclusions may be drawn from this table. First of all, the group that has long dominated New York City politics, native-born whites with native parents (third row of the table), now makes up less than one-fifth of the city's population, although in 2008 they contributed a quarter of eligible voters and almost a third of those actually casting ballots. Their vote share is larger than their voting-age-citizen and population shares because they are all citizens and, compared to other groups, they are older and better educated, have higher incomes, and are more likely to be homeowners. These demographic factors are all positively correlated with voting. Moreover, native-born whites with native parents have been long socialized into political participation. Their influence is enhanced by the fact that their immigrant "nearest neighbors," white immigrants, tend to vote like them. Immigrant first- and second-generation whites accounted for a

Table 7.2. Population by Immigrant-Origin Total, Voting-Age Citizens, and Voters in New York City, 2008

Immigrant Groups	Population	% of NYC Population	Voting-Age Citizens (VAC)	% of VAC	Votes Cast (VC)	% of VC	Turnout VC/VAC
White FB	732,000	9.0	406,191	8.4	129,169	5.0	31.8
White 2G	491,048	6.0	355,691	7.4	222,942	8.7	62.7
White NS	1,568,063	19.3	1,248,913	25.7	801,208	31.3	64.2
Ex-USSR*	*250,581*	*3.1*	*156,662*	*3.2*	*48,033*	*1.9*	*30.7*
Black FB	720,480	9.1	388,880	8.0	227,249	8.9	58.4
Black 2G	353,190	4.4	122,268	2.6	81,422	3.2	66.6
Black NS	1,016,948	12.5	711,197	14.6	399,241	15.6	56.1
West Indian*	*814,957*	*10.0*	*281,424*	*5.8*	*218,040*	*8.5*	*77.5*
Hispanic FB	868,642	10.7	317,574	6.5	152,218	5.9	47.9
Hispanic 2G	502,649	6.2	159,633	3.3	73,429	2.8	46.0
Hispanic NS	806,611	9.9	545,360	11.2	306,347	12.0	56.2
Dominican*	*449,371*	*5.5*	*155,220*	*3.2*	*64,144*	*2.5*	*41.3*
Asian FB	593,071	7.3	305,205	6.3	107,976	4.2	35.4
Asian 2G	448,615	5.5	266,055	5.5	56,751	2.2	21.3
Asian NS	23,820	0.3	23,820	0.5	0	NA	NA
Chinese*	*418,852*	*5.1*	*275,793*	*5.7*	*52,029*	*2.0*	*18.9*
Total FB	2,918,225	35.8	1,417,850	29.1	616,612	24.1	43.5
Total 2G	1,808,658	22.2	914,967	18.8	434,547	16.9	47.5
Total NS	3,417,728	41.9	2,531,576	52.0	1,509,082	58.9	59.6
New York City Total	8,144,611	100.0	4,864,393	100.0	2,560,241	100.0	52.6

FB = foreign born. 2G = one or two foreign-born parents. NS = native-born with two native-born parents.
* Combined FB and 2G population. NA = not available due to small sample size.
Source: 2008 Current Population Survey November Election Supplement.

significant share of the city's population in 2008 (15 percent) but smaller proportion of actual voters (13.7 percent), because they are less likely than native whites of native parentage to be citizens, speak English at home, have high incomes, or be attached to the political system. Nevertheless, their added electoral weight brought the total white share of the voters up to just under half.

Most white immigrant families have come from the former Soviet Union, specifically Russia, Ukraine, and Georgia, and the vast majority are Jews. Despite having experienced discrimination in the former Soviet Union, the first generation reached a high level of educational attainment before migrating and their children have done extremely well in New York City, often with the active help of old-line organizations established by the previous wave of Jewish immigrants. Paradoxically, this economically successful group is among the politically least engaged. While the exact reasons for this deserve further research, politics had a negative connotation for the first generation in the home country. They arrived in New York with an anticommunist orientation, but soon realized that the Republican Party, perhaps their natural ideological home, was not a route to political advancement. Meanwhile the regular Democratic organizations were ambivalent about the arrival of large numbers of Russian-speaking Jews, usually in declining outer-borough Jewish neighborhoods. They wanted the newcomers' votes, but incumbent office holders also wanted to hang onto their jobs.

The nonwhite half of New York City voters come from a kaleidoscope of racial and national-origin backgrounds. In 2008, native-born and immigrant blacks together made up the second largest racial-ethnic group in the electorate, at 25.2 percent. The city's black population is about evenly split between African Americans and those with immigrant ancestry, predominantly from the Anglophone West Indies and Haiti, although New York City has a growing West African population, which is about as numerous as those from Haiti. Because of their lower levels of citizenship, immigrant-origin blacks make up less than half of the black vote (43.6 percent in 2008), but have a stronger connection to the political system than the white immigrant-origin population, primarily because first-generation Anglo-Caribbeans did not come from authoritarian one party countries. The native black vote was half the native white vote in 2008, but the immigrant black vote was

almost twice the size of the immigrant white vote. In general, the historic mobilization of black voters for empowerment seems to have had
a spillover effect on immigrant blacks, leading to relatively high rates of
registration and voting.

West Indian voters come from democratically active and even fractious countries, sympathize strongly with African American opposition to racial discrimination and prejudice, and favor an active government. Many have found work in unionized industries and occupations
like hospital workers, transit conductors, or cable television installers.
Although West Indians are sometimes accused, with some basis, of
looking down on African Americans as being too dependent on the
U.S. welfare system, and they are clearly proud of their immigrant roots
and achievements, they vote like African Americans in most instances.
Only when one of their own is competing against an African American
incumbent do they part ways (Rogers 2006). As table 7.2 indicates, they
were enthused by the Obama candidacy and were one of the highest-
turnout groups in New York City in 2008.

Hispanic voters made up the third-largest segment of the electorate at 21 percent in 2008. Immigrant-origin Hispanics considerably outnumber native-stock Hispanics (largely those of Puerto Rican descent)
in the population at large. But this ratio is reversed among voters, with
immigrant-origin Hispanics accounting for only 42.4 percent of the
Hispanic total. Although many Puerto Ricans have lived in New York
City for three generations and all possess U.S. citizenship, Puerto Ricans
remain among the poorest and least educated New Yorkers. Their turnout rates are higher than those of immigrant-origin Hispanics and the
same as native blacks', but lower than those of native whitess.

The Hispanic immigrant communities of New York City are quite
diverse, including many from the Caribbean as well as Central and South
America. Dominicans are the largest and most effectively organized
of the Spanish-speaking newcomers. While they are still smaller than
the Puerto Rican population, they are growing while the Puerto Rican
population has been declining. In part because the Dominican Republic has had a robust tradition of political competition after the Trujillo
dictatorship and in part because Dominican political parties have been
active in New York (a recent president of the Dominican Republic grew
up in Washington Heights, the largest Dominican neighborhood in the

city), Dominican New Yorkers are actively engaged in city politics. Still, Dominicans cast fewer actual votes than their share of the potential electorate and for many of the same reasons that Puerto Ricans do, such as low levels of education, income, and English facility. The members of the rapidly growing Mexican population are too recent, too young, and too often noncitizens or undocumented to engage in electoral politics, but the community has formed organizations to press for issues of concern, their children are forming student organizations, and they will be an emerging force in the future (Smith 2005).

Many of the newest New Yorkers are from South and East Asia. About half of all Asians are from China (including Hong Kong and Taiwan), or overseas Chinese from other countries, and New York also has large populations of Indians and Koreans, as well as smaller populations of Filipinos, Bangladeshis, and Pakistanis. Broadly speaking, these groups have been economically successful but not particularly active in city politics, though a number of Asian candidates have recently gained office, including a Chinese American citywide official (Comptroller John Liu) and the first Chinese American female congressperson (Grace Meng). While little research has been done on this question, it is plausible that it reflects the first-generation Chinese experience with the Communist Party of China, together with the economic success of their children (achieved without reliance on help from the political establishment). Certainly the Democratic Party establishment has not been interested in mobilizing these groups. (For the most recent analysis of Asian American political engagement in U.S. as a whole, see Wong, Ramakrishnan, Lee, and Junn [2010]).

As Jennifer Hochschild (2010) has so perceptively observed, demography is not always political destiny, but it certainly provides raw materials from which urban political systems selectively mobilize or demobilize old and new immigrant ethnic groups. Demographic change between 1990 and 2009 continued to undermine the dominance of native-born whites with native-born parents, but rather than precipitating black-white conflict over racial succession, as in many other American cities, it led to greater fragmentation. Immigrants and their children from different racial backgrounds have been forming new constituencies while native-stock whites, African Americans, and Puerto Ricans are all in decline.

This has made assembling a citywide electoral majority ever more challenging. To be sure, racial polarization (whites versus nonwhites) has played an important role in all the mayoral elections between 1989 and 2009. The overwhelming Democratic advantage in voter registration should have meant that party allegiance would have enabled Democratic nominees to win citywide elections. In these mayoral races, however, enough white (and other) Democrats were willing to defect from Democratic candidates who were members of minority groups or received substantial support from them that Republican candidates won all the mayoral elections after the Dinkins victory in 1989. Still, because native and immigrant-origin white voters were no longer a majority of the electorate after 2000, white candidates could not use racial polarization as an effective strategy for assembling an electoral majority. Instead, they needed at least some cross-group coalition formation.

Through the 1980s, despite their falling share of the electorate, white native-stock people served not only as mayor (Edward Koch), but also comptroller (Jay Goldin) and city council president (Andrew Stein). They held four of the five borough presidencies (Stanley Simon in the Bronx, Howard Golden in Brooklyn, Claire Schulman in Queens, and Ralph Lamberti on Staten Island), the speakership of the city council (Peter Vallone, Sr.), and 28 of the 35 council seats. Several important institutional changes between 1989 and 1993 set the stage for major changes in this picture, however.

Steps in the Process of Immigrant Political Representation

In 1989, the U.S. Supreme Court ruled in *New York City Board of Estimate v. Morris* (489 U.S. 688) that one of the main organs of the city's government, the Board of Estimate (made up of the three citywide officials and the five borough presidents) was unconstitutional because each borough president had the same vote even though the borough populations varied widely. Seeing this ruling on the way, New York City established charter revision commissions in 1988 and 1989 that not only abolished the Board of Estimate and redistributed its powers to the city council and mayor, but also revised many aspects of city government, including enlarging the city council from 35 to 51 members and establishing a Districting Commission to redraw council boundaries with an eye toward enhancing minority representation (Benjamin and Mauro 1989) in the wake of the 1990 Census.[5] The redistricting of the city council in 1991, 2002, and 2012 has slowly but steadily increased the opportunities that minority and immigrant-origin candidates have for winning seats in that body.

The new district boundaries not only created new majority-minority districts for African Americans and Puerto Ricans, as required by the Voting Rights Act of 1965 as amended in 1982, but also carved out districts for many emerging communities, particularly the relatively concentrated West Indians of Brooklyn and Dominicans of northern Manhattan (Macchiarola and Diaz 1993). While the specific decisions were sometimes controversial (particularly fashioning a Chinatown district that combined the Chinese population with the affluent SoHo, Tribeca, and Battery Park City neighborhoods instead of the lower-income, largely Hispanic Lower East Side), redistricting set the framework for grassroots electoral mobilization within native-born minority and immigrant communities for the next several decades. Referendum voters adopted a two-term limit on service in the city council and other city offices in 1993 and reaffirmed it in 1996, creating open seats more frequently and making elections more competitive than when they were dominated by long-time incumbents.[6]

The first election after the charter reforms and city council redistricting in 1991 yielded a dramatic improvement of minority representation, from 20 to 40 percent. This included election of the first two immigrant candidates, Guillermo Linares, a Dominican activist in northern Manhattan's Washington Heights, and Una Clarke, a Jamaican community leader in central Brooklyn's Crown Heights. Two openly gay members were elected for the first time as well. However, only two of the 32 incumbents who ran for reelection were defeated, so the council leadership continued to be in the hands of Democratic Party regulars. In addition, several promising immigrant-origin candidates, such as Margaret Chin in Chinatown and Paula Chu in Flushing, lost.

Over time, the council has gradually come closer to the aspirations of those who drew the new district lines in 1991. Though immigrant-origin people made up 48 percent of the voting-age citizens and 41 percent of the voters in November 2008, only nine of the council's 51 members (17.6 percent) had immigrant roots after the 2009 municipal elections. These included three West Indians, four Dominicans, and two Chinese. This is a dramatic improvement even on 2005, however, particularly in the form of Margaret Chin's ultimate victory after 18 years of trying to win the council seat representing Manhattan's Chinatown. (Another 18 members were African American or Puerto Rican, giving minority representatives a bare majority of the total.) While the council still included ten Jews, nine Italians, six Puerto Ricans, four Irish, and two other white Catholics, it was gradually moving toward the demographics of the New York City voters, if not its residents.

While immigrant-origin representation still falls far short of parity with the presence of immigrant-origin voters in the electorate, it is a vast improvement over the zero representation that obtained until 1991. All the largest immigrant-origin groups, including West Indians, Chinese, and Dominicans, now have council representation. They are following the path of political upward mobility forged generations ago by the Irish, Italians, and Jews. For example, Yvette Clarke, daughter of Una Clarke, the first West Indian elected to the city council, defeated the son of the retiring African American congressman, Chris Owens, to represent central Brooklyn in the U.S. House of Representatives in 2006. In 2012, Grace Meng, the U.S.-born daughter of Taiwanese immigrants, became the first Asian American elected to Congress from New York, representing a newly drawn Queens district. The first Dominican assemblyman has taken a seat in the New York Senate and is also reported to be aiming for Congress to succeed Congressman Charles Rangel when he retires.

The large immigrant groups that have failed to win city council seats, Russians and South Asians, both face significant barriers. The Russians (as well as the growing Chinese community in southwest Brooklyn) face an obdurate Jewish and Italian Democratic political establishment, although Soviet-born Alec Brook-Krasny was elected to the state assembly in 2006 from a district that includes many Russian immigrants. Similarly the South Asians (many of Caribbean origin) of Richmond Hill and Ozone Park are not sufficiently numerous within one geographic concentration and their neighborhood is fractured by four council districts each represented by members of other, larger minority groups.

One might say, following Churchill, that this is not the beginning of the end, but it is certainly the end of the beginning for immigrant representation in New York City. If the underrepresented immigrant groups are to create more favorable electoral terrains for the future, they will have to get better results from a city council redistricting process currently dominated by incumbents from other groups as well as work harder on registering immigrant-origin voters and turning them out in local elections.

Mayoral Efforts to Make Immigrant Voters Part of a Majority Coalition

Given the still-marginal immigrant influence on the city council, the diversity of New York City's immigrant communities, and the continued political relevance of racial as opposed to immigrant pan-ethnic categories, the city council is not likely to put immigration at the top of its list of priorities, although it has adopted a number of immigrant-friendly measures. For example, the council forced the issue of providing translation services for non-English speakers at city agencies, and opined that federal immigration enforcement agents should not intrude on the city's jails. More generally, its stands in support of working-class and minority families tend to help immigrants.

The center of power in New York City remains in the office of mayor, however. As of 2012, this office defines and manages a $68 billion budget, of which $44 billion is raised from local taxation. (New York State provides most of the difference from revenues that it extracts from New York City.) To put this in perspective, New York City alone spends more than a third of the European Union budget. It is certainly comparable to small European welfare states like Sweden, Norway, Switzerland, or Austria. If immigrant-origin voters were seen to be a pivotal part of the electoral majority that brings a mayor into power, this might be more meaningful than electing a certain number of city council members who can make only marginal changes in the city budget.

As was previously mentioned, the potential liberal electoral majority comprised of native minority, immigrant, and white liberal voters failed to win any mayoral election since David Dinkins's victory in 1989. Giuliani effectively carried out conservative reforms such as reducing public assistance, cracking down on panhandlers and homeless people, focusing police action on criminal hot spots, and restraining taxing and spending. Among other consequences, his actions (and those of the New York City Police Department) heightened racial tensions in the city. Nonetheless, massive white support enabled him to swamp a white liberal challenger in the 1997 mayoral campaign.

Since term limits prevented Giuliani from running again in 2001, Democrats thought that the mayoralty would return to their hands, especially since the Republican nominee was slated to be Michael Bloomberg, a billionaire completely new to politics. Democrats, however, went through a bruising primary battle in which a white liberal, Mark Green, narrowly defeated Bronx Borough President Fernando Ferrer, a Puerto Rican who had the support of many African American political leaders, including Reverend Al Sharpton. The destruction of the World Trade Center on September 11, 2001, caused the Democratic and Republican mayoral primaries to be postponed and dramatically shifted the terms of debate in the city.

In the end, spending a record amount from his personal fortune on the campaign, Bloomberg prevailed narrowly over Green. Many of Ferrer's core supporters could not bring themselves to back Green, especially since he had tacked to the right in order to win the nomination. (Many white Democrats supported Green in the runoff primary and then switched to Bloomberg in the general election.) Table 7.3 shows the vote for Mayor Bloomberg according to the racial and ethnic composition of the city's election districts. (The first column is the share of the total vote contributed by each type of election district; the second is the share of the total vote for Bloomberg; and the third is the share voting for Bloomberg.) White areas of the city contributed the majority of the votes in the 2001 election and leaned toward Bloomberg, especially in Catholic but also in Jewish areas. Bloomberg and Green split the Hispanic and (small) Asian vote more or less evenly. Bloomberg thus won a racially polarized vote not only because of the disproportionate turnout of his white Catholic and Jewish supporters, but also because lower-turnout Hispanic and Asian minority groups divided their support and blacks, who supported Green, also had low turnout.

Bloomberg proved to be a popular and effective mayor in his first two terms, coping with serious budget problems by raising taxes rather than reducing the number of public workers and by restoring public confidence in the city's economic future. Under his guidance, the police

Table 7.3. New York City Mayoral Election Vote in 2001, 2005, and 2009 by Predominant Racial-Ethnic Composition of Election District

	2001 Total Vote	2001 Vote for MB	MB %	2005 Total Vote	2005 Vote for MB	MB %	2009 Total Vote	2009 Vote for MB	MB %
White Catholic			72.6			73.9			65.3
Share of total	22.3%	32.2%		20.5%	25.9%		20.8%	27.3%	
White Secular			47.3			68.0			63.8
Share of total	9.6%	9.0%		8.4%	9.8%		8.2%	10.5%	
Jewish			59.8			78.0			71.3
Share of total	20.3%	24.1%		18.9%	25.2%		19.5%	28.0%	
White Plurality			53.8			60.5			53.8
Share of total	5.2%	5.5%		4.9%	5.1%		5.2%	5.6%	
African American			22.7			45.9			19.9
Share of total	13.0%	5.9%		13.7%	10.8%		14.5%	5.8%	
Afro-Caribbean			23.6			50.1			21.0
Share of total	5.8%	2.7%		5.6%	4.8%		6.1%	2.6%	
Black Plurality			35.6			48.4			34.0
Share of total	2.8%	2.0%		2.9%	2.4%		3.0%	2.0%	
Puerto Rican			41.1			28.2			33.0
Share of total	7.2%	5.9%		9.3%	4.5%		7.7%	5.1%	
Dominican			38.7			27.9			31.3
Share of total	4.4%	3.4%		5.6%	2.7%		4.7%	3.0%	
Latin American			51.4			43.3			50.6
Share of total	1.5%	1.5%		1.6%	1.2%		1.5%	1.6%	
Latino Plurality			47.6			45.3			42.4
Share of total	4.7%	4.4%		5.1%	4.0%		5.0%	4.2%	
Chinese			51.5			62.7			58.5
Share of total	2.3%	2.4%		2.3%	2.4%		2.5%	3.0%	
Other Asian			54.6			58.4			52.5
Share of total	.7%	.7%		.7%	.7%		.7%	.7%	
Total	1,480,582	744,757	50.3	1,289,919	753,089	58.4	1,178,057	585,466	49.7

MB = Michael Bloomberg vote or share. White Secular = majority white election districts that are neither predominantly Catholic nor predominantly Jewish. White Plurality, Black Plurality, Latino Plurality = election districts in which the group is a plurality, but not a majority.
Source: Author's calculations from Board of Election results and U.S. Census data.

department continued to reduce crime rates without the high levels of racial conflict and harsh treatment of young minority offenders that had characterized the Giuliani administration, although the department's "stop and frisk" practices remained controversial. When Bloomberg ran for reelection in 2005, once more challenged by Ferrer, table 7.3 shows that he received increased support across the board except in Hispanic areas of the city, Ferrer's natural base. Not only did Bloomberg increase his core support in white Catholic and Jewish areas, he substantially increased his white liberal support and doubled his backing among African American and Afro-Caribbean voters. He also brought Asian voters to his side.

If he had left office at the end of his second term, Bloomberg would clearly have gone out at a high point. In the wake of the 2008 financial and economic crisis, however, he decided that the city's difficult situation required him to try for a third term. Since many city council members were also about to be termed out of office, they joined him in changing the limit from two to three terms. In his final 2009 reelection campaign, Bloomberg faced Democratic City Comptroller William C. Thompson, an African American with Afro-Caribbean ancestry and a long association with the Brooklyn Democratic county organization. Although Thompson is competent and articulate, many voters thought he held a weak hand against a popular incumbent who ultimately spent $107 million on his campaign. Many core Democratic interest groups therefore did not rally to Thompson's side and his campaign generated much less enthusiasm than Barack Obama's presidential campaign did just a year earlier. In the end, Bloomberg eked out a narrow victory.

In 2009, Bloomberg had less support in all the places where he had run strongly in 2005. Of course, against a black Democratic challenger, his support remained strongest in white Catholic, Jewish, and white liberal areas—and predominantly white areas again cast a bare majority of the votes. Bloomberg lost the greatest ground among African Americans and Afro-Caribbeans, where Thompson ran most strongly. These areas also made up a slightly greater percentage of the total voters than they had in 2005. But this was not enough to offset Bloomberg's gain in support in Hispanic areas, especially the Latin American immigrant areas of Queens, and he retained a majority in Chinese and other Asian immigrant areas as well.

This short history of mayoral competition underscores the fact that race, not national origin, remains the basic dividing line in New York City politics. Since the political behavior of white immigrant voters is quite similar to that of white Catholic and Jewish voters, their rising numbers have offset some of the native-white decline in the electorate. At the same time, the two groups together are gradually decreasing as a share of the total. The key to their continued dominance is that black, Hispanic, Asian, and white liberal voters remain divided, whether they are immigrant origin or not. This situation is not likely to change quickly, given the material and ideological differences among the groups and their tendency to compete with each other.

If immigrant voters are neither sufficiently cohesive nor a large enough part of the total electorate to swing elections on their own, they have still had an impact on mayoral policies. The immigrant vote (or rather specific parts of it) are sufficiently available and appealing to a dominant white electoral plurality seeking to create an electoral majority that even white Republican candidates have avoided taking anti-immigrant positions, adopted a pro-immigrant rhetorical stance, and enacted some specific measures that immigrant advocates set as high priorities. The mayoral executive orders barring police from inquiring about a person's legal status in most situations and the language access measures adopted are two cases in point.

Conclusion

The process by which new, rising immigrant ethnic groups succeed old, declining ones has been a long-term affair in New York City politics. Although Italians and Jews became a rapidly growing part of New York City's population between 1880 and 1920, New York did not elect its first Italian Democratic mayor until 1950 (and did not elect another Italian American mayor until 1993). It did not elect its first Jewish Democratic mayor until 1973. African Americans arrived in substantial numbers from the 1920s through the 1950s but did not elect their first mayor until 1989. Puerto Ricans, who began to arrive in substantial numbers in the late 1940s and 1950s, have not yet succeeded in electing a mayor, though the Democratic nominee in 2005 was Puerto Rican.

At this writing, the 2013 Democratic mayoral primary election looms four months ahead and the general election six. It will be the first in more than a decade not to feature either an incumbent or a Republican with sufficient appeal and financial resources to rally white Democratic voters to recreate the Koch-Giuliani-Bloomberg electoral coalition. (One white Democrat who might do so, former Congressman Anthony Weiner, has entered the race, but he was driven from office for emailing risqué pictures to women he did not know and faces high negative ratings in opinion polls.) The primary will be hotly contested. In recent polls, the leader is Council Speaker Christine Quinn, a white legislator from lower Manhattan, who happens to be a lesbian. She became speaker with support from the Queens and Bronx regular Democratic organizations and has also received some backing from Mayor Bloomberg. Former comptroller William Thompson seeks to consolidate black and Latino support, but this will be a difficult task because other contenders have previously received strong support from these constituencies. This includes Public Advocate Bill de Blasio, who has won the endorsement of a key labor union, 1199SEIU (a union of healthcare workers), and has an African American wife. The 2013 Democratic primary thus promises to be unusually competitive, with immigrant voters potentially playing an important role.

The 2009 election did feature one triumph of immigrant political advancement, the election of Taiwan-born City Council Member John Liu to the city's second-highest office, comptroller. In this position, he manages the city's huge pension funds, reviews all city contracts, and audits the operations and expenditures of all city departments. It is considered a stepping stone to the mayoralty. Liu did not win office on the basis of Chinese or even immigrant voters, since they constitute a relatively small slice of the electorate. With backing from the Queens County Democratic organization, the Working Families Party (a union–community organization progressive third party), and many African Americans and Hispanics, and with avid financial support from Chinese contributors, he put together a winning primary campaign against strong opponents and won the general election by a considerably wider margin than did Mayor Bloomberg. His current campaign for mayor, however, has been weakened by the recent conviction of two of his aides for violating campaign finance laws. Even though he does not currently rank high in public opinion polls, he is a past master at retail politics and campaigning and may ultimately prove to be a serious contender as well. Given that immigrants will make up about three out of ten voters in the fall 2013 elections, whoever does win will have had to mobilize substantial support from them.

NOTES

1. New York City is divided into five boroughs, each of which is a county. Each county has its own party organizations. Since 69 percent of the voters register as Democrats, that party is dominant and its nominees usually win general elections. The building blocks of the county party organizations are state assembly districts, from which the party's enrolled voters elect two to four district leaders who in turn elect a county party leader, or "boss." In many instances, district leader elections are uncontested. Each district leader has the backing of a local political club, whose members sometimes hold government jobs. The county party organizations have a great deal of accumulated experience in the law and practice of winning primary elections. The Democratic Party has been much less successful in controlling access to the mayoralty, with Republican-backed candidates winning in 1993, 1997, 2001, 2005, and 2009.

2. Many scholars have argued that New York's Democratic Party organizations have suffered significant decline (Sterne 2001; Wade 1990). While this may be true in terms of their capacity to mobilize voters, it is not true of their continuing role as gatekeepers to local office-holding, particularly in minority and immigrant neighborhoods (Jones Correa 1998; Sanjek 1998).

3. The U.S. Census asks separate questions about race and Hispanic origin. Hispanics can be any race, but all have been grouped together here and removed from the other categories. Parents' place of birth was asked through 1970.

4. Presidential elections draw the largest electorates, in this case 2.6 million voters. The November CPS often slightly overstates the number of voters, but in this case slightly understated it.

5. The author was a consultant to the Districting Commission, drafting the lines for review by commission members. The council was redistricted again after the 2000 census with relatively minor changes to the original lines, and has been redistricted once again in 2012 to reflect changes recorded in the 2010 census.

6. In early 2009, the mayor and council agreed to rescind term limits for the 2009 election, so that Mayor Bloomberg and council members could be reelected, but limits were reinstituted afterward.

REFERENCES

Benjamin, Gerald, and Frank J. Mauro. 1989. "Restructuring the New York City Government: The Reemergence of Municipal Reform." *Proceedings of the Academy of Political Science* 37 (3): 1–15.

Green, Charles, and Basil Wilson. 1989. *The Struggle for Black Empowerment in New York City: Beyond the Politics of Pigmentation.* Westport, CT: Praeger.

Hochschild, Jennifer. 2010. "International Migration at a Crossroads: Will Demography Change Politics before Politics Impedes Demographic Change?" Paper presented to conference on Citizenship in a Globalized World, University of New South Wales, Sydney, Australia, July.

Jennings, James. 1977. *Puerto Rican Politics in New York.* Washington, DC: University Press of America.

Jones Correa, Michael. 1998. *Between Two Nations: The Political Predicament of Latinos in New York City.* Ithaca, NY: Cornell University Press.

Lowi, Theodore. 1964. *At the Pleasure of the Mayor: Patronage and Politics in New York City, 1896–1956.* New York: Free Press.

Macchiarola, Frank J., and Joseph G. Diaz. 1993. "Decision Making in the Redistricting Process: Approaching Fairness." *Journal of Legislation* 199 (16): 199–224.

McNickle, Chris. 1993. *To Be Mayor of New York: Ethnic Politics in the City.* New York: Columbia University Press, 1993.

Mollenkopf, John. 1992. *A Phoenix in the Ashes: The Rise and Fall of the Koch Coalition in New York City Politics.* Princeton, NJ: Princeton University Press.

———. 2003. "New York: Still the Great Anomaly," in Rufus Browning, Dale Marshall, and David Tabb (eds.), *Racial Politics in American Cities.* 3d ed. New York: Longman.

Morawska, Ewa. 2001. "Immigrants, Transnationalism, and Ethnicization: A Comparison of this Great Wave and the Last," in Gary Gerstle and John Mollenkopf (eds.), *E Pluribus Unum? Contemporary and Historical Perspectives on Immigrant Political Incorporation.* New York: Russell Sage Foundation.

Rogers, Reuel R. 2006. *Afro-Caribbean Immigrants and the Politics of Incorporation: Ethnicity, Exception, or Exit.* New York: Cambridge University Press.

Sánchez, José R. 1996. "Puerto Rican Politics in New York," in Gabriel Haslip-Viera and Sherrie L. Baver (eds.), *Latinos in New York: Communities in Transition.* Notre Dame, IN: University of Notre Dame Press.

Sanjek, Roger. 1998. *The Future of Us All: Race and Neighborhood Politics in New York City.* Ithaca, NY: Cornell University Press.

Shefter, Martin. 1976. "The Emergence of the Machine: An Alternative View," in Willis D. Hawley and Michael Lipsky (eds.), *Theoretical Perspectives on Urban Politics.* Englewood Cliffs, NJ: Prentice-Hall.

———. 1994. "Political Incorporation and Political Extrusion: Party Politics and Social Forces in Postwar New York," in Martin Shefter (ed.), *Political Parties and the State: The American Historical Experience.* Princeton, NJ: Princeton University Press.

Smith, Robert C. 2005. *Mexican New York: Transnational Lives of New Immigrants.* Berkeley: University of California Press.

Smith, Rogers. 2003. *Stories of Peoplehood: The Politics and Morals of Political Membership.* New York: Cambridge University Press.

Sterne, Evelyn. 2001. "Beyond the Boss: Immigration and American Political Culture, 1880–1940," in Gary Gerstle and John Mollenkopf (eds.), *E Pluribus Unum? Contemporary and Historical Perspectives on Immigrant Political Incorporation*. New York: Russell Sage Foundation.

Wade, Richard C. 1990. "The Withering Away of the Party System," in Jewell Bellush and Dick Netzer (eds.), *Urban Politics New York Style*. New York: New York University Press.

Waldinger, Roger. 1996. *Still the Promised City?: African-Americans and New Immigrants in Postindustrial New York*. Cambridge, MA: Harvard University Press.

Walter, John C. 1989. *The Harlem Fox: J. Raymond Jones and Tammany, 1920–1970*. Albany: SUNY Press.

Wong, Janelle, Karthick Ramakrishnan, Taeku Lee, and Jane Junn. 2010. *Asian American Political Participation: Emerging Constituents and Identities*. New York: Russell Sage Foundation.

8

Immigrant Political Engagement and Incorporation in Amsterdam

FLORIS VERMEULEN, LAURE MICHON, AND JEAN TILLIE

Over the past 50 years, first- and second-generation immigrants have grown from less than 1 percent of Amsterdam's population to more than 50 percent (Wintershoven 2000; O+S 2010).[1] Given this profound demographic change, newcomers' political representation is especially relevant. How have immigrants entered the precincts of power in Amsterdam over the last two decades?[2] In exploring this question, we analyze the different processes of political incorporation of the city's three largest immigrant groups: Surinamese, Turks, and Moroccans. The results are, at first glance, puzzling. Surinamese and Moroccan immigrants have relatively low participation rates, but have had relatively high levels of political influence in certain periods, whereas Turkish immigrants have high participation rates, but have yet to gain influential executive political positions.

Not only do we describe these patterns of political incorporation, but we also attempt to make sense of and explain them. Several factors are at play, and it is the interaction among these factors that can explain the different patterns. In this chapter we focus especially on the effects of so-called group-based resources, such as ethnic organizations or strong ethnic identity, on immigrants' political engagement and incorporation and the way the Amsterdam context influences this relationship. Ethnic politics, and the use of group-based resources, can be a successful strategy for both political engagement and political incorporation as illustrated in the New York context (see Mollenkopf, this volume). We argue that in the current Amsterdam context, group-based resources have a double and opposite effect on two important dimensions of political incorporation; they stimulate political participation (because in Amsterdam it pays off for immigrant groups to mobilize and act collectively), but frustrate the attainment of influential positions for immigrant groups. Amsterdam political parties are crucial in understanding the negative effect of group-based resources on political incorporation. Using group-based resources is interpreted by the political parties as a form of ethnic politics, which is increasingly seen as highly problematic. Therefore individuals and groups who use group-based resources for political purposes, or those group-based resources which parties expect them to use, are frustrated in getting more influential political positions.

In order to explain the influential political position of some individuals of immigrant background, the political visibility of the group they belong to—as well as their individual skills as politicians and public administrators—are important. Political visibility, or the extent to which the immigrant group is visible in public debates (in a negative way), leads to increased political attention, which eventually provides more opportunities for individuals from that immigrant group to gain influential political positions (especially when the individuals do not have a strong link, or presumed link, with an ethnic constituency).

So the Amsterdam paradox is that groups with many group-based resources have higher rates of political participation, because of a receptive institutional environment, but at the same time have a more difficult time becoming politically influential because the established political elite evaluates ethnic politics as problematic and undesirable. By the same token, immigrant groups with fewer group-based resources, but which are seen by the public and eventually by the political parties as problematic, will get more attention, which can lead to more opportunities for some individuals of that group to gain political influence, even if the group itself has relatively low rates of political participation.

This chapter elaborates these points, beginning with background information on Surinamese, Turkish, and Moroccan immigrants in Amsterdam. It then examines the extent to which the three groups have been able to achieve political positions and influence. This is followed by an attempt to explain the differing positions of the three groups within the local political system.

Background on Surinamese, Turkish, and Moroccan Immigrants

Immigration from Surinam to the Netherlands has a long history, being intimately tied to the colonial relationship. The population of Surinam is comprised of several distinct ethnic groups, the largest being Afro-Surinamese or "Creoles" (descendants of African slaves) and the Indo-Surinamese or "Hindustanis" (descendants of contract laborers brought mainly from India to Surinam after the abolition of slavery in 1863). Before World War II, Surinamese immigrants in Amsterdam were predominantly children of the colonial elite or the Afro-Surinamese middle class studying or working in the capital city, Paramaribo. After the war, Surinamese migration became more ethnically diverse and economically driven. In the 1950s and 1960s, administrative personnel, teachers, and nurses arrived, still in small numbers, to work in the booming Dutch economy (Van Niekerk 1994). Surinam's approaching independence in 1975—and increased economic and political uncertainty—resulted in more people leaving the country. An exodus of more than 50,000 Surinamese took place over 1974 and 1975. As of 2010, about 9 percent of Amsterdam's population was of Surinamese origin.

The rapid population increase during the early 1970s caused serious social problems among Amsterdam's Surinamese immigrants as far as housing, unemployment, and mounting racism were concerned. The arrival of large numbers of low-skilled Surinamese workers after 1975 exacerbated the situation. High unemployment sparked by the Netherlands' worsening economy was keenly felt by this group. Deviant and even criminal lifestyles took root among unemployed Surinamese youth (Sansone 1992). The adverse media coverage reflected on the whole Afro-Surinamese population, which was associated with drug crime and violence. Resistance to Surinamese immigrants, tension, and discrimination within Dutch society became widespread in the 1970s (Van Niekerk 1994). But in the 1980s and 1990s, the socioeconomic position of Surinamese immigrants slowly improved. The level of discrimination against the Surinamese has also dropped considerably since the 1970s.

Both Turks and Moroccans arrived as (mainly male) guest workers in the late 1960s to take up low-skilled jobs in Amsterdam's heavy industry. After the economic crisis of the early 1970s, many became unemployed. At the same time, many sent for their families to join them. As a result of family reunification, both groups grew rapidly over the next decades. Moroccans now represent about 9 percent of Amsterdam's population, and Turks about 5 percent. Both groups are predominantly Muslim, making them a minority in a highly secular city and in a country where Islam is more and more cast in a negative light (Tillie 2008; see Uitermark, Duyvendak, and Rath, this volume). In public debates, Moroccans feature more visibly, being viewed as the most problematic minority group in Amsterdam. The media have constantly focused on negative incidents involving Moroccans and negative features of the Moroccan community: for instance, riots in the late 1990s between second-generation Moroccans and the police in an immigrant neighborhood, criminal activities like youth gangs, robberies, and other forms of petty theft involving people of Moroccan origin (Bovenkerk 2009), and the fact that filmmaker Theo van Gogh's murder in 2004 was carried out by a Dutch national of Moroccan descent. Headlines in newspapers and reports on television have stigmatized Moroccans, giving rise to labels such as criminals, problem youth, and religious extremists. One could argue that Moroccan immigrants have taken over the marginal position occupied by Surinamese in the 1970s. Indeed, Moroccans are presently the largest yet also the poorest immigrant minority group in the city (see table 8.1).

Table 8.1. Characteristics of the Largest Immigrant Groups in Amsterdam

	Size of immigrant group (2010)	% of Amsterdam population (2010)	Unemployment % (2007)	Average monthly family income in euros (2005)
Surinamese	68,881	9.0	9.7	1,700
Turks	40,370	5.3	12.1	1,550
Moroccans	69,439	9.0	11.8	1,310
Dutch	385,009	50.1	4.3	2,180

Note: The term "immigrant groups" includes those in the first and second generation.
Sources: O+S (2008, 2010).

Studying the Political Incorporation of Immigrants

Considering that political incorporation is a multifaceted process, several indicators ought to be used when measuring it. Following Ramakrishnan and Bloemraad (2008: 21), who differentiate between political presence and political weight, we look at immigrants' political presence or access to the political system (i.e., ability to participate in the political process and to be represented) as compared to their political weight or power and influence in the political system (i.e., rank within the local political hierarchy and the ability to make political decisions). Furthermore, it is important to acknowledge that political integration involves historical processes that develop over time (Lucassen and Lucassen 1997; Vermeulen 2006). Here we follow Hochschild and Mollenkopf (2009: 16) who argue that the political incorporation of immigrants is a process in which groups move from less to more incorporation, or vice versa. In their basic model Hochschild and Mollenkopf include different stages of political incorporation, (1) entry into the political arena, (2) involvement in the political arena, and (3) responsiveness of the political system to immigrants as well as immigrants' response to it. They explicitly mention that the process of political incorporation is not automatically linear, nor is there any guarantee that it will continue once started. The political incorporation process, in the model Hochschild and Mollenkopf put forward, encompasses views as well as interests, involves various forms of political activity, and includes changes caused by as well as changes that affect immigrants' political activity. In our analysis in this chapter we focus, on the one hand, on the entry and involvement of different immigrant groups in the Amsterdam political arena and, on the other hand, on the responsiveness "of and to" the political system by looking at the possibility for immigrant groups to actually influence policy outcomes.

In order to identify the level (or lack) of political incorporation in the different stages of the process described by Hochschild and Mollenkopf, we analyze three indicators of political activities of Turkish, Moroccan, and Surinamese immigrants in Amsterdam: voting, elected representatives, and appointed executive positions. We consider voting and elected representation to be the primary indicators of level of entry and involvement in the political arena (i.e., presence and representation), while the number of appointed executive positions is an indicator of the possibility to have political influence and impact (i.e., political weight and responsiveness of the political system). We draw on information we have gathered on the ethnic background of voters in local elections and the ethnic background of local representatives as well as executives on the city and city district level.

Of course the fact that representatives or executives have a certain ethnic background does not necessarily mean that they represent this particular group; they may have other political identities that are more important for their political activities than immigrant origin. As Hochschild and Mollenkopf (2009: 22) note, politicians of immigrant background face a classic dilemma. A representative from an immigrant group is expected to work on behalf of his or her whole group, regardless of whether its members are part of that person's constituency, whereas constituencies outside the immigrant group want their elected representative to show no ethnic favoritism. How immigrant politicians deal with this dilemma in Amsterdam is a question beyond the scope of this chapter and calls for further study. In what follows we confine ourselves to looking at the collective voting behavior of different immigrant groups and the extent to which individual immigrants have entered the precincts of power in Amsterdam.

Obviously our formal indicators of political engagement and political incorporation are limited measures. They ignore informal forms of political and civic engagement outside of formal electoral politics in civic organizations such as labor unions and protest activities, which can be important aspects of political engagement and incorporation. Immigrant organizations, for instance, can engage in demonstrations and protest activities, and the organizations have been used by government officials in the Netherlands to gather information on and build communication channels in dealing with intergroup relations between immigrants and majority residents. Immigrants may also participate in existing native-Dutch organizations. A recent study found that a large percentage of Surinamese, Turkish, and Moroccan immigrants are active as members, volunteers, or board members in nonprofit organizations in the Netherlands (SCP 2008; for Amsterdam, see Vermeulen 2005, 2006, and Vermeulen et al. 2010). Another recent study, on the political participation of Muslims in the Netherlands, found that

28 percent participated in an informal political activity and 59 percent indicated an interest in political matters (Roex et al. 2010). If studies show that many immigrants in the Netherlands, including Amsterdam, are engaged in various kinds of informal forms of political action, we are concerned here, as we have emphasized, with a different topic: the question of power and political influence, which leads us to focus on more formal forms of political engagement and incorporation.

Political Participation and Representation of Immigrants in Amsterdam

Amsterdam provides a favorable context for the political engagement and representation of immigrants for several reasons.

First, there are features of the political system in Amsterdam (and the Netherlands as a whole). Elections occur through a party list system, with pure proportionality and very low thresholds. Parties make lists of candidates to be elected, and seats are allocated to each party in proportion to the number of votes. Effectively, there is a threshold so that a party must receive a minimum percentage of votes to obtain seats. Given the extremely low thresholds in the Netherlands, in the 2002 Amsterdam elections, for example, only 2.22 percent of the votes were needed to win a seat in the local council. Another important feature providing a favorable context for minority groups is the ability to cast preferential votes, which means that on election day the voter not only chooses a party, but also votes for a specific candidate of that party. In constructing their lists of candidates before elections, each party decides on the order of candidates, though voters can select a listed candidate who will independently earn a seat upon getting enough votes. Direct election through preferential votes requires only about 1,600 votes depending on the overall turnout rates. The ability to cast a preferential vote means that minority candidates who are placed at low, seemingly hopeless positions on electoral lists might still win if a significant group of ethnic voters mobilizes for their election. The system of proportionality favors representation in terms of gender and social background (Farrell 2001) and the system of preferential voting increases this effect.

Second, in 1985, the Netherlands began allowing noncitizens to participate in local elections after five years of legal residence in the country. It is unnecessary to even register: the municipal administration automatically mails voter registration cards to all inhabitants entitled to vote.[3] In 2006, nearly 580,000 inhabitants (77 percent of the population) were entitled to vote in Amsterdam (Hylkema and Van Zee 2006: 3). The enfranchisement of foreigners has had a direct effect on electoral politics via participation in elections, as well as an indirect effect in that parties list immigrants to appeal to the foreign electorate.

As we elaborate below, the results of local elections between 1994 and 2010 show that Turks have profited the most from the favorable Amsterdam context and have the highest rate of political participation and political representation.

Voting

Figures on electoral turnout for immigrants—defined as individuals who are foreign born or have at least one foreign-born parent—for five consecutive local elections (1994–2010) demonstrate that immigrant turnout is almost always lower than overall turnout (see table 8.2).

The figures also reveal that Turks have greater participation in elections than Moroccans or Surinamese (Michon et al. 2007). Moreover, in some cases, their turnout rate has been comparable to—if not higher—than overall turnout (in 1994 and 2006). The Moroccan turnout rate

Table 8.2. Turnout of Immigrant Voters in Amsterdam, 1994–2010 (Percentages)

Voter's country of origin	1994	1998	2002	2006	2010
Surinam	30	21	26	26	26
Turkey	67	39	30	51	46
Morocco	49	23	22	37	39
Overall turnout	56.8	45.7	47.8	50.8	51.3

Sources: Tillie (2000); Michon and Tillie (2003a); Van Heelsum and Tillie (2006); O+S (2010).

has been substantially lower than the overall rate, while the Surinamese turnout rate has been the lowest among all immigrant groups in the city and shows little variation.

Elected Representatives

Amsterdam's 45-seat city council, the city's legislative body, has important powers: it sets the agenda, passes regulations, and controls the actions of the executive. The executive, formed by the mayor and his or her deputies, has to abide by the decisions of the council. The executive also needs the council's support, since coalitions can crumble if there is a lack of confidence in the executive. In such a scenario, coalitions must be rebuilt during the council's term in office, but if this is not possible, new elections must be called. The number of councilors of immigrant origin has risen gradually, as table 8.3 shows. The highest share of immigrants elected to Amsterdam's city council was in 2006, when a fifth of local councilors were either born abroad or were the children of immigrants. In 2010, however, the steady upswing was interrupted and, for the first time since 1990, the number of immigrants elected to the council decreased from the prior election—although bear in mind that, because Amsterdam's council is relatively small, minor fluctuations in the number of councilors translate into substantial statistical changes.

Compared to their share of Amsterdam's general population, Turks were proportionately represented in the city council between 1994 and

Table 8.3. Amsterdam City Councilors of Immigrant Origin, 1990–2010

	Election					
Origin of councilors	1990	1994	1998	2002	2006	2010
Surinam	3	2	4	2	3	2
Turkey	1	3	3	4	3	2
Morocco	0	1	2	1	2	3
Other	0	0	0	1	1	0
Total	4	6	9	8	9	7
As % of whole council (N=45)	9	13	20	18	20	16

Source: Michon et al. (2007).

2010. Moroccans have always been statistically underrepresented. Yet in 2010, for the first time, more Moroccans were elected to council than Turks. Although Surinamese were well represented in the city council (compared to their share of Amsterdam's population) in the 1990s, since 2002, they have been statistically underrepresented.

Currently, seven of Amsterdam's eight districts have elected councils.[4] In formal terms, the districts are commissions of the city council, and their role depends on what the city council decides to delegate them. District policies mainly concern the management of public space, spatial and economic planning, welfare, culture, sports, and recreation (Barlow 2000: 277). Up until the 2010 elections, Amsterdam had 14 district councils with a total of 322 elected councilors. In 2002, 15 district councilors were Turkish, 14 Moroccan, and 12 Surinamese (respectively, 4.7, 4.3, and 3.7 percent of all district councilors). In 2006, the numbers had risen to, respectively, 22, 20, and 19 (6.8, 6.2, and 5.9 percent).[5] As the figures make clear, Turks have not suffered from unequal representation in district councils over the past years whereas statistical representation of Moroccans and Surinamese lags behind their share in the population—although, it is worth noting, that by international standards, Moroccan and Surinamese representation on local councils is substantial (Mollenkopf and Hochschild 2010). For the Surinamese it is important to be aware that, in 2002, a remarkable 75 percent of the district councilors elected in Zuidoost— where a large part of the city's Surinamese population is concentrated—were Surinamese. In 2006, this percentage had decreased to 43 percent, but it shot up again in 2010. Not surprisingly, immigrant district councilors are generally concentrated in districts where the proportion of Surinamese, Turks, and Moroccans is highest.

In 2010, to give the most recent figures, 20 percent of all district councilors in Amsterdam were of immigrant origin; among them, Turks were most numerous and overrepresented (comprising 6 percent of all councilors), followed by Surinamese (comprising 6 percent of all councilors, almost 75 percent in Zuidoost), while Moroccans were underrepresented (comprising 3 percent of all councilors).

As previously suggested, we must be careful about drawing definitive conclusions from these indicators, as we do not have information on more informal forms of political engagement (e.g., protest activities) or political representation (e.g., informal consultation of immigrant leaders by local authorities). Furthermore the differences among the groups are not always that substantial or significant. This said, the data we presented indicate that in terms of formal political engagement and political representation Turkish immigrants in Amsterdam display higher rates than the Moroccan or Surinamese.

Political Influence of Immigrants in Amsterdam

When it comes to political influence the picture is rather different. We measure political influence of immigrants in Amsterdam by taking into account the number of individuals with an immigrant background in executive positions, which also provides an indication of the responsiveness of political parties to immigrant groups. Admittedly—and to repeat—caution is needed in interpreting the results since we lack information about informal forms of political influence; additional indicators are needed to fully measure the level of political parties' responsiveness to immigrant groups. However, we believe that the number of executive positions provides important insights into the patterns of political incorporation of immigrant groups in Amsterdam.

Executive Positions

By executive positions, we refer to the positions of mayor, deputy mayor at the city level, and district mayor or district deputy mayor at the city district level. The mayors of Dutch municipalities are not elected by either the population or the municipal council. Instead, they are appointed (for a period of six years) on the basis of the choices made by a commission of the council, which are validated by the Ministry of the Interior (mayors are then formally appointed by the queen). Dutch mayors, particularly in big cities, can be characterized as professional managers. Their main duty is to secure public order and provide leadership in the everyday executive functions of the city. In 2002, a strict separation between the council (the legislative body controlling the executives) and the mayor and deputy mayors (the executives) was introduced in the Netherlands. As a result, it is now possible for deputy mayors to be appointed who may or may not be on a party list—and this happens quite often. Deputy mayors are appointed by the winning coalition. A coalition refers to those political parties that agree to govern the city until the next elections and who together have a majority of all seats in the city council (at least 23 seats). The deputy mayors have different domains for which they are politically responsible. At the district level, the party list's leading candidate who wins the most votes in a district nearly always becomes district mayor. In other words, while the district mayor is elected, the mayor and the deputy mayors (whether at the city or district levels) are appointed.

Table 8.4 provides information about Amsterdam's executive position holders of Surinamese, Turkish, and Moroccan origin since 2002. The most well known, Moroccan-born Ahmed Aboutaleb, was the first (and only) city deputy mayor of Moroccan origin in Amsterdam (2004–2007). He subsequently became secretary of state of social affairs (2007–2008) and mayor of Rotterdam (in 2009). It is striking that there are many more Moroccan and Surinamese than Turkish executives. Amsterdam has had a city-level deputy mayor of Moroccan origin twice and a city-level deputy mayor of Surinamese descent three times, though never one of Turkish origin. The same holds true for district mayors. After the 2010 elections, two of the seven city district mayors were of Moroccan descent and one of Surinamese descent, whereas no city district mayor of Turkish descent was ever elected. Typically, the city district mayors of Surinamese descent have been elected in the heavily Surinamese Zuidoost district. These include Elvira Sweet, born in Amsterdam to Surinamese immigrant parents, who previously was manager of a large social welfare organization in the city and Suriname-born Marcel la Rose, who moved to the Netherlands to study and became president of Kwakoe, one of the largest Surinamese community-based organizations in Amsterdam, and then a local businessman in Zuidoost. Politicians of Turkish origin have been present as district deputy mayors, though to a lesser extent than Moroccans or Surinamese.

Overall, then, Turks have been most successful at gaining entry (access) into the Amsterdam political arena. Compared to Surinamese and Moroccans, they display higher voter turnout rates over time and, with the exception of the last (2010) election, have had higher rates of elected representation at the city and city district levels. The data,

Table 8.4. Number of Position Holders of Surinamese, Turkish, and Moroccan Origin in Amsterdam, 2002–2010

	Of Surinamese origin			Of Turkish origin			Of Moroccan origin		
	Deputy mayor	City district mayor	City district deputy mayor	Deputy mayor	City district mayor	City district deputy mayor	Deputy mayor	City district mayor	City district deputy mayor
2002	2	I	I	0	0	I	I	0	I
2006	I	I	I	0	0	I	I	2	3
2010	0	I	2	0	0	I	0	2	I

Note: Some of these positions are filled by the same individual during different periods of government. We have therefore counted positions rather than persons here.

however, also indicate that the position of Turkish representatives has weakened over time: their city council level presence has decreased and they fail to get appointed to executive positions. Moroccans and Surinamese, by contrast, show low rates of political participation and representation. However, Moroccans and Surinamese have been incorporated at the top of Amsterdam's political system—in executive positions—more successfully than have Turks, suggesting that the political system is responsive to their political demands.

As noted, the base of Surinamese political influence lies in Zuidoost, a district with many Surinamese and African immigrants. Up until 2006, politicians of Surinamese descent were able to use Zuidoost as a springboard to political positions at the city level, to become either city deputy mayor or city councilor. An example is Hannah Belliot. Born in Suriname, she came to study in the Netherlands and then worked as a teacher and director of a pedagogical institute in Amsterdam. She was elected district mayor of Zuidoost in 1998 after fierce protests by city district civil servants and local politicians of mainly Surinamese descent against the overrepresentation of "white" politicians in executive power in the district. She remained in this position until 2002. Belliot, who was called the "queen of Zuidoost" by many in the Surinamese community, was appointed city deputy mayor in 2002. Recently, the route from Zuidoost to the City Hall has become more difficult for city district politicians of Surinamese descent. One reason is that the

Surinamese community is no longer seen as problematic as it had been by Amsterdam politicians, who feel there is less need to have politicians of Surinamese origin on the city council's executive board.

Group-Based Resources as an Explanation for the Pattern of Political Incorporation

Differences between immigrant groups in terms of political mobilization and incorporation have often been explained by scholars as reflecting the groups' social and economic position (Verba et al. 1993; Jacobs et al. 2004). However, Turks, Moroccans, and Surinamese to a large extent have comparable social and economic positions in Amsterdam, thus failing to explain the diverging patterns we have described. Indeed, contrary to what the literature would lead us to expect, Surinamese, although having a somewhat better social economic position than the other two groups, display the lowest rates of political participation.

This is why we turn to the study of group-based resources, which, we argue, are critical in understanding the differing political participation rates among the three groups. We define group-based resources as resources that are present within minority groups, such as the strength of group identity, the level of group consciousness, the number of ethnic organizations, and the level of ethnic organizational membership. All these features can have an effect on the political behavior of minority groups, as has been suggested by other studies. For certain groups and in some contexts, it makes a significant difference whether immigrants identify themselves as a coherent group and have strong (ethnic or religious) group consciousness. Shingles (1981), for instance, posits that group consciousness among African Americans in the 1960s was associated with both a high degree of political efficacy and a low degree of government trust, which thereby increased their political activities. Other studies argue that immigrant groups lacking human capital and that are confronted with a hostile environment are especially likely to organize along ethnic lines in reaction to the unreceptive context (Portes and Rumbaut 1996). In particular, stigmatized minorities facing a hostile environment tend to develop a clearer perception of group interest, which can produce stronger group consciousness and more group-based resources that can be used for a collective political trajectory (Lee 2008). Group-based resources also affect the extent to which immigrants organize along ethnic lines and the number of immigrant organizations. More group-based resources lead to greater group consciousness, also typically leading to more immigrant organizations and immigrants joining ethnic organizations (Schrover and Vermeulen 2005; Vermeulen 2006).

Fennema and Tillie (1999, 2001) found a striking difference in the civic and political participation of immigrants in Amsterdam in the late 1990s: of all immigrant groups, Turks displayed the highest rates of political participation as well as the highest rates of political trust. The authors explained this difference by using a civic community model. Turkish immigrants are believed to be the most "civic" immigrant group in the city, as they have the highest organizational density and their organizations are tightly connected by a dense network of interlocking directorates (ibid.). Through this dense network of Turkish organizations (which is an important group-based resource), civic virtues are created; these virtues are transferred to a wider circle of the Turkish community in Amsterdam, which leads to a more active and politically interested group of immigrants. Other studies have also shown that the Turkish and Moroccan communities in the Netherlands contrast significantly in terms of community strength. The Turkish community is much more cohesive than the Moroccan, as it is characterized by strong ethnic networks and a high degree of internal social interaction. Turkish immigrants in the Netherlands primarily socialize with other Turkish immigrants, whereas a significant share of Moroccan immigrants have strong social ties with people of other ethnic backgrounds (Van Heelsum 2002; Dagevos et al. 2007; Crul and Doomernik 2003).[6]

Table 8.5 provides data on the organizational densities of the Moroccan, Turkish, Surinamese, and native Dutch groups in Amsterdam in recent years, indicating the number of organizations present for every 1,000 persons within each group.[7] The table shows that Turks and Surinamese have a higher organizational density than Moroccans, which corresponds with data for the 1980s and the 1990s (Vermeulen 2006). The most important difference between Turks and Surinamese is that the Turkish organizations are more closely linked together by transnational ideological movements, such as Milli Görüş or Fethullah Gülen, whereas the Surinamese organizations are more isolated from each

Table 8.5. Organizational Density of Surinamese, Turks, Moroccans, and Native Dutch in Amsterdam, 2002–2007

	Surinamese	Turks	Moroccans	Native Dutch
Density of ethnic organizations, 2002	14.2	15.9	8.7	24.2
Density of ethnic organizations, 2007	14.0	13.3	7.5	26.9
Percentage of immigrant population belonging to an ethnic organization, 2007	17%	44%	25%	–

Density = number of ethnic organizations per 1,000 immigrants.
Sources: Vermeulen et al. (2010); Dekker (2008: 91).

other and revolve around certain individuals (Fennema and Tillie 2001; Vermeulen 2006; Mügge 2011).

Table 8.5 also shows the percentages of active members of organizations and, more specifically, ethnic immigrant organizations. A significantly higher number of Turks than Moroccans and Surinamese participate in ethnic immigrant organizations, reflecting the high levels of ethnic civic participation among the Turks. The Surinamese are characterized by an active elite (and relatively high levels of political representation and organizations) but with a more passive immigrant constituency. According to these indicators, the Moroccans possess the lowest level of group-based resources.

These differences in group-based resources among the groups can lead to different patterns of political incorporation, as several recent Amsterdam examples illustrate. The first concerns the Nieuw-West[8] district's contest for first place on the dominant party's electoral list for the 2010 elections. Stakes were high: the leading candidate would undoubtedly become mayor of that district.Two young candidates of Moroccan descent campaigned for the position in what became a hard-hitting, tight competition. Influential national politicians tried to intervene (albeit unsuccessfully), attracting attention from local and nationwide media. Their common ethnic background notwithstanding, the competition boiled down to a race between individuals, two local politicians battling it out within the political framework of their social-democratic party, PvdA. Yet the Moroccan community, characterized by relatively weak group-based resources, ultimately had no significant influence on the election's outcome.

The second example concerns the collective initiative by a number of local politicians of Turkish background to improve the Turkish community's chances in the 2010 elections. These politicians formed a "Turkish network" that would approach the four main political parties a few months before the elections. Their aim was to increase awareness of the need to include more candidates of Turkish origin on the party lists, thus providing a list of "high potentials": individuals who would be able to hold a prominent place on a list and/or were qualified to become deputy mayor (Michon and Vermeulen 2010). This initiative, though unsuccessful in bringing about the desired electoral results, shows how the Turkish ethnic constituency was mobilized for political action.

The third example involves the Surinamese. In 2008 a deputy mayor of Surinamese descent had to step down because of political mistakes. The Surinamese elite demanded publicly that a new deputy mayor be of Surinamese descent. Several public meetings were organized by Surinamese organizations in which local politicians discussed this issue further; these events did raise local media attention but were eventually not effective. Although the Surinamese, in this case, mobilized to try to improve their political representation, in the end a new deputy mayor was appointed who was not of Surinamese descent.

To summarize, Turks in Amsterdam possess more group-based resources than the Surinamese and the Moroccans. Their networks within the ethnic community are stronger, and they have founded and maintained more immigrant organizations. There are also indications that Turks have used these group-based resources politically, by stressing common political goals, as exemplified by the Turkish election network we just mentioned and that politicians of Turkish descent have stronger relationships with immigrant organizations than do politicians of Moroccan descent. The group-based resources of the Turks also partly explain their higher rates of political participation and representation as they mobilize the immigrant constituency and preferential voting among co-ethnics.

Political Parties' Acceptance of Group-Based Resources

The group-based resources we have described help account for different patterns of political mobilization, yet they are, surprisingly, a disadvantage in the current Amsterdam context when it comes to obtaining influential political positions. Understanding the position of the political parties and the history of policies developed for immigrant groups in Amsterdam helps to explain this puzzle.

Since 1953, left-wing parties have consistently held more seats than the right in Amsterdam's municipal council, and the social democrats have remained dominant (Berveling 1994: 25). For the last 20 years, the social democratic PvdA has always come out first in elections, followed by the social-liberal D66, the right-wing VVD, and the green Groen-Links. Coalitions formed for the executive have changed regularly over the past years, though the PvdA has always played a pivotal role, deciding which other parties it would govern the city with (ibid.). In a majority of district councils, the social democrats have also held a dominant position.

The social-democratic party's dominance in Amsterdam has major implications for the mobilization of immigrants. Immigrants seeking political power or influence must be willing to interact with the PvdA. Likewise, immigrants' access to elected positions largely depends on choices made by this party concerning inclusion. While there have been some efforts by parties to include immigrants in Amsterdam's political process, such ventures were more prominent in the past than in recent years.

Insights from studies on candidate selection help to illuminate the dynamics behind the more limited efforts to include immigrants in the recent period. The procedure of candidate selection is more or less the same for all significant parties in Amsterdam: a selection committee auditions candidates, receives support statements from individuals or party groups, and then drafts a list of candidates. Party members consequently set the final candidate order, as they vote on each position on the electoral list. The composition and functioning of the selection committees is thus crucial. Studies have shown that it is precisely at this stage that obstacles to the inclusion of immigrants arise, as the committees are predominantly composed of white, middle-aged men who use limited means to scout candidates (Berger et al. 2001: 53; Leijenaar et al. 1999: 41, 105). While in the past, selection committees prioritized the inclusion of more immigrants on party lists (Berger et al. 2001: 58–60), this has not been the case more recently. A study conducted on the

2009 candidate selection process within the local branches of six parties in Amsterdam showed that selection committees were not encouraged to take ethnic diversity into account: none of the major parties had strict rules concerning the inclusion of immigrants (or women) (Michon and Vermeulen 2013). Parties officially stated that they wanted to include minorities, but were generally unsuccessful, and did not try to correct or vary the composition of their lists in order to achieve more balanced representation. The result of this was immediate: the number of councilors of foreign origin in Amsterdam decreased between 2006 and 2010 from nine to six.

We believe that the reduction in parties' efforts to include immigrants on their electoral lists is related to the more general suspicion toward immigrants and group-based politics recently displayed in the Netherlands' public and political debates. This is a shift from the past. In the 1980s, local integration policy in Amsterdam has been characterized as multicultural. Policy makers, for instance, used ethnic categorization to formulate and implement policy in order to improve the position of immigrants in Amsterdam. Immigrant groups were classified as official minority groups entitled to specific policy measures. These official minority groups became eligible for direct subsidies to establish and develop their own ethnic organizations. In addition, minority advisory councils were established for each group separately to advise local politicians about how to solve the problems of the different immigrant groups. In such a context, group-based resources were encouraged, strengthened, and stimulated by local government policy. Group consciousness, the number of ethnic organizations, and the membership of ethnic organizations all increased among the different immigrant groups in Amsterdam during this period (Vermeulen 2006). In general it was seen as legitimate to use group-based resources for political purposes.

However, during the 1990s, Amsterdam politicians were increasingly discontent with the multicultural ideals and results of the policies adopted. Slowly they began to change the multicultural elements of their policies—decreasing subsidies for immigrant organizations, diminishing the role of minority advisory councils, and formulating more general policies instead of specific projects for marginalized groups. By 1999, local authorities had officially changed a multicultural policy to a diversity policy. Within this diversity policy framework, the focus was now on social problems across the entire Amsterdam population, not just among specific target groups. The central aim of this diversity policy was for all residents to feel "at home" in their city and to ensure that everyone had equal opportunity to participate in society. The new diversity policy was intended to better serve the diverse Amsterdam population by focusing on differences among individuals instead of among groups: it clearly and explicitly did not target groups (Vermeulen 2008; Vermeulen and Plaggenborg 2009; Uitermark 2010). In practice this meant that specific immigrant groups could no longer count on specific policy attention. Policy makers tried to take ethnicity into account as little as possible when formulating and executing local social policy; subsidies for immigrant organizations were phased out and minority advisory councils abolished. In this new policy context, group-based resources have been increasingly seen as problematic as these resources are linked to specific target groups, which the new diversity policy was designed to move away from.

The backlash against multiculturalism in the Netherlands (Prins and Saharso 2010), including in Amsterdam, increased further in the first decade of the twenty-first century and resulted in fewer opportunities for group-based politics (Vermeulen and Plaggenborg 2009). At the organizational level, it has had especially negative consequences for the city's Moroccan organizations, as Moroccans lack group-based resources to maintain high numbers of immigrant organizations. In terms of political weight—specifically, access to politically influential positions—the backlash has also had negative ramifications for Turkish politicians, who have strong ties within their ethnic community and are seen by parties as representing group-based interests, and for the Surinamese group as well in which the elite also makes use of group-based resources for political purposes. However, paradoxically enough, the backlash against multiculturalism seems to have provided more opportunities for politicians of Moroccan descent. Similar to what studies in the United States show (Akpetar 2009), groups defined as "model minorities" tend to be ignored by political parties, with more attention going to the group that is perceived as most problematic. In the Amsterdam case, Moroccans have been seen as most problematic. Their group-based resources declined even further in the last decade. Yet while Moroccans as a (policy) category have not been targeted, individual politicians of Moroccan descent have been given opportunities by political parties to enter the precincts of power as long as they do not engage in overt ethnic politics and, at the same time, seek to come up with solutions for the perceived problems that Moroccan immigrants have been causing the city.

In principle then, Turks, Moroccans, and Surinamese face a similar set of institutions and structures (legal and electoral rules and the local party system) that frame their opportunities for political participation. And yet, recent developments in the political climate—what Koopmans and Olzak (2005) have called the discursive opportunity structure—impact the groups differently. On one hand, the integration debate's increasingly harsh tone is fixated on the position of Moroccans, who are believed to be more violent and show more delinquent behavior than other groups and have, as a consequence, become even more visible to the public eye. This negative perception is probably also what makes them more appealing as members of political parties, for both symbolic and political reasons. On the other hand, parties in Amsterdam are less keen on incorporating immigrants as groups. Group-based mobilization is no longer openly valued in the Dutch political arena, and this may affect the position of those who do mobilize mainly along ethnic lines, such as Turks, but to a certain extent also the Surinamese.

Conclusions

Amsterdam's three main immigrant groups—Surinamese, Turks, and Moroccans—display very different patterns and stages of political engagement and incorporation. An understanding of these patterns requires an examination of a combination of factors, including the institutional opportunity structure, the structure of immigrant communities, and political party attitudes.

The outcomes we have described lead to several conclusions about the current political position of these groups in Amsterdam. Turks have a well-organized community and, compared to other groups, participate most in the political process, but are excluded from executive positions. This situation, in our opinion, is due to political parties' wariness of strong ethnic communities and group-based political mobilizations as well as the fact that Turks are not perceived to be a problematic group, even though their socioeconomic position is similar to that of Moroccans and they, too, are Muslim. In other words: Turks in Amsterdam are not favored for executive positions because their community is seen to be strong and active, and their public image is not one of troublemakers. At the same time, their well-organized community, in combination with a favorable institutional opportunity structure, produces a statistical overrepresentation in city and district councils.

Moroccans do not mobilize as strongly as Turks in either organizational or political terms though they do attain many executive positions. We argue that this has to do with their visibility in public debates: political parties want to show that, by putting Moroccan role models at the forefront, they are tackling the problems Moroccans are seen to cause. Because political parties are reluctant to see strong group-based mobilization in politics, the Moroccans who obtain executive positions are party politicians who mostly refrain from ethnic politics.

Surinamese, who display a fragmented community and have an active elite, are well represented in Amsterdam's political arena, though they have lately lost ground in terms of executive positions. Surinamese were the most visible community in the 1980s and 1990s and their well-educated, active elite found its way into the political arena. Having lost visibility and the backing of a strong community, however, they also have lost political weight. This illustrates how groups may become less influential and less well represented over time (Hochschild and Mollenkopf 2009). In our opinion, this development could easily occur in the future for Moroccan politicians, who also lack the support of a well-defined, well-organized community. As for Turks, we think it is unlikely that they will disappear in high numbers from councils or district councils thanks to their community's strong civic mobilization. As we have shown, political parties in Amsterdam have a lot of leeway when it comes to candidate selection and the appointment of position holders. Still, the parties cannot altogether neglect the electoral power of the well-organized, dense Turkish community. At the end of the day, parties want to win votes and, from this point of view, a civic community is a political asset.

NOTES

1. In this chapter, the term "immigrant" refers to the Dutch-born second generation as well as the foreign-born first generation.
2. This chapter builds on Michon and Vermeulen (2013) by adding another group,
the Surinamese, to the analysis.
3. All inhabitants of the Netherlands are required to register with the city upon
moving into a municipality. Registration data are used, among other things, to
determine who is entitled to vote.
4. District Westpoort has no council due to the limited size of its population.
5. For elections prior to 2002, no comprehensive data are available.
6. Buijs and Nelissen (1994: 202–3) argue that the roots of this difference can be
found in the historical development of both countries of origin. The Turkish
nation-state is for many of its emigrants in the Netherlands a source of pride
and unity—a sentiment not shared by other groups when reflecting on their
country of origin. For many Moroccan immigrants in the Netherlands, the
Moroccan nation-state is characterized by corruption and social injustice. Lack
of national pride and the weaker social networks among Moroccans make for a
weaker community compared to that of Turks.
7. A Turkish, Moroccan, or Surinamese organization is defined here as an officially
registered not-for-profit, at least half of whose board members are born in,
respectively, Turkey, Morocco, or Suriname (i.e., are first-generation immigrants) (Vermeulen 2006). Organizations of second-generation Turkish and
Moroccan immigrants are classified in table 8.5 as "Dutch" because their board
members were born in the Netherlands. However, second-generation organizations in Amsterdam amounted to less than 1 percent in both 2002 and 2007
(Vermeulen et al. 2010).
8. Nieuw-West, one of Amsterdam's eight districts, has over 130,000 inhabitants,
about 17 percent of the city population. More than 59 percent of Nieuw-West's
residents are of immigrant background, which is slightly more than the 50
percent for the entire city; about 12 percent are of Moroccan background, compared to 9 percent for Amsterdam as a whole.

REFERENCES

Aptekar, Sofya. 2009. "Organizational Life and Political Incorporation of Two Asian
Immigrant Groups: A Case Study." *Ethnic and Racial Studies* 32: 1511–33.
Barlow, Max. 2000. "Amsterdam and the Question of Metropolitan Government," in
Leon Deben, Willem Heinemeijer, and Dick van der Vaart (eds.), *Understanding
Amsterdam: Essays on Economic Vitality, City Life, and Urban Form.* Amsterdam:
Het Spinhuis.
Berger, Maria, Anja van Heelsum, Meindert Fennema, Jean Tillie, and Rick Wolff.
2001. *Politieke participatie van etnische minderheden in vier steden.* Amsterdam:
IMES.

Berveling, Jacob. 1994. *Het stempel op de besluitvorming: Macht, invloed en besluitvorming op twee Amsterdamse beleidsterreinen.* Amsterdam: Thesis Publishers.

Bovenkerk, Frank. 2009. *Etniciteit, criminaliteit en het strafrecht.* The Hague: Boom Juridische Uitgevers.

Crul, Maurice, and Jeroen Doomernik. 2003. "The Turkish and Moroccan Second Generation in the Netherlands: Divergent Trends between and Polarization within the Two Groups." *International Migration Review* 37: 1039–64.

Dagevos, Jaco, Roelof Schellingerhout, and Miranda Vervoort. 2007. "Sociaal-culturele integratie en religie," in Jaco Dagevos and Mérove Gijsberts (eds.), *Jaarrapport Integratie SCP.* The Hague: SCP.

Dekker, Lisette, and Brahim Fattah. 2006. "Meer diversiteit in de gemeenteraden." *IPP Nieuwsbrief Zomer 2006*: 7–10.

Dekker, Paul. 2008. "Civil Society," in Andries van den Broek and Saskia Keuzenkamp (eds.), *Het dagelijks leven van allochtone stedelingen.* The Hague: SCP.

Eldersveld, Samuel J. 1998. "Party Change and Continuity in Amsterdam: An Empirical Study of Local Organizational Adaptation." *Party Politics* 4: 319–46.

Farrell, David. 2001. *Electoral Systems: A Comparative Introduction.* Basingstoke: Palgrave.

Fennema, Meindert. 2004. "Concept and Measurement of Civic Communities." *Journal of Ethnic and Migration Studies* 30: 429–47.

Fennema, Meindert, and Jean Tillie. 1999. "Political Participation and Political Trust in Amsterdam: Civic Communities and Ethnic Networks." *Journal of Ethnic and Migration Studies* 25: 703–26.

———. 2001. "Civic Community, Political Participation and Political Trust of Ethnic Groups." *Connections* 23: 44–59.

———. 2004. "Do Immigrant Policies Matter? Ethnic Civic Communities and Immigrant Policies in Amsterdam, Liège and Zurich," in Rinus Penninx, Karen Kraal, Marco Martiniello, and Steven Vertovec (eds.), *Citizenship in European Cities: Immigrants, Local Politics and Integration Policies.* Aldershot: Ashgate.

Garbaye, Romain. 2005. *Getting into Local Power: The Politics of Ethnic Minorities in British and French Cities.* Malden: Blackwell.

Hochschild, Jennifer, and John Mollenkopf. 2009. "Modeling Immigrant Political Incorporation," in Jennifer Hochschild and John Mollenkopf (eds.), *Bringing Outsiders In: Transatlantic Perspectives on Immigrant Political Incorporation.* Ithaca, NY: Cornell University Press.

Hylkema, Cor, and Wim van Zee. 2006. *Verkiezingen 2006, Gemeenteraad Amsterdam: Definitieve uitslag.* Amsterdam: Gemeente Amsterdam, Dienst Onderzoek en Statistiek.

Jacobs, Dirk, Karen Phalet, and Marc Swyngedouw. 2004. "Associational Membership and Political Involvement among Ethnic Minority Groups in Brussels." *Journal of Ethnic and Migration Studies* 30: 543–59.

Koopmans, Ruud, and Susan Olzak. 2004. "Discursive Opportunities and the Evolution of Right-Wing Violence in Germany." *American Journal of Sociology* 110: 198–230.

Lee, Taeku. 2008. "Race, Immigration and the Identity-to-Politics Link." *Annual Review of Political Science* 11: 457–78.

Leijenaar, Monique, Kees Niemöller, and Astrid van der Kooij. 1999. *"Kandidaten gezocht": Politieke partijen en het streven naar grotere diversiteit onder gemeenteraden.* Amsterdam: Instituut voor Publiek en Politiek.

Michon, Laure, and Jean Tillie. 2003. *Amsterdamse polyfonie: Opkomst en stemgedrag van allochtone Amsterdammers bij de gemeenteraads en deelraadsverkiezingen van 6 maart 2002.* Amsterdam: IMES.

Michon, Laure, Jean Tillie, and Anja van Heelsum. 2007. "Political Participation of Migrants in the Netherlands since 1986," paper presented at the ECPR Joint Sessions, Helsinki, May 7–12, 2007.

Michon, Laure, and Floris Vermeulen. 2009. "Organizing for Access? The Political Mobilization of Turks in Amsterdam." *Turkish Studies*, 10 (2): 255–75.

———. 2013. "Explaining Different Trajectories in Immigrant Political Integration: Moroccans and Turks in Amsterdam." *West European Politics* 36: 597–614.

Mollenkopf, John, and Jennifer Hochschild. 2010. "Immigrant Political Incorporation: Comparing Success in the United States and Western Europe." *Ethnic and Racial Studies* 33: 19–38.

Mügge, Liza. 2011. *Beyond Dutch Borders. Transnational Politics among Colonial Migrants, Guest Workers and the Second Generation.* Amsterdam: Amsterdam University Press.

Odmalm, Pontus. 2005. *Migration Policies and Political Participation: Inclusion or Intrusion in Western Europe?* Basingstoke: Palgrave.

O+S (Onderzoek en Statistiek Amsterdam). 2008. *Amsterdam in cijfers 2008.* Amsterdam: Dienst Onderzoek en Statistiek.

———. 2010. *Fact sheet: De diversiteit van de Amsterdamse bevolking.* Amsterdam: Dienst Onderzoek en Statistiek.

Portes, Alejandro, and Rubén Rumbaut. 1996. *Immigrant America.* Berkeley: University of California Press.

Prins, Baukje, and Sawitri Saharso. 2010. "From Toleration to Repression: The Dutch Backlash against Multiculturalism," in Steven Vertovec and Susanne Wessendorf (eds.), *The Multiculturalist Backlash: European Discourses, Policies and Practices.* London: Routledge.

Ramakrishnan, Karthick, and Irene Bloemraad. 2008. "Introduction," in S. K. Ramakrishnan and I. Bloemraad (eds.), *Civic Hopes and Political Realities: Immigrants, Community Organizations and Political Engagement.* New York: Russell Sage Foundation.

Sansone, Livio. 1992. *Schitteren in de schaduw: Overlevingsstrategieën, subcultuur en etniciteit van Creoolse jongeren uit de lagere klasse in Amsterdam 1981-1990.* Amsterdam: Het Spinhuis.

Schrover, Marlou, and Floris Vermeulen. 2005. "Immigrant Organizations." *Journal of Ethnic and Migration Studies* 31: 823–32.

SCP (Sociaal Cultureel Planbureau). 2008. *Het dagelijks leven van allochtone stedelin-gen Andries van den Broek en Saskia Keuzenkamp*. The Hague: Sociaal Cultureel Planbureau.

Shingles, Richard. 1981. "Black Consciousness and Political Participation: The Missing Link." *American Political Science Review* 75: 76–91.

Tillie, Jean. 2000. *De Etnische Stem, Opkomst en Stemgedrag van Migranten tijdens Gemeenteraadsverkiezingen, 1986–1998*. Utrecht: Forum.

Uitermark, Justus. 2010. *Dynamics of Power in Dutch Integration Politics*. Amsterdam: University of Amsterdam.

Van Heelsum, Anja. 2002. "The Relationship between Political Participation and Civic Community of Migrants in the Netherlands," *Journal of International Migration and Integration* 3: 178–200.

Van Heelsum, Anja, and Jean Tillie. 2006. *Opkomst en Partijvoorkeur van Migranten bij de Gemeenteraadsverkiezingen van 7 Maart 2006*. Amsterdam: IMES.

Van Niekerk, Mies. 1994. "Zorg en hoop: Surinamers in Nederland nu," in Hans Vermeulen and Rinus Penninx (eds.), *Het democratisch ongeduld: De emancipa-tie en integratie van zes doelgroepen van het minderhedenbeleid*. Amsterdam: Het Spinhuis.

Verba, Sidney, Kay Schlozman, and Henry Brady. 1993. "Race, Ethnicity, and Political Resources: Participation in the United States." *British Journal of Political Science* 23: 453–97.

Vermeulen, Floris. 2005. "Organizational Patterns: Surinamese and Turkish Associa-tions in Amsterdam, 1960-1990." *Journal of Ethnic and Migration Studies* 31: 951–73.

———. 2006. *The Immigrant Organising Process: Turkish Organizations in Amsterdam and Berlin, and Surinamese Organizations in Amsterdam, 1960–2000*. IMISCOE Dissertations Series. Amsterdam: Amsterdam University Press.

———. 2008. *Diversiteit in uitvoering: Lokaal beleid voor werkloze migrantenjongeren in Amsterdam en Berlijn*. The Hague: NICIS Institute.

Vermeulen, Floris, Martijn Brünger, and Robert van de Walle. 2010. *Vitaal, dynamisch maar toch kwetsbaar? Een onderzoek naar de ontwikkelingen van het maatschap-pelijk middenveld in Amsterdam*. Amsterdam: IMES.

Vermeulen, Floris, and Tim Plaggenborg. 2009. "Between Ideals and Pragmatism: Practitioners Working with Immigrant Youth in Amsterdam and Berlin," in Jan Willem Duyvendak, Frank Hendriks, and Mies van Niekerk (eds.), *City in Sight: Dutch Dealings with Urban Change*. Amsterdam: Amsterdam University Press.

Wintershoven, Lukas. 2000. *Demografisch eeuwboek Amsterdam: Ontwikkelingen tus-sen 1900 en 2000*. Amsterdam: Dienst Ruimtelijke Ordening Amsterdam.

PART V

How Are the Children of Immigrants Shaped by and Also
Changing New York City's and Amsterdam's Cultural Life?

Cities of migration are the birthplaces of new artistic and cultural forms.
Children of immigrants play a vital role in such innovation. They bring
all kinds of new ideas, outlooks, and practices into the cultural arena.
Influenced by their immigrant parents as well as the receiving society and
city, the second-generation children of immigrants find themselves in a
special position from which they may rework and challenge established
repertoires and invent new styles and forms of artistic expression. The
question is not so much *if* the second generation is a source of cultural
creativity and innovation. This seems to happen in all cities of immigration. The central questions are *how* and *why* they manage to do so. What
shapes the ways in which children of immigrants enter artistic fields?
How do they in turn shape the cultural scene in a city? To what effect?
And what lines of demarcation and exclusion remain? As the two chapters in this section show, the innovative force of migration on a city's arts
and cultural life can follow quite different pathways and lead to quite different patterns. The comparison of New York City and Amsterdam highlights that cultural innovation by the second generation not only produces hybridity and dynamism, but also reflects existing cleavages.

There are, to begin, some underlying dynamics that help to understand why the children of immigrants in both Amsterdam and New York
are often innovators in the arts. It is partly, as Philip Kasinitz notes in his

chapter, that they have what he and his colleagues have called a second-generation advantage—in this case, the ability to combine elements of their parents' and the receiving society's cultures in new and often original ways (see Kasinitz et al. 2008). Also, their position of being slightly outside the dominant culture may spark creativity and insight. Moreover, as he observes, immigrants and their children may go into the arts—often a risky enterprise—because they lack access to more conventional career paths.

Beyond these basic similarities, the two chapters by Philip Kasinitz, on New York, and Christine Delhaye, Sawitri Saharso, and Victor van de Ven, on Amsterdam, bring out striking differences between the two cities that are related to their place in the global art scene as well as historical and cultural factors that have affected the opportunities available to the second generation and discourses about diversity. Whereas the children of immigrants in New York have long had an influence on and contributed to mainstream American art venues, including in the visual arts, music, film, and theater, second-generation Amsterdammers are struggling to carve out their own niches and become accepted into an already established cultural scene. Not that the children of immigrants have had no influence on art and culture in Amsterdam. On the whole, however, they have had a difficult time obtaining the space and the opportunity to participate with the native Dutch establishment.

One aspect of history that is important in New York has to do with the experiences of second-generation Jews and Italians from the last great wave of immigration, from the 1880s to the 1920s, who made their artistic mark in the mid-twentieth century. This second generation had the good fortune, as Kasinitz shows, to come of age at a time when New York was the world's greatest center of cultural creativity—a hothouse for both mainstream and avant-garde culture. The New York second generation produced such "greats" as George Gershwin and Aaron Copland in music, Arthur Miller and Eugene O'Neill in theater, and a host of film producers, directors, and actors. That New York, in the past, easily absorbed the second generation into leading artistic positions, may well contribute to the receptivity to the second generation's contributions today—a period, it should be noted, when the city is still the nation's major center of popular and "high" culture and has a prominent position in the world, as well.

History has played a role in New York in another way, through the changes brought about by the African American civil rights movement of the 1950s and 1960s—and the subsequent lessening of barriers facing blacks, Latinos, and Asians in the performing and other arts. Certainly, there are far more opportunities than in the pre-Civil Rights era for black, Latino, and Asian actors in New York City's theaters and in television shows and films made in the city; the work of immigrant-origin artists is now shown in many mainstream museums located in New York. As Kasinitz observes, the contemporary second generation also faces less pressure to assimilate into the dominant American culture, and there is a greater appreciation and tolerance of culture and art from elsewhere. Indeed, immigrant-origin artists in various fields, from theater and film to classical and popular music, have been recipients of many national and citywide honors and awards.

The current ethos of multiculturalism, or cultural pluralism, in New York City today—and the public celebration of diversity—provide a receptive context for the immigrant and second generations in the arts. As Kasinitz and his colleagues have written elsewhere, while second-generation New Yorkers feel the sting of disadvantage and discrimination, "they move in a world where being from somewhere else has long been the norm [. . . and reap] the benefits of New York's long history of absorbing new immigrants" (2008: 360).

The extraordinary diversity of the city has played a role in the creative mixing of immigrant and native minority cultures in music, art, dance, and poetry—bringing different traditions together in ways that create new innovative energy (Kasinitz et al 2008: 355). Nowhere is this more true than in hip hop, which Kasinitz calls New York's most influential cultural export of the last three decades and describes as a creation (in its early New York years) of Afro-Caribbean, Latino, and African American youth. Kasinitz also cites the Broadway musical *In the Heights*, which is about Dominicans in upper Manhattan and was written by a New Yorker of Puerto Rican heritage.

Across the Atlantic, mass popular culture in Amsterdam has been heavily influenced by developments in New York as well as other global centers such as Paris, London, and Los Angeles. At the same time, the second generation has played a distinctive role. As Delhaye and her coauthors note, children of immigrants from colonial Indonesia combined country and rock 'n' roll, drawn from the United States, with the traditional Indonesian genre of *krontjong* to create Indorock, while Turkish and Moroccan rappers created their own Dutch blend of American-influenced rap, with Turkish and Arabic vocals. In contrast to second-generation New Yorkers, who are more oriented to changing and building on American mass popular art and styles, their Amsterdam counterparts have been bent on appropriating new forms and styles from elsewhere. Their popular music has been widely viewed as a departure from traditional, conservative Dutchness toward a modern, dynamic, and *international* field of arts and culture that is not exclusively branded with one national or ethnic marker. This is different from certain aspects of the everyday youth culture among Amsterdam youth of immigrant origin that Delhaye et al. describe as reinforcing ethnic divisions. Ethno-parties, for example, divide youth of immigrant origin along ethnic lines, although a boys' street culture has also emerged bringing together young men of Moroccan, Antillean, and Surinamese descent as well as native Dutch youth of lower socioeconomic origin.

Penetrating the domain of "high" arts has been more of a challenge for the second generation in Amsterdam than New York. To be sure, today's second-generation New Yorkers have hardly been fully incorporated into the city's "high" culture, which is such a significant part of New York's arts milieu and includes many of the world's most celebrated opera and ballet companies, museums, and orchestras as well as the center of the nation's theater life. They have, however, made noticeable inroads, perhaps most marked in classical music, where Asians (13 percent of New York City's population) are a fifth of the musicians in the New York Philharmonic Orchestra (Paarlberg 2012). The path to roles in the city's high culture seems to be easier in New York than in Amsterdam, partly owing to the history of incorporating an earlier second generation into the artistic mainstream as well as the positive discourse on and celebration of ethnic and racial diversity and advances made by racial minorities since the civil rights reforms of the mid-twentieth century.

Although Amsterdam has a rich history of immigration, as Leo Lucassen demonstrates in his chapter in this volume, the city is not, like New York, generally understood as a mosaic or melting pot of immigrants. Nor is ethnoracial diversity in art and culture as broadly accepted. Indeed, Amsterdam is seen as the heart of established Western high art— with the Rijksmuseum, Van Gogh Museum, and Royal Concertgebouw Orchestra considered national, and indeed world, treasures. This has left second-generation artists to set up their own niches at the margins or to try to gain access to the native Dutch establishment, which requires them to adapt to existing conventions in established fields—more so than in New York, which appears more open to second-generation innovation in the performing and visual "high" arts. In fact, New York's fame as a world center of creativity is linked to twentieth-century "modern" artists and performers—a good many of them children of earlier immigrants— whereas Amsterdam's reputation is strongly connected to Dutch artists from further back, Van Gogh in the nineteenth century and Rembrandt in the seventeenth century, when the United States did not even exist!

Delhaye and her coauthors also write of the compartmentalization of Amsterdam's "high" art scene into "white" and multicultural circuits, something that has not happened to the same degree in contemporary New York and that, they contend, has been reinforced by government subsidy programs. Changes are afoot, however, as some Amsterdam youth of immigrant origin are finding their way into formal art education institutes and mainstream theaters and films. Interestingly, classical musicians from Asia, coming in a small but steady flow since the 1970s, have gravitated to the Amsterdam conservatory and the world renowned orchestras, the Royal Concertgebouw Orchestra in particular. While initially viewed with some suspicion by the Dutch public and music establishment—it was sometimes suggested that they lacked creativity and sufficient emotional sensibilities—by now, Asians have been fully accepted in the highly cosmopolitan world of professional classical music performance. In general, the clearly demarcated worlds of ethnic, popular, and established culture may slowly be giving way to a more diversified milieu in Amsterdam—just as, across the Atlantic, the children of contemporary immigrants, in future years, will also no doubt be more widely represented at all levels of the arts in New York.

ROGIER VAN REEKUM AND NANCY FONER

REFERENCES

Kasinitz, Philip, John Mollenkopf, Mary C. Waters, and Jennifer Holdaway. 2008. *Inheriting the City: The Children of Immigrants Come of Age.* Cambridge, MA: Harvard University Press.

Paarlberg, Michael Ahn. 2012. "Can Asians Save Classical Music?" *Slate*, February 2.

9

Immigrants, the Arts, and the "Second-Generation Advantage" in New York

PHILIP KASINITZ

When we think of the culture of New York or Amsterdam, artistic innovation, high levels of cultural diversity, and a brusque but tolerant cosmopolitanism are often what come to mind.[1] These images are, of course, stereotypes. Yet they contain more than a grain of truth. Both cities have long been centers of cultural innovation. Both are hubs of artistic production and cultural industries (Kloosterman 2005). And in both it is widely acknowledged that ethnic diversity has something to do with this. The idea that demographic diversity and cultural creativity are connected is part of the way New Yorkers and Amsterdammers think about their cities and what sets them apart from other Americans or Dutch (see Lucassen, this volume; Kahn 1987; Bender 1987).

In New York, the idea that the city's role as a center of cultural innovation is related to its diverse population borders on a cliché and regularly appears in academic and popular descriptions of the city's cultural life (see Glazer and Moynihan 1963; Kahn 1987; Burns, Sanders, and Ades 2003). Some historians and cultural commentators have even pointed to New Amsterdam's Dutch mercantile origins as the source for the diversity that is part of the city's cultural DNA (Bender 1987; Binder and Reimers 1996). One can be skeptical about this: The portion of today's New Yorkers who can claim any meaningful connection to Dutch New Amsterdam is miniscule and it is highly questionable whether the city's distant Dutch origins can shed any meaningful light on its contemporary urban culture. Still, the influence of the tolerant Dutch, in contrast to Boston's Puritans and Virginia's plantation owners, is one of the stories New Yorkers have told themselves about what makes their city different since at least the days of Washington Irving in the early nineteenth century.

This chapter explores the role that New York's immigrants, and more importantly their children, have played in fostering cultural innovation in the arts, broadly defined. I focus primarily on two historical periods. The first section deals with the mid-twentieth century—roughly the period between 1920 and the early 1960s when the children of the huge migration of southern and eastern Europeans, who came to the city from about 1880 to 1924, were the demographically dominant group. The second part deals with the contemporary period, when once again a huge second genera-tion—this time the children of immigrants arriving since the late 1960s—has remade New York's social life and cultural institutions. These two sec-ond-generation cohorts faced quite different circumstances. They came of age in very different economies and at different political moments. Most of the earlier cohort were generally regarded as white, which afforded them opportunities not always available to the children of the post-1960s immi-grants, most of whom are regarded as persons of color. However, in this chapter I suggest that when it comes to issues of cultural creativity and artistic innovation today's children of immigrants are in many ways more similar to earlier second generations than is generally realized (see Foner 2000; Kasinitz et al. 2008). In making this case I draw on a wide variety and different types of examples. These are in no way meant to be exhaus-tive—indeed readers will no doubt find many of their personal favorites missing and for that I apologize. My hope is that these examples will help illustrate the processes by which immigrants and their children have played a disproportionate role in creating New York's distinctive culture. In this sense the newcomers are perhaps the quintessential New Yorkers.

One obvious reason why immigration has been linked to moments of cultural creativity and artistic productivity in New York and elsewhere is that immigrants bring with them different artistic traditions and cultural repertoires from various parts of the world. Not surprisingly, immigrants often remain strongly and sometimes nostalgically attached to the cul-tural forms of their homelands, and this has the effect of bringing many different traditions to the city. Yet the continuation of "old-country" forms is only a small part of the story of immigrant cultural activity. Much immigrant and second-generation cultural innovation is rooted in an ambivalent acknowledgement of their outsider status combined with an often headlong rush to embrace, but also an urge to re-create, "Americanness." As Charles Hirschman (2013) puts it, "not all immigrants look solely to the past to find meaning or to express their longings. This is particularly true for the children of immigrants and even some immigrants, who feel inspired by the possibility for innovative expression in American arts, culture and pastimes." This embrace of Americanness is often seen as "assimilation," and in some senses it is. But it is important to note how much of America's (and New York's) culture has been transformed in the process of being reimagined by newcomers. In the end, the retention of premigration traditions is less important to the process of immigrant cultural innovation than the transformative nature of the immigrant experience itself. Innovation is also related to what my colleagues and I have termed the "second-generation advantage." The children of immigrants, occupying a social and cultural space between the host society and that of their immigrant parents, are uniquely situated to selectively combine elements of both cultures in new and often innovative ways. Conversant in both cultures yet taking neither for granted, the second generation occupies a position that, if not always comfortable, is well suited to innovation. This can prove an advantage in daily life and particularly in fields, such as cultural production, in which creativity and innovation are highly valued (Kasinitz et al. 2008).

Immigrants and the Arts in the American Century

New York emerged as a world capital of artistic and cultural production in the mid-twentieth century. While this historical moment followed a long period of remarkably high immigration, it was actually a time when new immigration to the city was at an historic low (see Glazer and Moynihan 1963; Foner 2000). In the mid-twentieth century, the *children* of the great wave of eastern and southern European immigrants were becoming demographically, politically, and culturally dominant in New York City. Indeed, being the child of immigrants was so much the norm in mid-twentieth-century New York that the second generation in many ways set the tone for their contemporaries, including long-standing U.S. natives (many of whom, it should be remembered, were migrants from other parts of the United States).

Throughout the United States, immigrants and their children played a cultural role far out of proportion to their numbers (Hirschman 2005), and New York, where so much of the second generation in the United States was concentrated, became a hothouse for intellectual scenes, art worlds (Becker 1982), and cultural movements, both mainstream and avant-garde, as well as a center for the industry of cultural production (Kloosterman 2005; Scott 2000). New York gave the children of immigrants the cosmopolitan space in which to make these innovations. Despite nativists' worries that New York City was becoming a place apart from the rest of the nation, in the end the second generation repaid America with a new, broader, and perhaps better vision of itself.

In nineteenth- and early-twentieth-century America, immigrant cultural ways were often seen as a threat to the nation's traditions. Particularly suspect was the insidious influence of their partially Americanized children who felt entitled to produce art that drew on American themes. In 1935, writing in the *New York Times,* the eminent composer and music critic Virgil Thompson dismissed George Gershwin's (born Jacob Gershowitz, in Brooklyn to Ukrainian Jewish parents) *Porgy and Bess* as "straight from the melting pot. At best it is a piquant but highly unsavory stirring-up together of Israel, Africa and the Gaelic Isles." "I do not like fake folklore," Thompson continued, "nor bittersweet harmony, nor six-part choruses, nor fidgety accompaniments, nor gefilte-fish orchestration" (Melnick 1999: 73). Such sentiments were not unusual among critics at the time (see Schiff 1997).

Of course, Gershwin got the last laugh, albeit posthumously. Within a few decades, calling a work of art "straight from the melting pot" would no longer be an expression of scorn or derision. Once dismissed as a writer of sentimental popular tunes, Gershwin along with the more self-consciously high-minded Aaron Copland (born Aaron Kaplan, in Brooklyn of Lithuanian Jewish parents) and Leonard Bernstein (born in Lawrence, Massachusetts, to Russian Jewish parents) would come to symbolize twentieth-century America. Not only is Gershwin considered among the best of the "great American songbook" composers, his work is now firmly lodged in the concert and operatic repertoires. By contrast, Thompson's attempts to create a distinctly American modernism are, if not exactly forgotten, more often heard in academic music history classes than in concert halls.

Gershwin's triumph is part of a larger cultural shift. The mid-twentieth-century emergence of the United States and particularly New York as a broadly influential world leader in theater, painting, film, and popular and classical music occurred at the same time that the United States was fully absorbing the influences from the great immigration of the turn of the twentieth century—and perhaps more important, when those immigrants' American-born children were coming of age. These children of immigrants produced some of the most self-consciously "American" art, music, and theater ever created—despite the fact that self-appointed guardians of American high culture such as Thompson decried the foreign (or worse, "negro") influences they saw just below the surface. Consider the music of Irving Berlin (born Israel Baline, in Russia, emigrated as a child)—who wrote "God Bless America" as well as "White Christmas" and "Easter Parade" (Hirschman 2005; Most 2004)—or the self-consciously "American" themes in the plays of Arthur Miller (*Death of a Salesman*), Eugene O'Neill (*Desire Under the Elms*), and William Saroyan (*The Time of Your Life*). Interestingly, while a few of these works draw on immigrant and ethnic experiences—the phrase the "melting pot" itself comes from the title of Israel Zangwill's popular 1909 play—most often such themes are far below the surface.

In classical music, no composer before (or arguably since) has celebrated American themes and images as self-consciously as Copland. As his friend Alberto Ginastera wrote, "Copland has created American music in the same way Stravinsky did Russian music, or Falla Spanish, or Bartók Hungarian" (quoted in Rockwell 1999). American source material dominates his work, from cowboy tunes and folk music to his use of the Shaker hymn "Simple Gifts" in *Appalachian Spring*. As Copland himself noted in describing his choice of source material for the ballet, "When I wrote *Appalachian Spring* I was thinking primarily about Martha [Graham] and her unique choreographic style. . . . [S]he's unquestionably very American: there's something prim and restrained, simple yet strong, about her which one tends to think of as American" (Pollack 2000: 388). A second-generation immigrant and lifelong New Yorker with little experience west of the Hudson, Copland knew how improbable his engagement with the rural "American" landscape seemed to others. Asked how he could have so successfully captured the West in his ballet *Billy the Kid*, he quipped, "It was just a feat of imagination" (Pollack 2000: 325).

In the 1940s and 1950s, the Broadway stage was dominated by similar feats of imagination. To be sure, some of the second generation who created the landmark works of American naturalism and the Group Theater's "Method" acting style had grown up well aware of ethnic theater traditions. A vibrant Yiddish theater flourished in the immigrant communities of early-twentieth-century New York along with smaller but not insignificant Italian and German theater scenes. The largely eastern European origins of many central figures of mid-twentieth-century New York theater no doubt helps explain their affinity for, or at least familiarity with, Chekhov and Stanislavsky; at least one of the creators of the American version of the Method, Stella Adler, was the daughter of Jacob Adler, the closest thing the Yiddish theater had to an international superstar. Yet the style that the younger Adler, Lee Strasberg, and their Group Theater colleagues created in New York had little connection with the melodrama that dominated the Yiddish stage, and the themes in the works of second-generation (Jewish) playwrights Clifford Odets (*Waiting for Lefty*), Arthur Miller, and their contemporaries could hardly be more American.

Similarly, in Broadway musicals, the children of immigrants set shows like *Oklahoma*, *Annie Get Your Gun*, and *Carousel* in an imaginary rural American heartland far from any world they actually knew. For a form usually thought of as light entertainment, Broadway musicals have actually not been shy about facing issues of racial and ethnic conflict, but they have rarely done so in ways that had much to do with the lives of their largely second-generation authors or New York audiences. One of the earliest, the 1927 musical *Show Boat*, by Jerome Kern (the son of German Jewish immigrants) and Oscar Hammerstein (a then rare *grand*child of Jewish immigrants) deals with the tragic effects of segregation, albeit on a mixed-race woman "passing" for white in distant Mississippi. *Show Boat*'s depictions of blacks was certainly stereotypical—for later audiences, cringe-inducingly so. Yet by the standards of its day it took on the issue of race surprisingly directly.

Hammerstein's later work with Richard Rodgers (original family name Abrahams) continued to deal with race, although usually far from home; Americans needed to go all the way to the *South Pacific* to confront their biases. The closest Rodgers and Hammerstein came to telling a second-generation story was in *Flower Drum Song*, a 1958 musical in which the conflict between immigrant elders and the desires of a young, "hip" second generation is set in San Francisco's Chinatown. *Flower Drum Song* is based on a novel by the Chinese American author C. Y. Lee. Yet while the book tells a fairly dark tale stressing the tragic sides of displacement and exile, the upbeat musical shifts the focus to the love stories among the younger generation. Rodgers and Hammerstein made little attempt to accurately depict life in Chinatown. Indeed, beneath its sometimes crude stereotypes the musical might be seen as a 1950s New York Jewish assimilation story in Chinese garb. For this reason many Chinese American critics have objected to the play and the even more crassly stereotypical 1961 film version. Others, however, have seen *Flower Drum Song* as a guilty pleasure, which, for all of its faults, cast articulate and attractive young Asian American actors in leading roles (Berson 2002). In 2002 the story was rewritten for a new production, keeping most of the original music, by the Chinese American playwright David Henry Hwang (Lewis 2006).

About the same time as *Flower Drum Song* premiered, ethnic conflict on the streets of New York—albeit not involving the author's and composer's own ethnic group—finally came to the Broadway musical stage with *West Side Story*. Yet not until the early 1960s did eastern European Jewish "roots" truly come out of the closet in *Fiddler on the Roof*, a show that sentimentalized the Jewish *shtetl* and proved immensely popular with what was, by then, a largely third-generation audience.[2]

In his 2005 presidential address to the Population Association of America, Charles Hirschman (2005) noted the extraordinary influence that immigrants and their children have had on American culture, especially the arts in twentieth-century America. The impact on Hollywood is a prominent example—a place and an industry, it should be noted, that in the mid-twentieth century in many ways was a preserve of New Yorkers who had gone west. Although the immigrant influence on Hollywood is well known (see Buhle 2004; Winokur 1996), the numbers Hirschman presents are nonetheless stunning. Since the Academy of Motion Picture Arts and Sciences began awarding its Academy Awards (the "Oscars"), 17 directors have won the award for best picture more than once. Of these, nine were born outside of the United States (eight true immigrants and one long-term resident, David Lean, who never gave up his British citizenship). Four more were the children of immigrants. Only four were third- or third-plus-generation Americans. Although Hirschman does not make the distinction, of the foreign born two (Frank Capra and Elia Kazan) were members of what Rubén Rumbaut (1999) has termed the "1.5" generation—born abroad but brought to America as children and largely raised in the United States. Three of the foreign-born directors emigrated as young adults and began their careers in the United States while four (Lean, Billy Wilder, Fred Zinnemann, and Miloš Forman) began their careers abroad and came to Hollywood in part because it was a center of the film industry.

Yet while mid-twentieth-century Hollywood was dominated to an extraordinary degree by first- and second-generation immigrants, one would scarcely know this from what was on the screen. The art these immigrants created was often self-consciously "American," and immigrant experiences played little role in most Hollywood movies (see Gabler [1989] on the reluctance of Jewish immigrants and second-generation filmmakers to address ethnic themes). Of the 30 Oscar-winning films directed by Hirschman's immigrant and second-generation multiple Oscar winners, only two—Kazan's *Gentleman's Agreement* and second-generation John Ford's *The Quiet Man*—can be seen as addressing the issues of ethnic America. (Interestingly, of the four third-and third-plus-generation Americans on Hirschman's list, two won Oscars for films at least in part about ethnic conflict, George Stevens with *Giant* and Robert Wise with *West Side Story*, although in the latter case the award was shared with a second-generation New Yorker, Jerome Robbins [born Rabinowitz].)

Hollywood may represent an extreme case. It was, after all, a new industry in the years when the immigrant presence was highest. Immigrants often do well in new industries, where long-established social networks are less important and other groups have not yet effected the social closure that can limit newcomers' access (Light and Gold 2000). Still, the disproportionate immigrant influence on mid-twentieth-century American culture was not limited to film. The leading figures of the Broadway stage were even more likely to be the children of immigrants, as were many of the leading figures in popular and classical music, fiction writing, and painting.

Thus in looking at the twentieth-century experience of the children of immigrants in the American art world, we are left with two questions: Why were they so successful? And why was the art they produced so devoid—at least on the surface—of their own ethnic experiences?

Hirschman suggests several reasons. First, although the arts are potentially a highly rewarding field, they are also among the most risky. Immigrants and their children may have gone into the arts for the same reason other newcomers went into small business, crime, and other high risk careers—they lacked access to more conventional career paths. Also, the children of immigrants were often more open than other American artists to the influence of—and to collaborating with—"native outsiders," most notably African Americans. Second-generation musicians were among the first whites to fully appreciate jazz and to blend jazz with European traditions. Indeed, Benny Goodman and Artie Shaw (born Arthur Jacob Arshawsky), both huge stars in the 1930s, integrated their bands with African American musicians at a time when this entailed real professional risks and prevented them from touring in the South. At the same time, as whites, Goodman and Shaw were able to "cross over" to a mass audience and reap the rewards of jazz's new popularity far more than their African American colleagues (Hirschman 2005: 612). In the pop music of the 1950s and early 1960s, the collaboration between largely second-generation white song writers and producers and largely African American performers is another example of second-generation/black cultural fusion.

Finally, as Hirschman suggests, "perhaps there is something about being slightly outside the dominant culture that gives the edge of insight to an artist." Drawing on W.E.B. Dubois's notion of "double consciousness," Hirschman notes that "marginality, or the experience of navigating across multiple cultures, can be psychologically uncomfortable and even incapacitating. However, for some, it is an asset that sparks creativity and inspiration. Immigrants may see new possibilities for entrepreneurship, a greater awareness of cultural nuance, and greater insight into how art can capture the essence of emotions and lived experience. In a society that has relatively few cultural touchstones, immigrant artists (and others who live in multiple cultural worlds) have been free to define 'Americanness' in novel ways" (2005: 612–13). Members of the second generation, even more than their immigrant parents, occupy this intermediate position between cultural systems. This position may be psychologically challenging, but it can lead to great art. And when a city like New York in the mid-twentieth century (or today) is dominated by young people in that position, their way of seeing things may become the dominant sensibility of artists and their audiences, even those not themselves members of the second generation.

Many mid-twentieth-century immigrant and second-generation artists may now seem overly concerned with producing art that was truly "American." Yet it is worth remembering that they faced intense pressure from mainstream institutions to reject old country ways. As Leonard Covello, a leading educator in East Harlem, famously recalled of his own second-generation childhood, "We were becoming Americans by learning how to be ashamed of our parents" (quoted in Iorizzo and Mondello 1980: 118). Eugene O'Neill's highly autobiographical *Long Day's Journey into Night* contains a chilling father/son, immigrant/second-generation confrontation. In a heated argument, the son insults what he sees as his father's Irish peasant ways. The father retorts that the son should not be insulting Ireland "with the map of it on your face." The son coldly replies, "Not after I wash my face" (O'Neill 1956: 83). Although many second-generation artists worked in settings in which being the child of an immigrant was the norm, there was still considerable stigma attached to origins in the immigrant ghetto. Many sought either to embrace all that was "American"—or, particularly in the case of visual artists like Mark Rothko (born Marcus Rothkowitz) and Frank Stella, to embrace forms of abstraction and universalism that seemed beyond any national or ethnic particularity.

Social scientists today often celebrate the protective solidarity of the ethnic enclave (Portes and Manning 1986; Zhou 1992), but in the mid-twentieth century immigrant origins were often a source of embarrassment for second-generation New Yorkers, eager to break out of the ghetto, if only to encounter the ghetto next door. This may be one reason for the stunning speed with which the second generation, then, as now, adopted English and lost the parental language. Consuming and creating American art was another part of the process.

While a full-fledged celebration of ethnicity in the arts would have to wait until the 1960s, many earlier second-generation cultural producers engaged in a kind of winking acknowledgement of their immigrant backgrounds; they often created a kind of inside joke, and insider soli-darity, for their ethnic audiences even while crossing over to the main-stream. One early example of this ethnic humor was Groucho Marx, in his tuxedo, standing in an upper-class drawing room, turning to the camera and asking in song, "Did someone call me *schnorrer*?" (Yiddish slang for a sponger). This must have prompted peals of laughter from Jewish viewers while going by too fast to get much notice from others. This is certainly not a celebration of ethnic culture or an attempt to pre-serve old country ways, but it suggests an outsider's sensibility as well as perhaps a whisper of solidarity to co-ethnics in the audience.

By the 1960s, a more than winking acknowledgement of ethnic-ity, but rather a full- fledged style of ethnic humor, became part of the American cultural landscape. Ethnic humor—most often Jewish, but sometimes Irish or Italian—expressed the second generation's half insider and half outsider status in relation to both the dominant cul-ture and the immigrant community. The songs and comedy routines were performed in English, although much of the humor came from an exaggerated accent. Indeed, some of what made performers like Dean Martin (born Dino Crocetti), Pat Cooper (born Pasquale Caputo), Sid Caesar, Mel Brooks (born Melvin Kaminisky), and Milton Berle (born Milton Berlinger) funny came from their (perhaps loving, perhaps bit-ter) parodies of their immigrant parents.

At the same time, second-generation humorists also struck a chord with co-ethnics by introducing ethnic content into mainstream Ameri-can contexts—such as when, in the late 1940s, the musician and paro-dist Mickey Katz found he could get laughs by simply translating Amer-ican standards and folk songs into Yiddish (e.g., "Hain afen Range"). Here again, it is precisely the second generation's intermediate posi-tion—and their juxtaposing ethnic referents and mainstream cultural icons—that created the humor. Katz may have been ahead of his time. Popular in ethnic venues, he was never embraced by a mainstream audience, and was boycotted by many radio stations and producers, most of them Jewish, for perpetuating stereotypes and the language of the ghetto (Kun 1999). By the 1960s a mainstream audience was more accepting when humorist Alan Sherman rewrote well-known popular songs with lyrics that gently parodied the Jewish ethnic experience. It must be emphasized, however, that this kind of ethnic humor did not perpetuate old-country ways or viewpoints. For a pre–World War II, Yiddish-speaking audience a translation of "Home on the Range" would simply have been a translation; for their American-born children, however, the juxtaposition was funny. The viewpoint on which ethnic humor relies, like ethnicity itself, is a made-in-America creation. It is in many ways an ironic form of assimilation.

Immigrants and the Arts in Contemporary New York

Today's New York is once again a city in which the children of immigrants are a dominant demographic group. Among young adults, the 1.5 and second generation now outnumber long-time natives as well as immigrants who arrived as adults. Those we usually think of as mainstream Americans—native whites of native parentage—now make up less than a fifth of adult New Yorkers under age 30. It is too early to say what this demographic shift means for the city's cultural future, but the signs suggest that a likely possibility is another, albeit quite different, period of cultural innovation. Of course today's immigrants and their children, unlike those in the mid-twentieth century, are often encouraged to retain, and indeed to celebrate, their cultural roots. In contemporary New York, there is less pressure on immigrants to assimilate and a greater tolerance and appreciation of art from elsewhere. The generally successful assimilation and cultural influence of the descendents of the earlier immigrants, as well as the broad acceptance of at least some versions of multiculturalism in the wake of the African American civil rights movement, has created a climate less hostile to newcomers' cultures. Whether the children of the post-1965 immigrants will achieve the artistic prominence of the previous second generation is an open question. Yet there are reasons to expect they might, in part because of an underlying similarity with the past. As before, the "between two worlds" experience of the children of immigrants can promote cultural innovation.

It is revealing that today's immigrant and second-generation artists are far less likely to change their ethnic names than in the past. In a world of officially recognized multiculturalism, an exotic name and immigrant identity can actually be a resource, helping ease access to performance venues and funding opportunities. Immigrant artists do sometimes complain, and rightly so, about being ethnically typecast or limited to certain "representative" roles (Rodriguez 2006). But inclusion, even in an ethnic category, is still probably better than exclusion.

Today, in no other arena, save perhaps cuisine (see Gabaccia 2000), is the immigrant contribution to America now so generally acknowledged as positive as in the arts. The notion that immigrants weaken or debase the nation's cultural and artistic production, once a common feature of nativist discourse, is rarely heard in the United States today. Few give a second thought to the large number of immigrant and second-generation performers in American concert halls or on the American airwaves, and almost no one questions the Americanness of works by immigrant and second-generation artists. As in times past, some immigrant artists continue to work in and explore the artistic traditions of their homelands, yet unlike in the past, today these efforts often gain a positive reception from the American host society.

Ironically, the most "foreign" and "exotic" types of art are those that often have the easiest time finding support and audiences from outside the ethnic community. Prominent awards, such as the National Endowment for the Arts' "National Heritage Awards"—specifically designed to promote the preservation of America's cultural patrimony—often honor immigrants working in folk art forms from around the world. While cultural conservatives have pilloried the endowment for supporting art that pushed the envelope on issues of sexuality or religion, supporting Ethiopian liturgical singing, Korean folk dancing, and Peruvian religious painting as part of preserving the *American* cultural heritage is accepted without controversy. In the arts at least, the notion of America as a multicultural nation seems widely taken for granted. Traditional art forms practiced by immigrants find their way into New York's school curricula, museums, and mainstream concert venues. They often find a mainstream audience. As in cuisine, having access to "authentic" foreign artistic experiences without having to leave home is seen as one of the benefits of living in the city.

However, the price of preserving "authenticity" can be artistic conservatism and stagnation. Art that clings strictly to traditional forms and seeks to preserve heritage away from the context from which it sprang often takes on an unchanging fly-in-amber quality. And since it rejects addressing the world of migrants in favor of a timeless, imaginary homeland, it generally has only a limited, nostalgic appeal to immigrants, and even less for their American-born children. In 2009, there were 23 private music schools teaching Western classical music and jazz in the Chinese enclaves of Queens, Brooklyn, and Manhattan listed in New York's Chinese-language business directories. Many are thriving, as largely second-generation children study piano and violin, although only two schools were listed that teach traditional Chinese music (Lu 2013).

As in the past, immigrant and second-generation artists tend to have their greatest influence when they indirectly draw on old-country traditions and techniques or self-consciously leave old-country ways behind. Indeed, the very act of creating art in the American context transforms it, in both obvious and subtle ways. Cultural forms in immigrant communities may start out traditional but they inevitably change their meanings as the creators respond to their new life situations. Luis Guarnizo and his collaborators present an example of such activity in their observations of Colombian National Day in Flushing Meadows Park in Queens. This event, promoted as a celebration of Colombian culture, features Colombian music, dance, and folk costumes. Yet its meaning is different than if the same event were held in Bogotá. The New York context has transformed it into a New York ethnic celebration—one that in many ways resembles the celebrations of other ethnic groups, complete with the appearance of New York's mayor and city council leaders (Guarnizo and Diaz 1999). New York politicians come to these events to gain support from immigrants; the politicians' presence, in turn, reinforces the immigrant community's legitimacy as one more tile in the "gorgeous mosaic."

The West Indian Labor Day Carnival is the largest ethnic parade in New York City, annually drawing one to two million people to Brooklyn's Eastern Parkway. While Carnival is the most visible West Indian symbol in the city, most West Indian New Yorkers come from nations without Carnival traditions. Costume designers and musicians from Trinidad come to New York and help organize the bands. But most participants are from other parts of the Caribbean and, over the years, have paid less attention to the organized, Trinidad-style *mas* bands. Perhaps this development was inevitable, as the ethnic identity being expressed in the event has changed in the New York context (Kasinitz 1992, 2004).

Although migrant community leaders often favor the static preservation of homeland artistic traditions, the producers of culture, even
those rooted in folk forms and folk traditions, usually express ideas that
come from the dynamic immigrant context. From the outside, cultural
products may look like the continuation of traditions, but viewed from
within the artistic traditions of the homeland, the art of immigrant
communities often represents radical departures. When the Mighty
Sparrow, Trinidad's greatest living calypsonian (who lives part of the
year in Queens) wrote a song to celebrate New York's Carnival, the mel-
ody and arrangement were pure Trinidad. Yet the ideas expressed by
the lyrics were very New York. Sparrow sang not about continuity with
the past, but recounted the immigrants' joy in forgetting the past, cut-
ting ties, and creating a new self in the city of opportunity:

> You can be from St. Cleo, or from John-John
> In New York, all that done,
> They haven't to know who is who
> New York equalize you.
> Bajan, Grenadian, Jamaican, "toute monde,"
> Drinking they rum, beating they bottle and spoon.
> Nobody could watch me and honestly say
> They don't like to be in Brooklyn on Labor Day! (quoted in Kasinitz
>   1992: 150)

Immigrant cultural production and celebration can be grounds for
sustaining transnational connections, but also express new ideas that
respond to new conditions. They may even do both at the same time as
Douglas Massey and Jorge Durand (1995) show in their book on Mexican
retablos, Miracles on the Border. These religious folk paintings are usually
commissioned by migrants to thank patron saints for deliverance from
the dangers and misfortunes that migrants endure. They are the product
of folk artists using the most traditional of forms. Yet the statements the
retablo painters make in their creations are about issues of transnational
family life, balancing home and work lives that straddle international
borders, and the opportunities and heartbreaks of assimilation.

Another, more prosaic, example of similar dynamics is the mural on
the wall at a taqueria in Brooklyn not far from my home. The restaurant

is in a neighborhood where a polyglot community of new immigrants and older white working-class residents has begun to blend into a gentrifying area; the clientele is a mix of Mexican and other immigrants and middle-class black and white New Yorkers. Much of the décor is typical of this sort of place—including a map of the Estado de Puebla, photos of old Mexican movie stars, and a painting of mariachis. But the large mural that takes up most of the room is striking. The work of local artists Tashiro and Javier del Helguerro (aka Javier Pinator), the mural depicts an immigrant New York variation on the story of the founding of the Aztec capital, Tenochtitlan. A band of Aztecs, wearing a mix of indigenous costumes drawn from both ancient sources and popular culture—including a shaman with jaguar-cloaked assistants and a tall warrior with a fanciful headdress—look out over the water at a tiny island, on which the eagle with the snake in its mouth is about to land. But the body of water is not a lake in central Mexico. It is New York harbor. Behind the island stands the Statue of Liberty, with the Brooklyn Bridge, World Trade Center, and Empire State Building in view. In a good-humored way this Aztec "discovery" of New York makes a serious point about Mexican settlement in New York, emphasizing that Mexicans are here, that they are staying, and that they are Mexicans *and* New Yorkers.

If artists in immigrant communities often repackage traditional and folkloric forms to say new things and serve new purposes, artists in high-culture settings, many of them second generation, often take the idea further, using folkloric references or traditional forms and techniques in new and often ironic ways. At least one academically recognized artist—whose work has been shown at the Guggenheim Museum in New York and the Reina Sofia in Madrid—has taken up the same theme portrayed on the wall of the taqueria. Felipe Galindo (aka Feggo) has for more than a decade made the Mexicanization of New York the theme of his humorous works on paper and short films, which he calls the *Manhatitlan* project. These works juxtapose stereotypical Mexican themes with a New York context—a matador faces off with yellow taxi cabs, an Olmec statue rides the subway, *voladores* hang from the peak of the Empire State Building. Galindo's *Manhatitlan Codex* tells a story of immigration to New York in the style of a pre-Columbian Aztec codex to explore, in the words of his Manhattan gallery's website, the concepts of homeland, migration, and globalization. A similar use of immigrant themes can be seen in the work of Dulce Pinzón, a Mexican-born photographer now living in Brooklyn, who has depicted Mexican immigrant workers in New York doing their jobs while dressed in American superhero costumes: a window washer dressed as Spider-Man, for example, a restaurant delivery man dressed as Superman, and a nanny dressed as Wonder Woman.

In 2007 the Queens Museum of Art organized a "Generation 1.5" exhibit featuring artists who had emigrated when they were children. All were academically trained, most were quite avant-garde, and some had exhibited in leading museums. While their work could hardly be further from the folkloric traditions of their homelands, many deliberately used images and techniques from those traditions to comment on their own hybrid identities. For example, in *Jihad Pop*, Seher Shah, a Pakistan-born New Yorker used (according to the catalog copy) "layered motifs derived from architectural references and religious imagery [that] interact within iconic Islamic spaces such as the interior courtyard. These energized realms are at once utopian and nostalgic" (Finkelpearl and Smith 2009). In this case, as in many others, when traditional forms are used to address nontraditional situations the immigrant artist is creating something very new.

Whereas immigrants and their children in the mid-twentieth century benefited from the fact that film and theater then were new industries, open to outsiders, this is no longer true in these fields. Popular music, however, with its relatively low costs of entry, young audiences, and insatiable appetite for the "next big thing," is a different matter, and here immigrants and their children continue to play a leading role. Space does not permit an adequate discussion of New York's vibrant and dynamic Latin music scene. Suffice it to say that salsa, the dominant Latin style of the 1970s, was a New York creation. While its origins lie in Cuba and Cuban dance bands that became popular with multiethnic New York audiences in the 1950s, the most influential figures in salsa were largely New York–born and –raised Puerto Ricans.[3] In New York, they mixed Puerto Rican and Afro-Cuban traditions with big band swing, other forms of jazz, and rhythm and blues. The majority of the performers were Latino, but influential salsa musicians have also included African Americans and Jews (and in one case, a Filipino), many of whom grew up in or near Puerto Rican communities in New York (Boggs 1992; Manuel 1995) More recently reggaeton, a Puerto Rican dance music form, has taken root among the New York second generation, where it mixes freely with hip hop, Jamaican dancehall, and Dominican musical styles (Rivera et al. 2009).

Hip hop is arguably New York's most influential cultural export of the past three decades. From its origins in housing projects in the South Bronx in the late 1970s, hip hop's combination of music, dance, poetry, clothing styles, and graffiti has become a leading cultural form for youth and youthful rebellion all over the world. It has a particular appeal to young people who see themselves as marginal, including the immigrant second generation in Europe.

Yet while hip hop is usually perceived as an African American form, in its early New York years it was at least as much the creation of Afro-Caribbean and Latino youth. Many of the most prominent New York rappers have been 1.5- and second-generation immigrants: Kool Herc (from Jamaica), Biggie Smalls (parents from Jamaica), Wyclef Jean and Pras (from Haiti), and Nicki Minaj (from Trinidad) just to name a few. Only after it had taken root on the West Coast and later in the South did hip hop come to be seen as essentially African American, a development that, paradoxically, probably made it more marketable to young whites (see Flores 2000; Rivera 2003; Hinds 2004). Whatever the precise role of Latino and Caribbean youth in hip hop's origin and development, in using African American imagery they were not, I would argue, assimilating or even "downwardly assimilating" (Portes and Zhou 1993) into black America. Hip hop was not about adopting African American ways. It was a coming together of second-generation and African American youth to create something new.

I was first struck by this culture-creation process in an interview with a young man from the Bronx, whose parents were from Belize, in doing research for a study of second-generation New Yorkers (Kasinitz et al. 2008). When I asked if he belonged to any ethnic clubs or organizations, he seemed confused by the question. He had no interest in Belizean associations or church groups, although there are many in New York. After a minute he tentatively offered that he was president of the City College hip hop club. He explained how this multiethnic, Caribbean-African-American-Latino-Asian group was, for him, about far more than music but about a cultural style, a lifestyle, and even a sort of cultural politics. He spoke proudly of his Bronx neighborhood, one of the seedbeds of hip hop. It is an area many would see as a minority ghetto. Yet he saw it as diverse and cosmopolitan. "We got everything . . . black American, Caribbeans, Puerto Ricans, Dominicans, South Americans, a few Asians, Guyanese . . . everything. Except whites," he added. For him, the culture of the young people in the neighborhood—and their music, hip hop—was cosmopolitan, representing a move away from his parent's ethnic parochialism.

Hip hop artists routinely change their names, although not because they are ashamed of their parents. I am not sure why Clive Campbell, the Jamaican-born, Bronx-raised DJ who has a good claim to having been the inventor of hip hop, became Kool Herc. Or why Christopher Wallace (born in Brooklyn of Jamaican parents) took the name of a character in an African American gangster novel and recreated himself as Biggie Smalls and later as the Notorious B.I.G. The hip hop artists' reinvention of themselves no doubt has something to do with joining a larger, multiethnic, if generally nonwhite, hip hop world. Caribbean American rappers toss in an occasional line of patois and Latinos make an occasional, Groucho-like aside to Spanish speakers in their audiences. But, by and large, hip hop is an American invention—in its early days a New York invention—bringing together young people from a wide variety of backgrounds. From the outside hip hop looks very "ghetto"—but for many who make and consume it, hip hop is also about leaving and transcending the limitations of the ethnic enclave. As Baz Dreisinger notes, "Hip-hop is a classic American rags-to-riches saga, yes, but it's also a postcolonial immigrant story—as much Henry Roth as Horatio Alger" (Dreisinger 2012).

Nor, it should be noted, is hip hop's celebration of gangsters and criminality all that novel. That the rappers who play at being gangsters establish their "street cred" by flaunting associations with real gangsters—sometimes with disastrous consequences—is an echo of an earlier second-generation story. Think of Frank Sinatra or the actor George Raft, who sometimes had their pictures taken with real-life mobsters. Like mid-twentieth-century Broadway and Hollywood, hip hop is a new industry, open to ambitious outsiders. High risk, it can also, for the lucky very few, be highly lucrative. And if the industry's business side has more than its share of criminals, hustlers, and disreputable hangers-on, that too has precedents in the mid-twentieth-century entertainment industries.

Perhaps the most conspicuously multicultural hip hop artist today is rapper/producer Wyclef Jean. His work celebrates his Haitian origins while freely mixing in African American, Jamaican, Trinidadian, Latin American, South Asian, and a host of other elements in a way that could probably have come together only in New York. Some criticize Jean's recent work for having become something of a multicultural variety show, and indeed, it has been suggested that hip hop more generally is a form that has seen its best days. Who can say? Yet clearly hip hop came out of a period of immense cultural vitality. I think it is no coincidence that it was also a place and time in which so many children of immigrants were coming of age.

Sometimes the new second generation makes its artistic statement on a previous second generation's home turf. Today's children of immigrants had their "Fiddler on the Roof" moment in 2008 when the Broadway play *In the Heights* won the Tony Award for the year's best musical. *In the Heights* is a sentimental (some would say corny) story about the struggles of immigrants and their second-generation children in an upper Manhattan Dominican neighborhood. In many ways it is a throwback to the "feel good" musicals of an earlier era. Musically it draws on hip hop, Latin music, and Broadway show tunes in about equal measure. While it tells a Latino immigrant story it does so in a very New York way. Compared to Gershwin, Bernstein, or Sondheim, the show's creator, 28-year-old New York–born Puerto Rican Lin-Manuel Miranda is much less reluctant to let his ethnic roots show. At the same time, like his predecessors, he refuses to be constrained by those roots. He clearly feels entitled to draw on the art of the old country, the New York streets, *and* New York's own middle-class (middlebrow?) traditions to make something entirely new. That is the essence of the second-generation advantage.

Conclusion

It is never easy to examine the social origins of something as inherently individual as artistic creativity or cultural innovation. Yet we all know that there are times and places where cultural creativity comes into flower, and cities with diverse populations and cosmopolitan outlooks tend to be fertile grounds for artistic achievement (see Kahn 1987). In the mid-twentieth century, New York City was clearly such a place. At that time the children of immigrants set the cultural tone for the city, at least among the young.

Obviously the situation faced by today's second generation differs in many ways. But there are also many similarities that should not be overlooked. As in the past, many contemporary observers worry that the second generation is "torn between two worlds." One hears this from critics of multiculturalism, but also from within immigrant communities. The fact that the second generation draws on a variety of different cultural repertoires makes many people uneasy, but this is also a great strength. If the example of mid-twentieth century New York teaches us anything it is that, given the right social and economic climate, cultural "in-betweenness" can be a source of resilience and creativity. Nowhere is this more clear than in the arts. Perhaps when it comes to culture, the question facing diverse cities like New York (and Amsterdam) is not whether immigrants and their children are clinging to old-country ways or assimilating into the "leading culture," but rather how the culture and the cultural products created by the newcomers are transforming how we understand the city and the larger society. The process of immigrant and second-generation incorporation is not always easy and it is sometimes painful. But if the past is any guide, it may produce some great art.

NOTES

1. I wish to express my deep appreciation to Nancy Foner, Robert Kloosterman, John Mollenkopf, Bowen Paulle, Mary C. Waters, Sharon Zukin, and two anonymous reviewers for their helpful comments on this chapter.
2. The 1922 hit *Abie's Irish Rose* provides an unusual counterexample of a much earlier Broadway play dealing with immigrant themes. However, that play, the story of a romance between a second-generation Jewish man and his second-generation Irish bride who wed over the objections of both of their immigrant families, is less about immigrant origins than a celebration of how assimilation—and love—can overcome immigrant parochialism.
3. Of course, as U.S. citizens, Puerto Ricans are not technically immigrants in New York, and the timing of Puerto Rican migration, peaking in the low-immigration 1950s, does not fit the periodization of this chapter. However, the cultural processes for this group are in many ways similar.

REFERENCES

Alba, Richard, and Victor Nee. 2003. *Remaking the American Mainstream: Assimilation and Contemporary Immigration*. Cambridge, MA: Harvard University Press.

Becker, Howard. 1982. *Art Worlds*. Berkeley: University of California Press.

Bender, Thomas. 1987. "New York as a Center of 'Difference.'" *Dissent* 34 (4): 429–36.

Berson, Misha. 2002. "A 'Drum' with a Difference." Theatre Communications Group. http://www.tcg.org/publications/at/2002/drum.cfm.

Binder, Frederick, and David Reimers. 1995. *All the Nations Under Heaven*. New York: Columbia University Press.

Boggs, Vernon W. (ed.). 1991. *Salsiology: Afro-Cuban Music and the Evolution of Salsa in New York City*. Westport, CT: Greenwood Press.

Buhle, Paul. 2004. *From the Lower East Side to Hollywood*. London: Verso.

Burns, Ric, James Sanders, and Lisa Ades. 2003. *New York: An Illustrated History*. New York: Knopf.

DiMaggio, Paul, and Patricia Fernandez-Kelly (eds.). 2010. *Art in the Lives of Immigrant Communities in the United States*. New Brunswick, NJ: Rutgers University Press.

Dreisinger, Baz. 2012. "Ready or Not." *New York Times Book Review*, October 21.

Finkelpearl, Tom, and Valerie Smith (eds.). 2009. *Generation 1.5*. New York: Queens Museum of Art.

Firestone, Ross. 1993. *Swing, Swing, Swing: The Life and Times of Benny Goodman*. New York: Norton.

Flores, Juan. 2000. *From Bomba to Hip-Hop*. New York: Columbia University Press.

Foner, Nancy. 2000. *From Ellis Island to JFK: New York's Two Great Waves of Immigration*. New Haven, CT: Yale University Press.

Gabaccia, Donna. 2000. *We Are What We Eat: Ethnic Food and the Making of Americans*. Cambridge, MA: Harvard University Press.

Gabler, Neal. 1988. *An Empire of Their Own: How Jews Invented Hollywood*. New York: Anchor Books.

Gans, Herbert. 1992. "Second Generation Decline: Scenarios for the Economic and Ethnic Futures of the Post-1965 American Immigrants." *Ethnic and Racial Studies* 15 (2): 173–93.

Glazer, Nathan. 1997. *We Are All Multiculturalists Now*. Cambridge, MA: Harvard University Press.

Glazer, Nathan, and Daniel P. Moynihan. 1963. *Beyond the Melting Pot: The Negroes, Puerto Ricans, Jews, Italians, and Irish of New York City*. Cambridge, MA: MIT Press.

Gordon, Milton. 1964. *Assimilation in American Life: The Role of Religion and National Origins*. New York: Oxford University Press.

Gorelick, Sherry. 1981. *City College and the Jewish Poor: Education in New York, 1880–1924*. New Brunswick, NJ: Rutgers University Press.

Guarnizo, Luis E., and Luz Marina Diaz. 1999. "Transnational Migration: A View from Colombia." *Ethnic and Racial Studies* 22 (2): 397–421.

Halter, Marilyn. 2002. *Shopping for Identity: The Marketing of Ethnicity*. New York: Schocken.

Hinds, Selwyn. 2003. *Gunshots in My Cookup*. New York: Atria.

Hirschman, Charles. 2005. "Immigration and the American Century." *Demography* 42: 595–620.

———. 2013. "The Contribution of Immigrants and Their Children to American Culture." *Daedalus* 142: 26–47.

Hollinger, David. 1995. *Postethnic America: Beyond Multiculturalism*. New York: Basic Books.

Howe, Irving. 1976. *World of Our Fathers: The Journey of Eastern European Jews to America and the Life They Found and Made*. New York: Simon & Schuster.

Iorizzo, Luciano, and Salvatore Mondello. 1980. *The Italian-Americans*. Boston: Twayne.

Jablonski, Edward. 1996. *Harold Arlen: Rhythm, Rainbow, and Blues*. Boston: Northeastern University Press.

Kahn, Bonnie Menes. 1987. *Cosmopolitan Culture: The Gilt-Edged Dream of a Tolerant City*. New York: Atheneum.

Kasinitz, Philip. 1992. *Caribbean New York: Black Immigrants and the Politics of Race*. Ithaca, NY: Cornell University Press.

———. 2004. "New York Equalize You? Continuity and Change in Brooklyn's Labor Day Carnival," in Millia Reggio (ed.), *Carnival: Culture in Action, The Trinidad Experience*. New York: Routledge.

Kasinitz, Philip, John Mollenkopf, and Mary C. Waters. 2002. "Becoming American/ Becoming New Yorkers: The Experience of Assimilation in a Majority Minority City." *International Migration Review* 36 (4): 1020–36.

Kasinitz, Philip, John Mollenkopf, Mary C. Waters, and Jennifer Holdaway. 2008. *Inheriting the City: The Children of Immigrants Come of Age*. Cambridge, MA: Harvard University Press/Russell Sage Foundation.

Kloosterman, Robert C. 2005. "Come Together: An Introduction to Cities and Music." *Built Environment* 31 (3): 247–57.

Kun, Josh. 1999. "The Yiddish Are Coming: Mickey Katz, Anti-Semitism, and the Sound of Jewish Difference." *American Jewish History* 87: 343–74.

Lewis, David H. 2006. *Flower Drum Songs: The Story of Two Musicals*. Jefferson, NC: McFarland.

Light, Ivan, and Steven Gold. 2000. *Ethnic Economies*. San Diego: Academic Press.

Lu, Weiting. 2013. "Confucius or Mozart? Community Cultural Wealth and Upward Mobility Among Children of Chinese Immigrants." *Qualitative Sociology* 36, forthcoming.

Manuel, Peter. 1995. *Caribbean Currents: Caribbean Music from Rumba to Reggae*. Philadelphia: Temple University Press.

Massey, Douglas, and Jorge Durand. 1995. *Miracles on the Border: Retablos of Mexican Migrants to the United States*. Tucson: University of Arizona Press.

Melnick, Jeffrey. 1999. *A Right to Sing the Blues: African Americans, Jews and American Popular Song*. Cambridge, MA: Harvard University Press.

Most, Andrea. 2004. *Making Americans: Jews and the Broadway Musical*. Cambridge, MA: Harvard University Press.

O'Neill, Eugene. 1956. *Long Day's Journey Into Night*. New Haven, CT: Yale University Press.

Pollack, Howard. 2000. *Aaron Copland: The Life and Work of an Uncommon Man*. New York: Henry Holt.

Portes, Alejandro, Maria Patricia Fernandez-Kelly, and William Haller. 2005. "Segmented Assimilation on the Ground: The New Second Generation in Early Adulthood." *Ethnic and Racial Studies* 28: 1000–40.

Portes, Alejandro, and Robert Manning. 1986. "The Immigrant Enclave: Theory and Empirical Examples," in Suzanne Olzak and Joanne Nagel (eds.), *Competitive Ethnic Relations*. Orlando, FL: Academic Press.

Portes, Alejandro, and Rubén Rumbaut. 2000. *Legacies: The Story of the New Second Generation*. Berkeley: University of California Press.

Portes, Alejandro, and Min Zhou. 1993. "The New Second Generation: Segmented Assimilation and Its Variants." *Annals of the American Academy of Political and Social Science* 530: 74–97.

Rivera, Raquel. 2003. *Puerto Ricans from the Hip Hop Zone*. New York: Palgrave Macmillan.

Rivera, Raquel, Wayne Marshall, and Deborah Pacini Hernandez (eds.). 2009. *Reggaeton*. Durham, NC: Duke University Press.

Rockwell, John. 1999. "Sounds of America: A Biography of a Composer Whose Music Captured the Diversity of a Continent." *New York Times Book Review*, March 14.

Rodriguez, Richard. 2002. *Brown: The Last Discovery of America*. New York: Viking.

Roediger, David R. 1991. *The Wages of Whiteness: Race and the Making of the American Working Class*. New York: Verso.

Rumbaut, Rubén. 1999. "Assimilation and Its Discontents: Ironies and Paradoxes," in Charles Hirschman, Philip Kasinitz, and Josh DeWind (eds.), *The Handbook of International Migration: The American Experience*. New York: Russell Sage Foundation.

Schiff, David. 1997. *Gershwin: Rhapsody in Blue*. New York: Cambridge University Press.

Scott, Allen J. 2000. *The Cultural Economy of Cities*. Thousand Oaks, CA: Sage.

Waters, Mary C. 1999. *Black Identities: West Indian Dreams and American Realities*. Cambridge, MA: Harvard University Press.

Winokur, Mark. 1996. *American Laughter: Immigrants, Ethnicity, and 1930s Hollywood Film*. New York: St. Martin's Press.

Zhou, Min. 1992. *Chinatown: Portrait of an Ethnic Enclave*. Philadelphia: Temple University Press.

10

Immigrant Youths' Contribution to Urban Culture in Amsterdam

CHRISTINE DELHAYE, SAWITRI SAHARSO, AND VICTOR VAN DE VEN

Amsterdam's cultural life has been changed in a variety of ways by the children of immigrants. Taking our lead from Ulf Hannerz (1992), in this chapter we look at Amsterdam's culture from a processual perspective. Cultures are always in a state of flux, and this is obviously the case in contemporary globalized societies such as the Netherlands, which not only face growing internal diversity owing to, among other things, processes of professionalization and specialization but have also witnessed large-scale inflows of people from abroad.

In seeking to shed light on the complex and varied ways that the children of migrants have influenced Amsterdam's urban public culture, we are concerned with "culture" on three levels: everyday youth culture, mass popular culture, and the arts that are recognized and supported by the more highly educated sectors of society, often referred to as "high culture." We conceive of these different levels as partially overlapping and loosely bounded sets of cultural expressions, which notwithstanding their fuzzy boundaries, differ not only in content but also with regard to the way that cultural expressions are formally codified and disseminated.

In addition to documenting the many, and profound, ways that the children of migrants have affected Amsterdam's cultural landscape, a central question in our analysis is the *cultural interconnectedness* that has developed at the three different levels out of the interactions among

Amsterdam's varied ethnic groups, including the long-established native-born Dutch. By "interconnectedness" we mean, following Robert Park and Ernest Burgess, "a process of interpenetration and fusion in which persons and groups acquire the memories, sentiments, and attitudes of other persons and groups and, by sharing their experience and history, are incorporated with them in a common cultural life" (Park and Burgess 1921, cited in Alba and Nee 1997: 828). The concept of "common culture" as we use it refers not to some kind of overarching homogeneous culture but to a certain degree of integration that has emerged out of different, often contradictory, sets of values.

Everyday Youth Culture

In everyday life, Amsterdam youth of immigrant origin have developed a wide array of cultural practices. While much urban youth culture in Amsterdam has been developing—and is divided—along ethnic and socioeconomic lines, an urban street culture has brought together boys of different ethnic backgrounds. Indeed, gender figures prominently in everyday youth culture. Evidence from a number of qualitative studies suggests that girls develop an everyday youth culture among their co-ethnics in contrast to boys, who are more likely to cross ethnic boundaries in the process.

The Party Scene

There is a lively party scene in Amsterdam among youth of immigrant origin, with clubs organizing ethno-parties aimed at specific ethnic groups. The ethno-party scene is the result of both exclusion and self-exclusion: youth are drawn to parties with co-ethnics among whom they feel comfortable, while they avoid parties where they sense they are not welcome and would meet with discrimination and, for young women, where they are forbidden to go by their parents. Simone Boogaarts's (2009) study of the Turkish, Moroccan, and Asian party scene in Amsterdam and Rotterdam revealed that Asian parties, which are in decline, are no different from youth parties among native-Dutch Amsterdammers, except that they are frequented by Asians, mostly Chinese, who say they go because they like to be among other Asians. Turkish and Moroccan parties attract large crowds, and religion and social control play important roles in who attends and how they are run. Those attending Turkish parties dance to their favorite Turkish music, a major reason why Turkish youth go. In explaining why they go to Turkish parties, young men also mentioned discrimination by other clubs; young women said that their parents permitted them to go only to Turkish clubs. Moroccan parties stand out in that they are organized in the afternoon or early evening, are sometimes sex-segregated, and do not serve alcohol—which is why parents allow their daughters to frequent them. As among Turkish young people, Moroccan men in Boogaarts's study said they were drawn to Moroccan clubs because of discrimination in other clubs.

Girls: Beauty and Sharing Experiences

Girls' subcultures revolve around girls sharing secrets with their best friends in the privacy of their bedrooms or are about socializing with a small group of friends. The inability to discuss cultural or religious difference hampers friendships across cultural lines. This comes out in Linda Duits's (2010) ethnographic study of girls at two primary schools in Amsterdam.[1] Friendships between girls who wore the hijab and those who did not were rare. This was not necessarily because the girls' experiences were so different—actually, they had a lot in common—or because Muslim girls wearing the hijab were rejected. Girls who did not wear the hijab believed it should be respected because "it is their religion" or because "it is her choice," or because "everyone has a right to be herself." Choices involving religion or authenticity were not to be questioned; religious difference was a topic that was placed beyond the reach of debate. But the fact that the religious differences among them could not be talked about inhibited the development of confidentiality between girls of different religious backgrounds; as sharing experiences was central to their subculture, they felt they had little to say to each other.

Fashion and ideals of beauty are important in girls' subculture. For many young Muslim girls, religion seems to be perfectly compatible with fashion as they display a variety of fashionable styles of Islamic dress in the streets of Amsterdam. Carefully combining stylish hijabs with other fancy clothing items, these young Muslim girls create their own versions of sporty, urban, ladylike, or other trendy looks. Their heightened visibility in the public sphere not only contributes to the diversity of the Amsterdam street fashion scene, but also openly counters the stereotype of veiled Muslim women as oppressed, backward, and dull (Moors 2009; Mossinkhoff and Corstanje 2011).

What young women consider to be beautiful body shapes is also influenced by their ethnic background. Deborah de Rooij's (2004) study of beauty ideals among young Afro-Surinamese women in Amsterdam shows that being overweight is a non-problem for them; a real woman should have "meat on her bones," they believe.[2] Reflecting the popularity of Western black culture, Afro-Surinamese young women admire and adopt the styles of black media icons. Frizzy hair is accepted among these woman, but many dye their hair or use hair straightening techniques, which are, however, integrated into a "black style." Skin color is a contested issue. Although the women in De Rooij's study said they were satisfied with their dark complexions, some used skin whiteners and the ideal was light-colored skin. Their ideal skin tone was not that of white Claudia Schiffer nor dark-skinned Sudanese model Alek Wek, but of light-skinned Tyra Banks. To be a good-looking woman in their view, however, is primarily to be immaculately dressed. In short, the young women did not evaluate themselves in terms of white Western beauty images, but derived their beauty norms from their black Surinamese environment and Western images of black beauty.

Another study (Kropman 2007) offers additional clues about attitudes to weight and body type among Amsterdam youth. This study also found that Afro-Surinamese girls viewed plumpness as attractive, while a slim body was the beauty ideal among native Dutch girls.[3] Moroccan and Turkish girls were divided on the subject. Some preferred a slim figure while others thought that some curves make a body feminine. Notions of beauty—which are so central to girls' youth culture—appear to pull girls of different ethnic background apart rather than unite them.

Boys: Street Culture

Whereas intimate friendships across ethnic lines are not likely to develop among girls of immigrant origin, an urban street culture in Amsterdam, dominated by Moroccan young men in the western part of the city and by Antillean and Surinamese young men in the southeast, seems to transcend ethnic lines, involving youth of different immigrant origins as well as native Dutch youth from lower-socioeconomic backgrounds. For example, a street language has developed that is a mixture of Moroccan, Surinamese, and Dutch.

Several ethnographic studies in Amsterdam reveal the dynamics of urban street culture and its variants in particular neighborhoods and among different ethnic groups. Jan Dirk de Jong's study of the group culture of boys of Moroccan descent who hang out on the streets of Amsterdam Overtoomseveld (a district in Amsterdam-West) shows how they developed their own street culture that endorsed certain types of (serious) delinquent behavior. The boys developed this street culture, De Jong argues, in reaction to growing up as "foreigners" (children of immigrants) in a disadvantaged urban neighborhood. The boys form a loose network—"gang" or "group" suggests more cohesion than is the case—and boys from different ethnic backgrounds, for example, Surinamese, are occasionally accepted if they share the group's values and display the required tough behavior (De Jong 2007: 136). The boys feel connected to Moroccans like themselves in other parts of Amsterdam, but their strongest identification and first loyalty is to their own neighborhood. They speak proudly of Westside, of which Overtoomseveld is a part, and consider themselves to be superior to boys from other parts of Amsterdam-West such as Osdorp (De Jong 2007: 103–9). The real outside groups, if not the enemy, are the (native) Dutch and the police. The boys' world turns around money: making money by hustling—they reject low-paying jobs—and spending money on expensive clothes and consumer goods. The boys earn respect by threatening to use violence; they constantly challenge each other and often physically fight to establish their rank in the pecking order (De Jong 2007: 149–84). In another ethnographic study—of young people in southeast Amsterdam—Paulle (2005) describes the pernicious effects of street culture on the school life and career prospects of boys, including those of Antillean, Surinamese, and African origin. The street culture in and around the school is open to those who accept peer group values and show the expected behavior, which involves the use of street language (a combination, as noted, of Surinamese, Dutch, and Moroccan), an overly masculine attitude, gangsta rap lyrics denigrating females, and carrying weapons.

In Amsterdam's everyday youth culture there is thus little cultural interpenetration or fusion among different ethnic groups. The party scene appears to be divided along ethnic lines. In girls' subcultures, religious difference is experienced as a bright boundary that is hard to cross and girls are not united around shared beauty ideals (Alba 2005). The only subculture where fusion and a boundary shift have occurred is street culture. in which youth of immigrant origin and native Dutch youth of lower socioeconomic origin mix (Alba 2005). This street culture reflects a shared consciousness based on underclass experiences and group loyalty, and involves an opposition to mainstream Dutch society. The violence and sexism in this street culture are reminiscent of the oppositional culture that has been described among some native black and Latino youth in the United States (Portes and Zhou 2003) and white working-class boys in Britain (Willis 1977).

Radio FunX

Despite limited ethnic blending in actual social settings, a shared street culture flourishes through local (social) media. To a large extent this development is generated by FunX, a radio station partly financed by public funds that was founded in 2002 to cater primarily to ethnic youth and to provide a media outlet for new types of popular urban music. FunX broadcasts in the Randstad (the region that spans the four largest cities in the Netherlands, Amsterdam, Rotterdam, The Hague, and Utrecht), airing a mix of programming for the entire region and local shows. Because it is government funded, there are restrictions on the amount of music it can air; a substantial part of its schedule is filled with talk radio, in which discussions of popular culture blend with more serious topics like politics, sexuality, and employment. All issues are presented from a multicultural point of view and in a tone that relates to the ethnically mixed target group.

FunX has become highly popular among Amsterdam youth, both ethnic and native.[4] In addition to daily broadcasting, the radio station has launched an interactive website and makes active use of social media. An important ingredient in the station's success is the staff, whose ethnic mix reflects the station's target demographic (interview with Sanne Breimer, chief editor of FunX Amsterdam, June 9, 2011). Recently, FunX became one of the many victims of government cutbacks in the cultural field. In June 2011 a proposal was presented to end national government financial support by 2012 as part of a larger plan to terminate publicly funded ethnic-based programming in the Netherlands through the local media (Ministerie OCW 2011: 5). In response to the financial cuts, new collaborations arose between Fun X and Dutch public broadcasting organizations; in addition, some local governments decided to support specific urban programs on Fun X.

Mass Popular Culture

Eclecticism versus "Traditionalism"

Migration has had an impact on the Dutch popular cultural landscape in various ways since the end of World War II. The huge inflow from Indonesia in the years soon after the war gave rise to the musical genre that subsequently has been labelled Indorock. From the mid-1950s to the late 1960s, Dutch Indonesian bands, such as the Tielman Brothers and the Blue Diamonds, loomed large in the local rock 'n' roll scene. Combining country and rock 'n' roll (partly influenced by American groups like the Everly Brothers) with the traditional Indonesian musical genre *krontjong*, the Indorockers proved important in the popularization of rock 'n' roll in the Netherlands. Their virtuoso guitar skills were acclaimed abroad, mainly in Germany (Ter Borgt 1997: 46–47).

The second wave of postcolonial migration in the 1970s from Suriname added a distinct Afro-Caribbean flavor to the Dutch musical spectrum. That Afro-Surinamese influence has been highlighted in Amsterdam's annual Kwakoe Festival, named after a slave in Suriname celebrated for having freed himself. The Kwakoe Festival started in 1975 as a soccer tournament for Surinamese who weren't able to spend the holiday in their homeland. It evolved into the city's third-largest annual event, with 250,000 visitors from all different backgrounds. As a result of a structural financial deficit caused by a decline in government funding and a top-heavy organizational structure, the Kwakoe Festival was canceled in 2011 for the first time. The cancellation caused a stir in the local media, not the least due to alleged racist remarks by the festival's interim manager, Paul Stiekema (Meershoek 2011).[5]

In the 1980s another musical genre, hip hop, emerged on the Amsterdam scene. From its origins in 1970s New York (see Kasinitz, this volume), hip hop evolved into a global phenomenon, borrowing from other musical genres, producing transnational crossovers, and spinning off numerous local subgenres, often with ethnic-inflected elements. In Amsterdam the Osdorp Posse (a white Dutch hip hop crew, named after a district in Nieuw-West) proved groundbreaking in this process as pioneers of Nederhop: hip hop with Dutch lyrics. Their explicit, literally translated gangsta rap gained the group vast media coverage and popularity, mainly among native white middle-class youth. Initially, ethnic youths considered rapping in Dutch less credible than U.S.-style rap, which they saw as more authentic (Krims 2000: 156). The Osdorp Posse were also accused of "playing ghetto" by the media and young people, both native and ethnic. As the Posse matured, they were able to establish and maintain a credible underground image; their style, inspired by American acts like Public Enemy and NWA, was acclaimed throughout the national hip hop scene. A decade after their debut album, *Osdorp Stijl* (Osdorp Style, 1992), it became common for ethnic youths to rap in Dutch as well, often blending in elements and catchphrases from their (parents') native tongues: Arabic, Turkish, or Papiamento. At present Nederhop, which has become a blend of Dutch and many ethnolinguistic elements, has eclipsed Dutch American style rap, both among artists and the public.

The rise of *urban*—a black pop music genre that gained popularity beginning in the early 2000s—has brought a new dynamic to the Amsterdam hip hop scene. It fueled the articulation of tendencies toward "old school" or "true school" traditionalism, on the one hand, which remains loyal to U.S. rap of the 1980s and 1990s in musical style and lyrical themes, and the "new school" eclecticism of *urban* on the other, which is less purist and blends styles and themes from different genres like pop, electroclash, and dance music. One of the most important voices in this new genre is De Jeugd van Tegenwoordig (Today's Youth, the JVT), an Amsterdam hip hop act, formed by two native-Dutch rappers (one of whom attended Rietveld, the prestigious Amsterdam art school) and one Surinamese. Their debut single, "Watskeburt?" (a self-invented neologism for "What's up?"), topped the Dutch charts. They remain enigmatic "black sheep" owing to their self-mockery and bizarre interviews, as well as their playing down of traditional rap values like masculinity and stardom. Yet they maintain a credibility among young Amsterdammers due to their musical abilities and original style. For years the JVT has been performing at major pop music festivals, winning countless awards and opening for Snoop Doggy Dogg in the Netherlands. The fresh approach of the JVT set an example for other multicultural acts associated with the *urban* culture, which attracts an ethnically mixed audience (Nabben 2010: 142–47).

As for the more traditional "true school" hip hop, gangsta rap and politically engaged rap with lyrics about racial inequality and life on the streets are popular among ethnic youths in economically disadvantaged Amsterdam boroughs such as Nieuw-West and Zuidoost. To them hip hop provides a "cosmopolitan" access to a world music culture and a relationship with African American musical genres (McCorkel 2009). Ethnicity comes to the fore among many artists performing in these styles. It is not uncommon for Turkish and Moroccan rappers to use Turkish or Arabic vocals. They also often create aggressive lyrics that depict the hardship of street life, which is perhaps not surprising given that Moroccans, Turks, and Surinamese are among the most marginalized ethnic groups in Amsterdam. Whether or not some boroughs of Amsterdam can be compared to the Bronx or South Central Los Angeles, rap music offers a model of identification for many ethnic youth (Kooijman, 2008: 112–17; Brooks and Conroy 2010). American black expressive culture, with its particular political history, resonates in the lives of ethnic youths in Amsterdam, a phenomenon that has been described as hip hop's *connective marginalities* (Osumare 2001: 171–72). Although hip hop originates in American culture, many of its themes—like class, culture, and historical oppression—are, for some Amsterdam youth, highly relevant. In 2007 Dutch Moroccan rapper Salah Edin caused a stir by portraying himself on the cover of his album *Nederlands Grootste Nachtmerrie* (Holland's Biggest Nightmare) in a manner similar to the mug shot of Mohammed B., the youth who murdered filmmaker Theo van Gogh. The rapper's intention was to show the way the average Moroccan youth is viewed and treated by Dutch society:

> In some ways I resemble him. We are the same age, Moroccan, Muslim, and engage views of distrust and fear on the street. I felt the same

frustration and anger. If it weren't for the music I might have ended up in a similar way. (Salahedine 2011)

In a genre identified with those of African ancestry, such as hip hop, being black can be an asset for an artist, lending legitimacy to his or her creative endeavors. However, by the same token, a focus on ethnicity or racial themes can be seen as a gimmick or unrelated to the Dutch context, as Dimitri Madimin, an artist, promoter, and curator of Surinamese Indonesian descent, explained:

> A friend of mine is a black artist born in a middle-class environment in Holland who thematizes Malcolm X in his work. That just doesn't convince me. I mean, it is so far removed from the world he or I grew up in. And it is also too restricted in my opinion. Instead of focusing on his "blackness," maybe he should focus more on himself or Dutch society. (interview with Dimitri Madimin, April 16, 2011)

In sum, no matter how the artists relate their art to ethnicity and/or race, the Amsterdam hip hop scene has been blooming thanks to the successful blending of the American genre with Dutch lyrics and Arabic, Turkish, Indonesian, and Papiamento slang.

Cultural Entrepreneurship and Street Credibility

Urban youth cultures among the children of immigrants in Amsterdam—including hip hop—are bound up with cultural entrepreneurship, through which young artists introduce new themes and styles to the Amsterdam cultural scene. Contrary to the romantic idealization of the avant-garde artist as a struggling bohemian or misinterpreted genius, money and fame are important measures of success for hip hop artists (Rose 2006: 216–19). They can even be the primary goals. Melvin Wix, a DJ and prominent gatekeeper of Amsterdam urban culture, explained:

> For kids with a deprived background, bling [flashy jewelry, but also designer clothes and luxury goods] and status are indicators of success. And even though Amsterdam lacks *real* ghettos and *heavy* poverty, many minority kids are raised from a similar perspective. They go for

the gold! The attitudes of hip hop, skate culture, and nightlife were a true eye opener to me! I soon adopted the same freedom of expression. My parents came as immigrants from Suriname—for them making it was a goal in itself. They taught me to stay out of trouble and adopt a strong working ethic. Being creative and developing your cultural and artistic needs were values my parents could not pass on to me, but I have never really given up on my parents' values. (interview, June 9, 2011)

Young artists involved in popular urban and street culture have also been engaged in cultural entrepreneurship because they feel excluded from mainstream institutions. Conventional cultural organizations and the educational system are both mainly the sphere of long-established Dutch. In the process of allocating government subsidies for arts institutions, cultural forms rooted in urban and street culture are not always recognized. Moreover, many successful street culture artists look down on (ethnic-based) subsidies. The general feeling is that artists should be self-sufficient. Said Wix, the DJ:

If you are structurally dependent on grants, there might not be enough demand for your ideas. We learned at an early stage that we could make a quick buck with club nights, providing the financial freedom to further develop ourselves, and have a great night as well! (interview, June 9, 2011)

Street culture has triggered a strong do-it-yourself (DIY) attitude among many youngsters of immigrant origin as well as a desire to create, and attend, institutions that foster artistic talents among and stimulate contributions from ethnic minorities. The Surinamese comedian Howard Komproe said of the early days of hip hop in Amsterdam, "We had nothing, and there was nothing in our youth, so we had to create everything from scratch." Speaking of how cultural institutions and art schools eventually developed for minorities, he explained, "At the Academy of Drama I didn't feel at home; hip hop culture and comedy were not merited as professional genres. The board and curriculum were very 'white' in those days" (interview, April 29, 2011). Dimitri Madimin commented on the Rietveld, Amsterdam's Academy of Arts, "There were no black kids at Rietveld in my days [the 1990s], I was pretty much the only one. And even today the mix of students doesn't reflect the changing population"(interview, April 26, 2011). It is only in the last decade or so that "urban-inspired" educational programs have been set up on a large scale. Many are located in community centers and run by self-taught peer group teachers, who try to make a living out of their artistic interests and want to inspire young people with shared talents and ambitions. The pioneers of these programs acknowledge the importance of their mentors for their own development, and in turn feel obliged to "adopt" promising protégés and give them a platform (Kammer 2011).

While some of these pioneers have become part of the established cultural world, street credibility and a connection with their urban roots remain important to them. Artists of ethnic descent are caught in a bind. On the one hand, they need to "keep it real" in order to maintain their status and popularity within their peer group. Komproe, Madimin, and Wix all find it important to stay in touch with the younger generation that is still "on the streets." This affiliation also helps them to keep pace with the latest trends and fashions. In turn they use their status as gatekeepers to provide a platform for talented youths. On the other hand, the desire to become successful—and to enjoy and benefit from their success—may alienate artists from their roots on the streets. However, many artists have concluded that being successful and "authentic" are not inevitably incompatible as long as the artist is aware of and sensitive to the potential conflicts.

Comedy as a Force against Intercultural Barriers and Ethnic Tensions

Another mass popular culture genre in which youth of immigrant origin have become very influential is comedy. In addition to a long-standing Dutch tradition of "one-man shows," often combining sketches and songs, an "American," open-microphone style of stand-up has become popular in Amsterdam's clubs and theaters and on television. The new breed of comedians includes many with an ethnic background, mainly Surinamese, Antillean, and Moroccan. Their linguistic skills often were shaped within hip hop and street culture, and so was their style of performance. The highly popular Suriname-born comedian and television host Jörgen Raymann is considered their godfather. His primetime Friday night comedy/talk show (broadcast live on national public television) proved important for the popularization of this style of comedy: the weekly show closes with a five-minute performance by a stand-up comedian. The connection with street culture is stressed by hip hop DJs, who mix musical intermezzos between various performances and comedy routines.

The Moroccan Najib Amhali, presently one of the most in-demand comedians in the Netherlands, is acclaimed for his beatbox (vocal percussion) performances. He has mastered the skill of making fun of both natives and immigrants. His flawless Dutch provides legitimacy with a native Dutch audience. Although some ethnic comedians cater solely to "their own" crowds, the most successful ones can count on a substantial native Dutch following as well. A paramount component of their success is cultural bridging. By showing immigrants' perception of their new homeland, ridiculing the "strange" practices they brought with them, as well as referring to stereotypes the native Dutch and ethnic minorities have of each other, minority comedians can parody ethnic tensions with the goal of reducing them. What is funny to some, of course, can be insulting to others. It is one thing when comedians from ethnic minority groups use ethnic humor to lampoon their own culture; it is another when a native Dutch comedian does this. This difference gives ethnic minority comedians more leeway in their use of ethnic humor, and makes it likely that they—not Dutch comedians— will be the ones doing the cultural bridging.

Beside bridging cultures, the youth of immigrant origin are also introducing a relaxed and informal atmosphere to formal Amsterdam art venues. At the Meervaart, a theater in Nieuw-West, a Caribbean comedy night, inspired by Chris Rock's shows in New York City, has gained popularity among native Dutch as well as those with ancestry in the Caribbean. The all-night program, combining comedy with food, DJs, and live music, is a format unfamiliar to "white" venues. Andreas Fleischmann, head of programming at the theater, said, "The native Dutch find the atmosphere *gezellig* [warm, cosy]. The Suriname comedians appeal to a wide ethnic audience because of their self-mockery, cultural bridging capacities, and high comfort factor" (interview, May 31, 2011). Performing comedian Howard Komproe observes, "Comedians can be seen as twenty-first-century jesters. They present heavy issues in a light fashion" (interview, April 29, 2011). At the same time, many ethnic comedians do not want to be stigmatized as mere clowns and seek to present themselves in more serious ways, turning to acting, music, or writing. While they serve as a bridge between cultures, they are also breaking the barriers between artistic genres in the Amsterdam domain of mass popular culture.

High Culture

Artists of immigrant origin have also influenced high-culture settings and the "high arts" in Amsterdam, although in a less clear-cut way. The domain of the high arts is a highly codified one, and unsettling or changing the codes requires considerable effort. This has especially been the case in more recent times as attitudes toward ethnic minorities have hardened.

Cultural Policy

During the 1960s and 1970s, the Dutch arts scene was characterized by experimentalism and cosmopolitanism. In this period, the Netherlands, and especially the city of Amsterdam, became well known throughout the world for its liberal and free climate. The city hosted a growing number of artists, from Colombia, Mexico, Iceland, and Israel, among others, many of whom were in the Netherlands for political reasons. Being "foreign" in those days was not an issue in the art world (Lopez 2002). According to artist and art historian Franck Gribling, the diversity among artists working in the Netherlands, and the variety of cultural traditions on which they drew, resulted in innovative ideas and styles and new modes of expression, which in turn contributed to the cultural vitality of Amsterdam. Within this climate of renewal and at the same time critique of established institutions, artist collectives and experimental arts institutes were founded (Gribling 2004). It should be noted that Turkish artists were also attracted to the open, experimental climate of Amsterdam and had begun to arrive as early as the 1950s. According to the Dutch Turkish artist Nur Tarim, who arrived in 1977, Amsterdam was appealing because of its free and "hip" atmosphere (Welling 2004).

In the 1980s, the political and cultural climate changed. "Foreignness" became a dividing principle as the term "allochthone" (referring to people born outside, or having at least one parent born outside, the

Netherlands) was adopted and increasingly used as a rationale for various policies that targeted colonial and labor migrants, such as Surinamese, Antilleans, Turks, Moroccans, and Moluccans, and which came to affect other non-Western citizens as well (Lopez 2002). As far as cultural matters were concerned, a separate subsidy system for "allochthone *kunstenaars*" (immigrant artists) was established on the national as well as on the Amsterdam city level. This target-group policy was based on the idea that artists from minority groups were in need of extra encouragement to improve the quality of their work. Consequently, foreign artists were subjected to assessment procedures that were different from those used for their Dutch colleagues. Indeed, the budgets allocated to minority artists were rather large, and the threshold for eligibility was deliberately kept low. As there was no discrimination made between amateurish projects and professional ones, the separate systems turned out to prevent some migrant artists from being perceived as full-fledged professionals (Lavrijsen 1992).

Already in the late 1980s (in Amsterdam) and the early 1990s (at the national level), the separate funding systems were stripped down because governments wanted the "allochthone artists" to be integrated into the regular funding structure. However, it was not until 1999 that the secretary of state for education, science, and culture, Rick van der Ploeg, came up with concrete new measures related to cultural diversity. Van der Ploeg's explicit aim was to enhance cultural diversity both in the artistic supply and the audience. To achieve these goals, the plan was to set aside 10 percent of the entire national budget for culture to invest in diversity initiatives. In addition, every organization would have to spend at least 3 percent of the subsidies it received to reach a more diverse public or create a more diverse program. Van der Ploeg's cultural policy elicited strong reactions from artists' unions, individual artists, cultural critics, and to a lesser degree from politicians, who argued that aesthetic quality should be the only standard considered in the subsidy and influence of artistic production. Although most of the proposed measures have been softened in implementation and Van der Ploeg's successors gradually removed the issue of diversity from the political agenda, the consequences linger. Until now, artists of migrant descent often are not seen as artists on the same level as those of native Dutch origin. Because many cultural intermediaries in the mainstream felt pressured to reach diversity targets set by politicians, concepts such as multicultural or cultural diversity have strong negative connotations, and cultural diversity policies are still distrusted by some established institutes, which see those policies as compromising their own high-quality standards (Taner 2011).

New Cultural Institutions

Owing to barriers they faced in the "white" established Dutch art institutions, on the one hand, and their desire to develop an independent organizational structure, on the other, "allochthone" artists began to create their own cultural institutions. In the field of theater several companies and production houses have been set up with the goal of exploring the multiethnic and multicultural character of contemporary Dutch society, thereby drawing on other artistic repertoires than the Western canon. At the beginning of the 1980s, Amsterdam's first intercultural production house, Cosmic Theatre, was founded by Antillean artists Felix Peter de Rooy and Norman de Palm to support artists and collectives in the production of new work. In 1986, De Nieuw Amsterdam (DNA) was set up as the city's very first multicultural theater company. Following its lead, Made in da Shade, a pioneering urban and multimedia theater, was founded in 1992. Theater Compagnie RAST, a fusion of Turkish and Kurdish theater groups, started in 1999, supported by Van der Ploeg's diversity policy. In 2009, Cosmic Theatre and Made in da Shade merged into an organization known as MC, which has been one of Amsterdam's leading multicultural production companies. Characteristic of these companies is the way they transformed theatrical venues into urban multimedia performance sites. However, because of recent severe cuts in arts funding in the Netherlands, competition among cultural organizations has become fierce. DNA, Rast, and MC all saw their national government subsidies cut dramatically for the 2013–16 period. According to the national funding organization, a major reason is that the theater groups' performances do not always meet expected artistic standards (Fonds Podiumkunsten 2012). In response, the city of Amsterdam has provided support for these institutions to enable them to survive, in some cases after reorganizing.

The Long March toward the Mainstream

Although the founding of these "diverse" institutions has resulted in the compartmentalization of Amsterdam's art scene into "white" and multicultural circuits (Delhaye 2009), it also has raised issues of identity and belonging in an artistic setting, and offered a platform (and employment) for a growing pool of young, talented artists. A number of young people of immigrant origin have made their way into and graduated from formal art education institutes. Others have moved into the professional art circuit through informal trainee projects (Jenniskens 2009). Still, the number of artists with a migrant background who have successfully made it into the mainstream is small. In the booklet *NEW! 20 Years Multicultural Theater*, published in 2006 to mark the twentieth anniversary of the multicultural company DNA, leading figures in Amsterdam's multicultural theater scene noted that few performers and directors of immigrant background have been able to move into the mainstream. In the preceding 50 years, no actor of immigrant background had received a Dutch theater award. This lack of recognition led to the establishment of the Cosmic Award to honor artists of non-Dutch descent for their artistic achievements (De Gruyter 2006).

There are some signs of change. The new breed of young actors of immigrant background more easily navigates between various professional milieus than the earlier generation did. These young artists, performing as they do in the "diversity" circuit as well as crossing over into different niches of Amsterdam's mainstream, are gradually reducing the barriers that closed off the ethnic cultural domains. They are acting in film as well as on stage, where they now more frequently play side by side with Amsterdam's greatest actors. In an overview of the 2010–11 Amsterdam theater season, the renowned critic Loek Zonneveld (2011) especially praised Nasrdin Dchar and Sadettin Kirmiziyüz, two young actors of Moroccan and Turkish descent, respectively, for the highly professional and inspiring way they brought their family histories on stage. Interestingly, both solo shows drew on the actors' parental backgrounds in order to explore how these histories impacted the actors' own identities. Dchar and Kirmiziyüz have indicated that the problematic contemporary climate in Dutch society with regard to non-Western

migrants was an important reason why they created the shows. Kirmiziyüz explained,

> Ten years ago my background was not an issue to me. I was simply a
> Dutchman. It is a cliché, but then came 9/11. All of a sudden, your back-
> ground became a great problem. "You are Turkish? You are Muslim?"
> When on top of this Theo van Gogh was murdered, people reacted in
> such a way, so many things were said that at a certain moment I thought:
> now I want to say something too. (quoted in Heuven 2011)

Nasrdin Dchar's solo show was written by one of the most successful Dutch writers for stage and screen, Maria Goos. Immigrant themes
such as acquiring a sense of belonging within the Western and the Muslim world also feature in many works by Adelheid Roosen, another
famous female Dutch playwright. As for Dchar, he is a recognized actor
not only on stage, but in film now as well. In 2011, he won the Golden
Calf, the top Dutch film award, for best actor for his performance in the
road movie *Rabat*.

Undeniably, Amsterdam's established cultural institutions as well as
various Dutch artists are gradually absorbing immigrant cultural influences, thereby slowly pulling down the walls behind which their cultural expression has been confined. This development is occurring not
only in the domain of theater; it is also evident in literature, music, and
the visual arts, though to varying degrees. As a recent evaluation report
of the Amsterdam cultural field noted, the city's large established institutions are still reluctant to integrate cultural and ethnic diversity in
their programming or explore the potentials of diversity (Taner 2011).
Or in the words of Hannerz, the mainstream cultural institutions have
not yet succeeded in keeping the cultural flow open. The immigrants'
children raised in the Netherlands gradually seem to be gaining more
access and the ability to use a broader range of the mainstream cultural
apparatus to contribute to cultural innovation in Amsterdam, although
they still have to fight the many conventions preserving the status quo.

Conclusions

In analyzing developments in everyday youth culture, mass popular culture, and high culture, we have shown how in each of these arenas youth of immigrant origin have had a significant impact on Amsterdam's cultural life. Of particular concern has been how the dynamics of what we call *cultural interconnectedness* have played out as the interactions among different ethnic groups, including the native Dutch, have led to the creation of new cultural styles, forms, and institutions.

In everyday youth culture, it is primarily in street culture that the processes of interconnection have taken place. Amsterdam street culture is now dominated by young men of Moroccan, Antillean, and Surinamese descent. Youth of other ethnicities, including native Dutch youth, can be included, provided that they have a command of the street codes and behavior. Street culture is macho, sexist, and celebrates toughness. As an expression of the urban male lower-class experience it bears a resemblance to the oppositional subcultures found in America among native black and Latino youth and in Britain among white working-class youth. As we have shown, Radio FunX also plays a critical "interconnecting" role. With its ethnically mixed staff and multicultural programming, it has been able to reach and unite youth of different ethnic backgrounds.

In mass popular culture, we find hybrid eclecticism in cultural production, both among performers and the audience. Within the flourishing urban music scene of Amsterdam's multicultural acts, native Dutch and those of various ethnic backgrounds entertain the same crowds, with a style that is based on a range of influences, from hip hop to electroclash and dance music. Ethnicity can bring inspiration to popular music artists, but is not considered a theme that divides. Hostility toward traditional, predominantly white Dutch, cultural institutions is rare but not unkown. Especially within the "old school" hip hop scene, youths tend to articulate their hostility toward mainstream society and the Dutch.

Young popular artists of immigrant descent have also injected a strong DIY mentality into the Amsterdam art scene. They are playing a crucial role in bridging different cultures. Like no others, comedians of immigrant descent have been able to parody narrow-minded opinions toward different cultures as well as aspects of both their own and native Dutch culture, in this way contributing to mutual understanding and the overcoming of ethnic tensions. Moreover, by performing in a relaxed and informal atmosphere, they have transformed a number of formal art venues into informal performing spaces—a transformation welcomed by Dutch audiences.

In the domain of "high arts," cultural production and dissemination in Amsterdam have been heavily influenced by cultural policy on the national as well as municipal levels. Various diversity schemes to bring immigrants' cultural output into the mainstream did not have the intended effect. The diversity schemes often ended up stigmatizing artists of immigrant origin as less than fully fledged creators and, it has been argued, offered mainstream cultural institutions a justification for not seriously engaging with cultural diversity, which they view as compromising their own high-quality standards (Taner 2011). Deeply ingrained codes and conventions regulating the operation of high art institutions constrain the development of cultural interconnectedness.

For their part, artists of immigrant origin have been able to establish new institutions that offer opportunities to raise issues of cultural identity and articulate them in multicultural and multidisciplinary ways. However, the founding of these "diverse" institutions has led to a compartmentalization of the Amsterdam culture apparatus. Some artists may have intended and some still aim to cater to their own crowd, but many more want to connect with broader audiences. What is clear is that the children of immigrants, raised and educated in the Netherlands, are navigating across various niches in Amsterdam's mainstream and multicultural circuit, thereby exploring and fusing diverse artistic repertoires and making themselves much more visible to various audiences as well as important cultural gatekeepers. Entry into the core of the established institutions, on full and equal terms, however, undoubtedly will be harder to achieve.

NOTES

1. She followed 32 girls aged 11–12 from their last months in primary school to their first months in secondary school.
2. De Rooij interviewed 16 young women aged 14–21 years. The interview consisted of a questionnaire to measure the respondents' evaluation of their own body and open questions about their beauty ideals, and the young women were

invited to react to images of top models with different skin colors. Each interview ended with a photo shoot.

3. The study consisted of a quantitative part that included questionnaires, physical tests, and fitness tests obtained from 1,044 pupils from 18 secondary prevocational schools in the Netherlands and a qualitative part that consisted of observation, a questionnaire, and interviews with 82 girls (mean age 13.8 years) of different ethnic backgrounds (the girls attended a secondary prevocational school in Amsterdam). In one part of the qualitative study, the interviewees were asked to grade and comment on the pictures of six women.

4. FunX is lobbying against the method of measuring the average number of listeners (CLO), an important figure used in determining subsidies and selling airtime for commercials. According to FunX the current method, in which a selected panel is supposed to register weekly listening behavior on paper, is outdated and mainly suited to a middle-aged white crowd. Based on the CLO, FunX is a marginal station in terms of the number of listeners, yet "counter-research" conducted in 2010 for FunX by Synovate shows that the station is the second most popular station in Amsterdam in the age group 15–35 (FunX's target demographic) and the number one station in the age group 15–25.

5. Paul Stiekema allegedly shouted racist remarks at one of the festival's black employees in an argument over the license for an alternative, smaller version of the Kwakoe Festival after the cancellation. The accusation was made by one of the promoters of the substitute festival, who claimed she overheard the exchange. Stiekema, in turn, accused her of slander and claimed that she was bitter because her company had provided the festival tents the year before, but was turned down in 2011.

REFERENCES

Adriaanse, Aram, Chris Keulemans, and Jens Besse (eds.). 2006. *Nieuw. 20 jaar multicultureel theater*. Amsterdam: International Theatre & Film Books.

Alba, Richard. 2005. "Bright vs. Blurred Boundaries: Second-Generation Assimilation and Exclusion in France, Germany and the United States." *Ethnic and Racial Studies* 28 (1): 20–49.

Alba, Richard, and Victor Nee. 1997. "Rethinking Assimilation Theory for a New Era of Immigration." *International Migration Review* 31 (4): 826–74.

Boogaarts, Simone. 2009. "Gedwongen of vrije keuze? Uitsluitingsmechanismen in de etno-party scene." *Migrantenstudies* 25 (1): 88–104.

Brook, Siobhan, and Thomas Conroy. 2010. "Hip-Hop Culture in a Global Context: Interdisciplinary and Cross-Categorical Investigation." *American Behavioral Scientist* 55 (1): 3–8.

De Gruyter, Werner. 2006. "Knuffelnegers en witte mannen: Zes cultuurmakers van allochtone komaf geven hun visie op de Nederlands kunstwereld." *Boekman* 69: 30–36.

De Jong, Jan D. 2007. *Kapot moeilijk. Een etnografisch onderzoek naar opvallend delinquent groepsgedrag van "Marokkaanse" jongens*. Amsterdam: Amsterdam University Press.

Delhaye, Christine. 2009. "Towards Cultural Diversity in Amsterdam's Arts," in Liza Nell and Jan Rath (eds.), *Ethnic Amsterdam: Immigrants and Urban Change in the Twentieth Century*. Amsterdam: Amsterdam University Press.

De Rooij, Deborah M. 2004 *"Ooh, me bil staat mooi in die broek!" Over schoonheid en etniciteit bij Afro-Surinaamse jonge vrouwen*. Master's thesis, VU University Amsterdam.

Dohmen, Anne. 2011. "Ik maak geen programma's voor negers." *NRC Handelsblad*, September 10/11.

Duits, Linda. 2010. "Kiezen om normaal te zijn: Normen en waarden in multiculturele meisjescultuur." *Pedagogiek* 30 (1): 9–25.

Fonds Podiumkunsten. 2012. "Meerjarige activiteitensubsidies 2013–2016." http:// www.fondspodiumkunsten.nl/toekenningen/meerjarige_activiteitensubsidies_2013-2016/, accessed on October 25, 2012.

Gribling, Franck. 2004. "Fremdkörper. Het vreemde als noodzakelijke katalysator van de Cultuur." www.Denieuwe.nl/Vreemd/artikelen/FranckGribling.html, accessed on October 26, 2004.

Hannerz, Ulf. 1992. *Cultural Complexity: Studies in the Social Organization of Meaning*. New York: Columbia University Press.

Heuven, Robbert van. 2011. "Culturele identiteit en theater." *Trouw*, April 8.

Jenniskens, Anneke. J. 2008. *De positie van culturele diversiteit in de kunst- en cultuursector van Gemeente Amsterdam*. Master's thesis, Utrecht University.

Kammer, Claudia. 2011. "Hiphoppers maken werk van hun talent." *NRC Handelsbad*, June 9.

Kooijman, Jaap. 2008. *Fabricating the Absolute Fake: America in Contemporary Pop Culture*. Amsterdam: Amsterdam University Press.

Krims, Adam. 2000. *Rap Music and Poetics of Identity*. Cambridge: Cambridge University Press.

Kropman, Wouter. 2007. *Obesity. A Cultural Concern? A Study of the Influence of Culture on the Prevalence of Obesity among VMBO Students in the Netherlands*. Master's thesis, VU University Amsterdam.

Lavrijsen, Ria. 1992. "Allochtone kunstenaars en beleid." *Boekmancahier* 13: 349–53.

López, Sebastian. 2002. 'Identity: Reality or Fiction?' in Rasheed Araeen., Ziauddin Sardar, and Sean Cubitt (eds.), *The Third Text Reader on Art, Culture and Theory*. London/New York: Continuum.

Meershoek, Patrick. 2011. "Moddergevecht om afblazen Kwakoe." *Het Parool*, July 18.

Ministerie OCW (Ministerie van Onderwijs, Cultuur and Wetenschap). 2011. *Uitwerking regeerakkoord onderdeel media*. The Hague: Ministerie van Onderwijs, Cultuur and Wetenschap.

Moors, Annelies. 2009. "Islamic Fashion in Europe: Religious Conviction, Aesthetic Style, and Creative Consumption." *Encounters* 1 (1): 175–201.

Mossinkoff, Marco, and Charlotte Corstanje. 2011. "From Segments and Lifestyles to Communities-light: Identifying Islamic Sub-cultures in the Netherlands." *Journal of Islamic Marketing* 2 (2): 154–64.

Nabben, Ton. 2010. *High Amsterdam: Ritme, Roes en Regelmaat in het Uitgaansleven.* Amsterdam: Rozenberg.

Osumare, Halifu. 2001. "Beat Streets in the Global Hood: Connective Marginalities in the Hip Hop Globe." *Journal of American and Comparative Cultures* 24 (1/2): 171–81.

Park, Robert. E., and Ernest Burgess. 1921. *Introduction to the Science of Sociology.* Chicago: University of Chicago Press.

Paulle, Bowen. 2005. *Anxiety and Intimidation in the Bronx and the Bijlmer: An Ethnographic Comparison of Two Schools.* Amsterdam: Amsterdam University Press.

Rose, Tricia. 2006. "Voices from the Margins: Rap Music and Contemporary Cultural Production," in Andy Bennett, Barry Shank, and Jason Toynbee (eds.), *The Popular Music Studies Reader* London: Routledge.

Salahedine. 2011. http://www.salahedinonline.com/seo/index.php/artists/salah-edin. html, accessed December 19, 2011.

Taner, Gorgun. 2011. *Amsterdam, Kunst en cultuurstad van wereldklasse.* Amsterdam: Gemeente Amsterdam.

Ter Bogt, Tom. 1997. *One, Two, Three, Four . . . Popmuziek, Jeugdcultuur en Stijl.* Utrecht: Lemma.

Van den Berg, Nanda. 1994. "De kunst van het weglaten. De positie van allochtone beeldend kunstenaars." *De Gids* 157 (1): 69–78.

Welling, Wouter. 2004. "Een tentoonstelling in historisch perspectief. 3 juni 1988. Ismet Birsel opent Turkse kunstenaars in Holland," in Rosemarie Buikema and Maaike Meijer (eds.), *Kunsten in Beweging. Cultuur en Migratie in Nederland 1980–2000.* The Hague: Sdu Uitgevers.

Willis, Paul. 1977. *Learning to Labour: How Working Class Kids Get Working Class Jobs.* New York: Columbia University Press.

Zonneveld, Loek. 2011. "Het Verhaal van de Ander," in *Terugblikken Theaterseizoen 2010–2011.* Amsterdam: Stichting Vakblad voor de Podiumkuns.

CHRISTINE DELHAYE is Lecturer in Cultural Theory and Cultural Policy in the Department of Art, Religion, and Cultural Studies at the University of Amsterdam, where she is also Chair of the Master's Program in Cultural Studies. A specialist in the sociology of arts and culture, she has published widely on fashion, fashion exhibitions, and visual culture. Her research interests also include urban culture and cultural diversity in global societies.

JAN WILLEM DUYVENDAK is Full Professor of Sociology at the University of Amsterdam, having previously been Director of the Verwey-Jonker Institute for Social Issues and Professor of Community Development at Erasmus University Rotterdam. Currently, his main fields of research are belonging, urban sociology, "feeling at home," and nativism. His latest books include *The Politics of Home: Nostalgia and Belonging in Western Europe and the United States* (Palgrave, 2011) and *Crafting Citizenship: Understanding Tensions in a Multi-Ethnic Society* (with Menno Hurenkamp and Evelien Tonkens; Palgrave, 2012).

NANCY FONER is Distinguished Professor of Sociology at Hunter College and the Graduate Center of the City University of New York. She is the author or editor of more than a dozen books, including *One Out of Three: Immigrant New York in the Twenty-First Century* (Columbia University Press, 2013), *In a New Land: A Comparative View of Immigration* (New York University Press, 2005), and *From Ellis Island to JFK: New York's Two Great Waves of Immigration* (Yale University Press, 2000), winner of the 2000 Theodore Saloutos Award of the Immigration and Ethnic History Society.

DAVID DYSSEGAARD KALLICK is Senior Fellow of the Fiscal Policy Institute and Director of the institute's Immigration Research Initiative. He is the principal author of numerous reports for the institute, including *Working for a Better Life: A Profile of Immigrants in the New York State Economy* (2007), *Immigrants and the Economy: Contribution of Immigrant Workers to the Country's 25 Largest Metropolitan Areas* (2009), and *Immigrant Small Business Owners: A Significant and Growing Part of the Economy* (2012).

PHILIP KASINITZ is Professor of Sociology at the Graduate Center of the City University of New York. He is the author of *Caribbean New York: Black Immigrants and the Politics of Race*, the editor of *Metropolis: Center and Symbol of Our Time*, coeditor (with Mary C. Waters and John Mollenkopf) of *Becoming New Yorkers: Ethnographies of The New Second Generations*, and coauthor (with Waters, Mollenkopf, and Jennifer Holdaway) of *Inheriting the City: The Children of Immigrants Come of Age*, which received the 2009 Mirra Komarovksy Book Award from the Eastern Sociological Society and the 2010 Distinguished Book Award from the American Sociological Association.

ROBERT C. KLOOSTERMAN is Professor of Economic Geography and Planning at the University of Amsterdam. He is Honorary Professor in the Bartlett School of Planning, University College, London and held the Francqui Chair at the Faculty of Business Studies, Hasselt University (Belgium) in 2012. He has published extensively in English-language journals on urban issues such as labor-market developments in urban areas (especially Amsterdam), migrant entrepreneurship, and more recently on cultural industries, notably Dutch architectural design. He has served as an advisor to the Dutch national government, a number of Dutch cities, and the OECD.

LEO LUCASSEN is Professor of Social History at the Institute for History of Leiden University. His research and writing focus on global migrations, settlement processes, urban history, and state-led social engineering. His recent books include *Migration History in World History: Multidisciplinary Approaches* (with Jan Lucassen and Patrick Manning; Brill Publishers, 2010), *The Encyclopedia of Migration and*

Minorities in Europe: From the 17th Century to the Present (with Klaus Bade et al.; Cambridge University Press, 2011), and *Living in the City: Urban Institutions in the Low Countries, 1200–2010* (with Wim Willems; Routledge, 2012).

LAURE MICHON is a Senior Researcher in the City of Amsterdam's Bureau for Research and Statistics and holds a Ph.D. in social science from the University of Amsterdam. Her dissertation (*Ethnic Minorities in Local Politics*, 2011) examined ethnic minority politicians' access to politics in Amsterdam and Paris, the development of their careers over time, and their discourses on representation. She has contributed chapters on the political participation of immigrants in the Netherlands and France, the political representation of immigrants in Amsterdam and Paris, and the political mobilization of Turks in Amsterdam to various edited volumes.

JOHN MOLLENKOPF is Distinguished Professor of Political Science at the CUNY Graduate Center, directs its Center for Urban Research, and coordinates its interdisciplinary concentration in public policy and urban studies. His work explores the intersection of urban politics, urban policy, urban development, and immigration in comparative perspective. His latest book is *The Changing Face of World Cities* (2012), coedited with Maurice Crul. He is a member of the MacArthur Foundation Research Network on Building Resilient Regions, the advisory board of the Netherlands Institute of City Innovation Studies, and the selection committee of the Zeit Foundation's doctoral fellowship in migration.

JAN RATH is Professor of Sociology and Chair of the Department of Sociology and Anthropology at the University of Amsterdam, where he is also a researcher at the Institute for Migration and Ethnic Studies (IMES) and the Center for Urban Studies. A member of the IMISCOE Research Network, he is European Chair of International Metropolis. He is the author or editor of numerous articles, reports, and books on the sociology, politics, and economics of postmigration processes, including *Unravelling the Rag Trade: Immigrant Entrepreneurship in Seven World Cities* (Berg, 2002), *Immigrant Entrepreneurs: Venturing*

Abroad in the Age of Globalization (Berg, 2003), *Ethnic Amsterdam* (Amsterdam University Press, 2009), and *Selling Ethnic Neighborhoods* (Routledge, 2012).

ROGIER VAN REEKUM holds a postdoctoral position at Erasmus University Rotterdam. He has written a dissertation based on a study of public and political debates on Dutch identity and citizenship in the Netherlands as part of the research project "Citizenship, National Canons, and the Issue of Cultural Diversity: The Netherlands in International Perspective." He has published a number of articles on the politicization of nationhood, diversity, and migration in the European context, and is an editor of *Krisis,* a journal on contemporary philosophy.

SAWITRI SAHARSO is Professor of Intercultural Governance at the School of Management and Governance at the University of Twente and the Department of Sociology of the VU University Amsterdam. Her research fields include the governance of migration, religious diversity and citizenship within a European comparative perspective, migrant youth, and gender and migration. She is editor of *Comparative Migration Studies.* Her recent publications include "The Settlement Country and Ethnic Identification of Children of Turkish Immigrants in Germany, France, and the Netherlands: What Role Do National Integration Policies Play?" (with Evelyn Ersanilli; *International Migration Review* 2011).

JEAN TILLIE is Professor and Head of the Political Science Department at the University of Amsterdam. He is also the Coordinator of the European FP7 EURISLAM project, which focuses on the social and cultural integration of European Muslims. Recent publications include "Different Effects of Ethnic Diversity on Social Capital: Density of Foundations and Leisure Associations in Amsterdam Neighborhoods," (with Floris Vermeulen and Robert van der Walle; *Urban Studies,* 2012) and a chapter, with Laure Michon, on voter turnout and party choices among immigrants in Karen Bird et al. (eds.), *The Political Representation of Immigrants and Minorities: Voters, Parties and Parliaments in Liberal Democracies* (Routledge, 2011).

JUSTUS UITERMARK is the Gradus Hendriks Professor of Community Development and Assistant Professor of Sociology at Erasmus University Rotterdam. His work focuses on cities, governance, and social movements. Among his recent publications is *Dynamics of Power in Dutch Integration Politics: From Accommodation to Confrontation* (University of Amsterdam Press, 2012).

VICTOR VAN DE VEN is a Research and Teaching Assistant in the Department of Cultural Studies at the University of Amsterdam. His main fields of interest are popular culture, youth culture, and music culture. He has been working in the field as a professional disc jockey and producer for more than 15 years.

FLORIS VERMEULEN is Assistant Professor in the Department of Political Science and Codirector of the Institute for Migration and Ethnic Studies (IMES) at the University of Amsterdam. A main area of his research is the civic and political participation of immigrants at the local level, including the role of immigrant organizations. His work has been published in journals such as *Urban Studies*, the *Journal of Ethnic and Migration Studies*, and *Turkish Studies*.

MARY C. WATERS is the M.E. Zukerman Professor of Sociology at Harvard University, where she has taught since 1986. She is the author or editor of numerous books and articles on immigration, ethnicity and identity, race relations, and young adulthood, including *The Next Generation: Immigrant Youth in a Comparative Perspective* (with Richard Alba; 2011), *Inheriting the City: The Children of Immigrants Come of Age* (with Philip Kasinitz, John Mollenkopf, and Jennifer Holdaway; 2008), and *Black Identities: West Indian Immigrant Dreams and American Realities* (1999).

INDEX